AF469918

SAVOUR THE MOMENT

SAVOUR THE MOMENT

The Life and Work of Alan Ingham

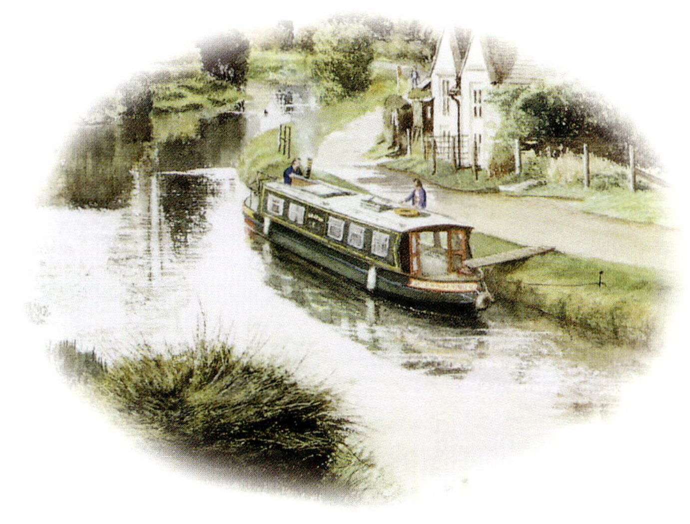

ALAN INGHAM

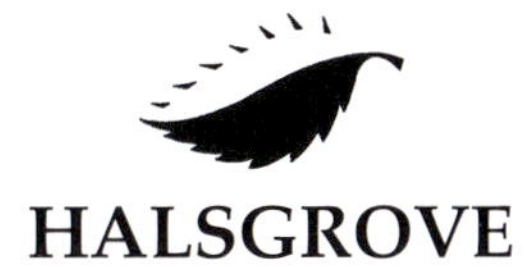

HALSGROVE

First published in Great Britain in 2005
Copyright © The Estate of Alan Ingham, 2005

All rights reserved. No part of this publication may be reproduced, stored in a retrieval system, or transmitted in any form or by any means without the prior permission of the copyright holder.

British Library Cataloguing-in-Publication Data
A CIP record for this title is available from the British Library

ISBN 1 84114 391 X

HALSGROVE
Halsgrove House
Lower Moor Way
Tiverton, Devon EX16 6SS
T: 01884 243242
F: 01884 243325
email: sales@halsgrove.com
website: www.halsgrove.com

Printed and bound by D'Auria Industrie Grafiche Spa, Italy

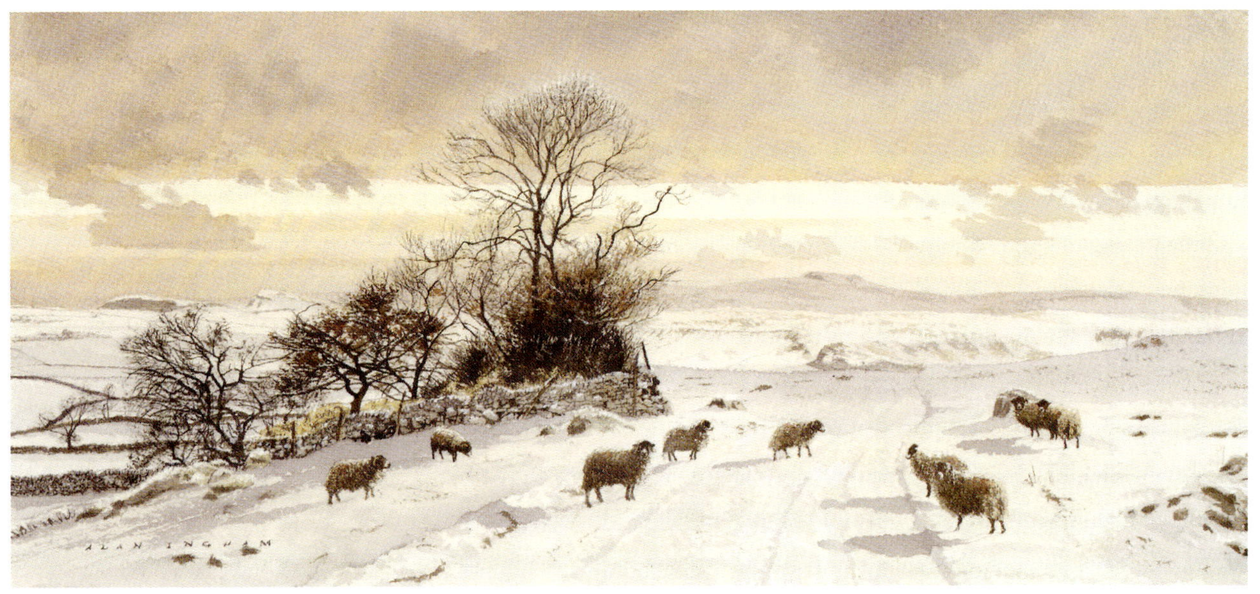

On Winskill Moor, Settle, North Yorkshire, 1989.

Contents

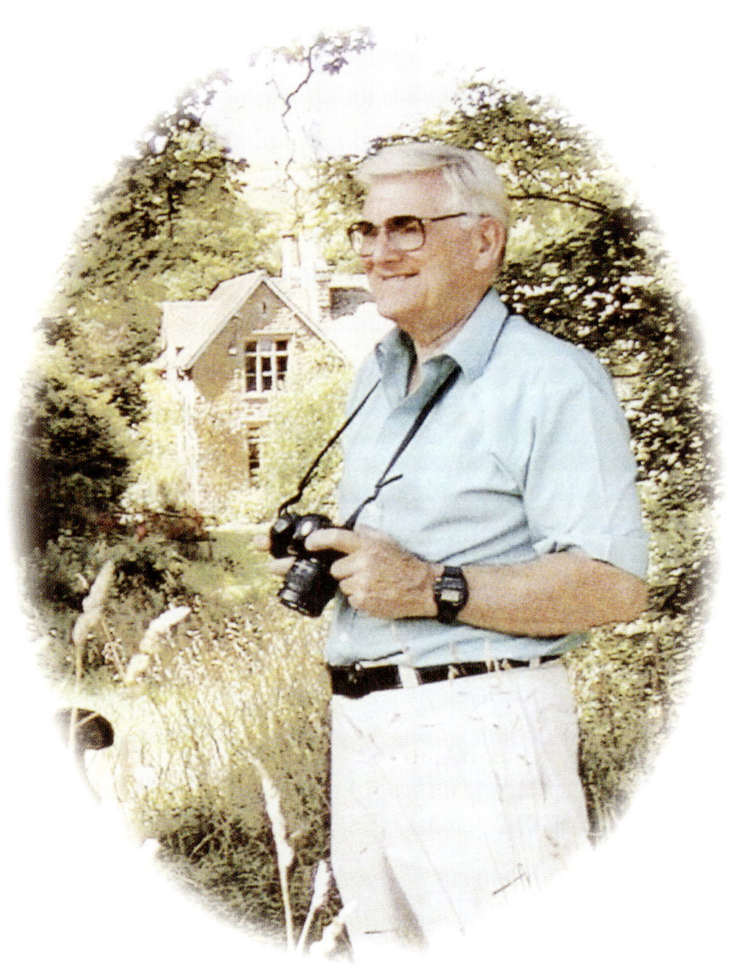

Foreword

Completed by Alan Ingham shortly before he died in 2002

Born in Skipton, North Yorkshire in 1932, I attended Ermysted's Grammar School and, from the age of thirteen, the Royal Naval College, Dartmouth.

In the Royal Navy I specialised as a hydrographic surveyor and worked in the Home Waters (chiefly Scotland), New Zealand, Fiji and other islands of the South Pacific, the east coast of Africa and the islands of the Indian Ocean. In 1965 I retired in the rank of Lt Commander and became a lecturer at the North East London Polytechnic. During this time my work included the writing of two text books on surveying at sea and projects in North and South America, Europe and South Africa.

An interest in drawing had been evident from my schooldays. Landscape was the favourite, later extended to an interest in ships, and 'party piece' caricatures of family and friends, teachers, etc.

The years as hydrographer and then lecturer afforded little time for the serious pursuit of other interests, and it was not until the 1970s that my urge to paint emerged again.

I started by exhibiting my work at fêtes and other events, then in galleries locally and, later, at the Mall Galleries in London. Throughout the 1980s I exhibited at the Granby Gallery in Bakewell and pursued my publishing ambitions in cards, calendars and prints through Royle Publications.

In 1984, I retired from the Polytechnic to turn to painting full time.

In 1989 I approached the Halcyon Gallery and its publishing company, Washington Green. My first limited edition prints *Easter Miracle* and *November Skies* were published in 1990 and, at the time of writing, the total exceeds seventy. My book *Under A Watercolour Sky* was published in 1996, and provided a showcase for much of this work to date.

Now, after many fruitful years I have been forced by poor health to change my pace of work. But one has to be very unlucky to have to stop painting altogether due to the fortunes of age or health. I revel in a state of mellow contentment, no longer striving to lead the field but still determined against the odds to capture the beauty, magic and light of nature. I am happier in my artistic endeavour than ever before.

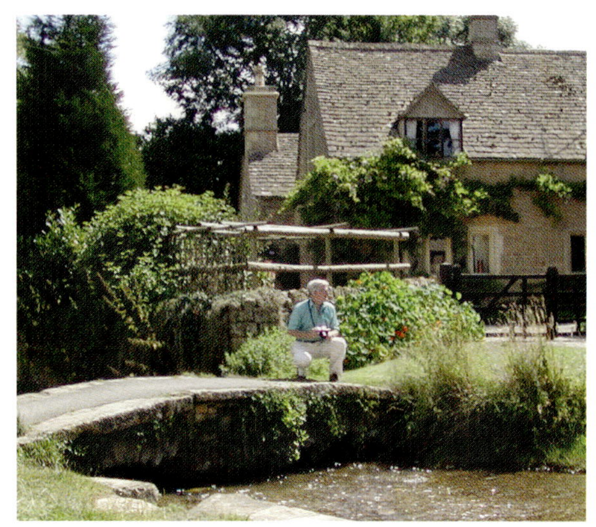

The Amateur Years and Cariactures

1940s–1960s

The Early Years

My early years in a north-country mill town in the 1930s and '40s are, today, a jumble of hazy memories...

Dad, a cabinet maker on £3 a week; Mum, just a housewife – mums did not go out to work in this proud community; me, a pupil in the local infants' school...

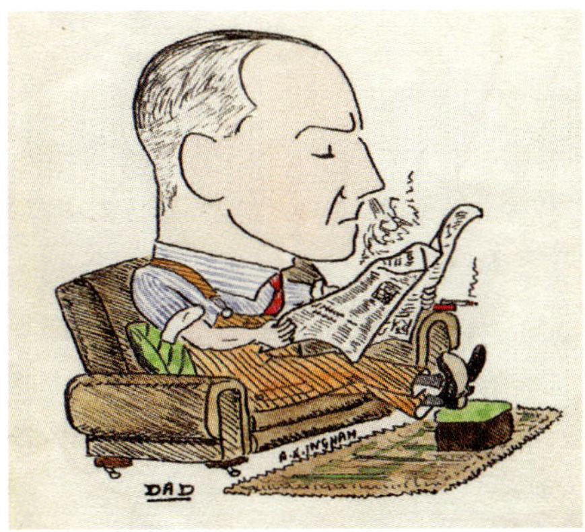

Dad, Caricature, Pen, Ink and Wash, 1948.

Aged forty-four, in relaxed mood at the end of a working day, with cigarette and News Chronicle, *on leatherette settee and velveteen-covered pouffe.*

Summer days in the fields or on the 'rec', playing cowboys and indians with the gang, riding my scooter backwards or jumping off a swing at its highest point to see who could jump the furthest (but succeeding only in coming a cropper!)

The Second World War seemed far away to a seven-year-old at home in the Yorkshire Dales. Dad was unfit for military service, so he was conscripted to work, knee-deep in mud, erecting huts to house the expected hordes of prisoners-of-war. He was also enrolled in the AFS (Auxiliary Fire Service) and joined the rota of night watches, playing cards and dominoes and waiting for the occasional barn or haystack fire ('keep it going, George, 'til we've finished this hand...')

For the kids, the war brought its own pleasures: Dinky toy aircraft and tanks to be endlessly swopped; balsa-wood models of Spitfires, Buffaloes and Yaks to be whittled and painted (I remember the Russian Yak fighter was to be painted in 'drab' and I never did find a shop where drab paint was sold); converting a scout hat into an Anzac one with brim turned up on one side, marching along singing *Roll Out The Barrel*...

Our 'rec' was right by the main Edinburgh to London LMS railway line. Troop trains stopped to take water onboard from the pump nearby, and the Canadian, American and even British soldiers threw nylons for our sisters, cigarettes for our dads and emergency rations and chocolate for everybody into our eager hands.

Soldiers billeted in Skipton fell prey to our badgering for cap badges and uniform buttons. Richard Green, heart-throb and star of Robin Hood films was one of them, and even his portrait on advertisements for Brylcream in the barbers' shops were not safe from us.

Evacuees from London's East End with a funny way of speaking were lodged in our homes: their fathers, to a man, were fighter pilots, allegedly, and we were intensely jealous of them.

At the age of twelve, then at Ermysted's Grammar School, goodness only knows what possessed me to decide on a career in the Navy and take a scholarship to the Royal Naval College at Dartmouth. I suppose

I liked the uniform and, for most of the war, had listened with awe to my friend's uncle telling of life at sea as a signalman. (He had actually been on the bridge of Lord Louis Mountbatten's ship HMS *Kelly* when she was torpedoed in the Mediterranean). I also liked to be different, and in a place mid-way between the east and west coasts, the Navy was different!

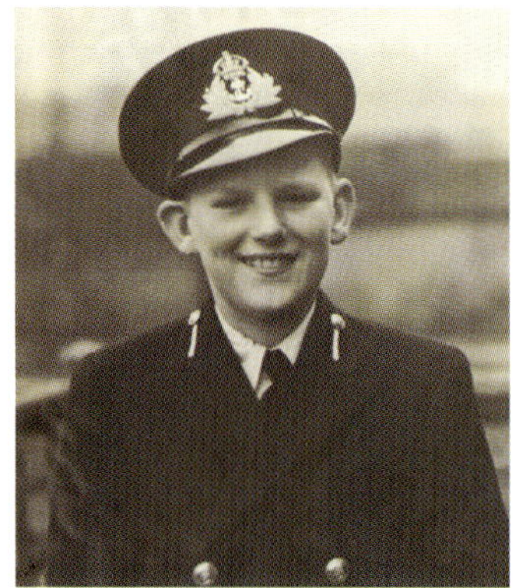

Cadet-to-be, 1 May 1946.

My uniform arrived from Messrs Gieves the day before I was due to go to college, and I just had to try it on. The next day the jaunty tilt of my cap was promptly corrected.

Whatever my motives, as far as fighting for king and country was concerned, my timing was immaculate, for when I eventually reported at the college on 2 May 1946, the war had been over for some nine months.

College life offered a wealth of opportunities to pursue my boyhood hobbies. Art and model-making were actively encouraged, and painting in watercolour became a major interest.

The house journal and the college magazine gave space to my sketches, cartoons and caricatures, while the house plays called for scenery painters and programme designers. Paper and pencil, paints and brushes were usually close at hand, often at the expense of my participation in team sports.

As for sports, my only strengths lay in the gym (not particularly good, but keen), dinghy sailing (ditto) and rowing (single sculls). I appeared to be growing up a loner.

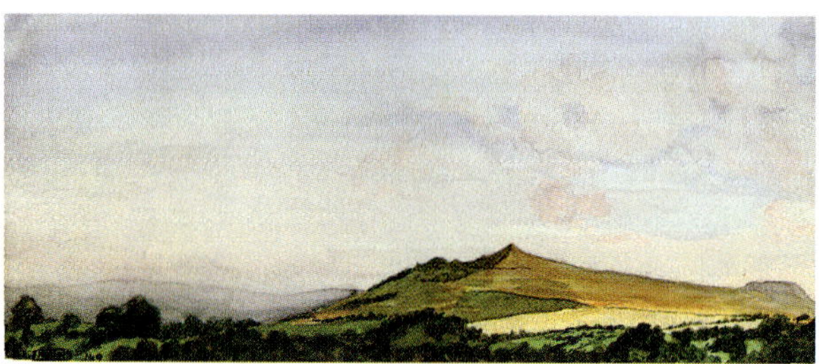

Sharphaw Hill, Skipton, North Yorkshire, Watercolour, 1946.

An early attempt at landscape painting in watercolour. My hometown nestles under this distinct, though minor peak in the Pennines.

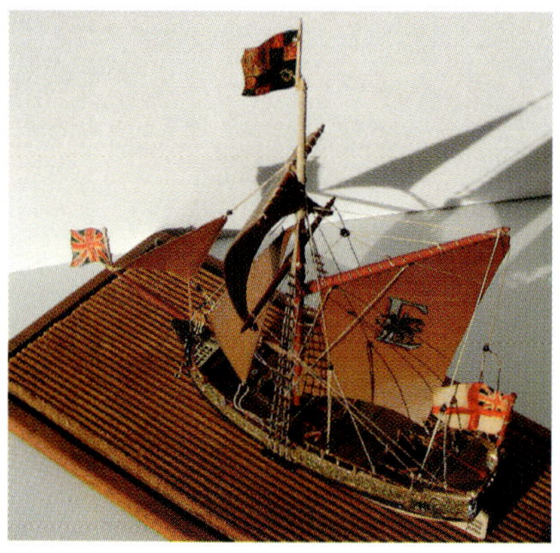

Stuart Royal Yacht c1650. Model, 1947.

Not all my work is faithful to the subject. The ship is seventeenth century, but the flags are strictly twentieth: the mainsail bears a monogram for my mother, Elizabeth, and the heraldic Griffin represents my college house, Grenville.

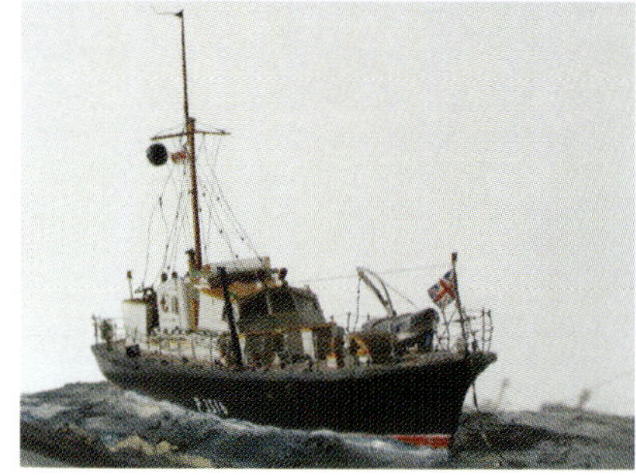

HM Surveying Motor Launch P3516. Model, 1958.

At 190mm in length, the same size as the yacht model, this contemporaneous model of my first command is correct in every detail.

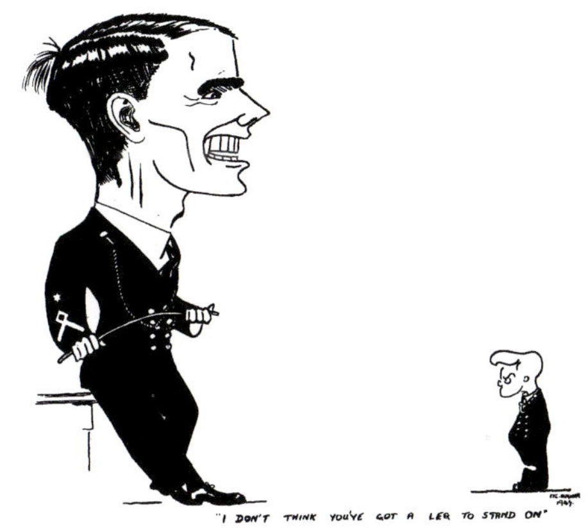

'I don't think you've got a leg to stand on'. Cartoon, Pen and Ink, 1949.

Punishment by caning was an accepted practice in almost all schools, and this cartoon from the Britannia expresses the junior cadet's hopeless indignation when his story fails to impress the all-powerful House Cadet Captain.

Meanwhile, on the Home Front, aged fifteen, I found my future wife, Rose. Over half a century on, she is still my heart-and-soulmate.

At that time, my best friend from grammar school days was Peter Whalley. Having met Rose at a youth club dance, our intrepid sailor turned to Pete to act as intermediary to arrange a date. He was thorough, I'll say that: not only did he fix the date, he came with us to the pictures!

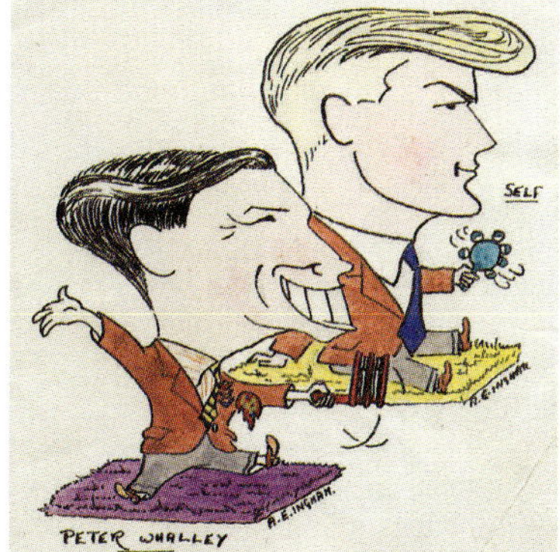

Peter and Me (my best mate). Caricature, Pen, Ink and wash, 1948.

We were speedway fans in those days.

(Eventually, Pete and I drifted along our separate ways, he to National Service in the RAF and I to the fleet as a midshipman. We were destined not to meet again for fifty years, and when we did, it was as if the friendship had never been interrupted. Even today, Pete comes with us often on a 'date', but now his wife Pat comes along as well.)

College days came to an end in 1950, to be followed by two training cruises in the Second World War heavy cruiser, HMS *Devonshire*.

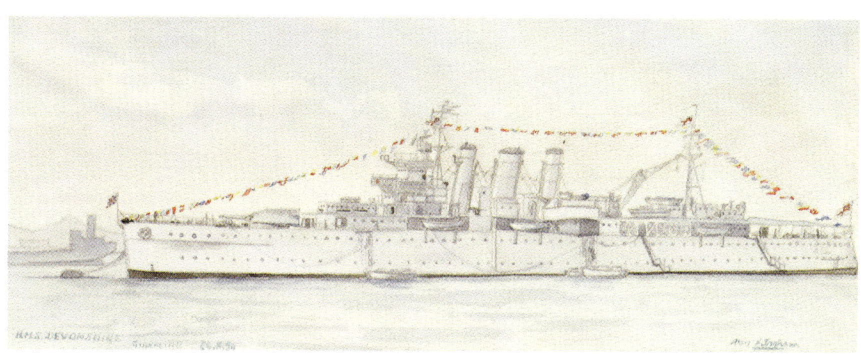

HMS Devonshire. Watercolour, 1950.

Cadets on the training ship were kept very busy indeed, scrubbing decks, painting the ship, running the ship's motorboats, lowering and hoisting the cutter and whaler, and taking part in every sort of exercise. 'Expected to behave like officers, to obey the orders of able seamen, and given the privileges of neither' was our moan.

It was a great adventure, though, and my very first venture out of England. The ship sailed from Devonport to Glengarriff, around the coasts of Ireland and Scotland, to Oslo, the Norwegian fjords, on to the Lofoten Islands, Narvik and the Arctic ice barrier. For the second cruise, we visited twelve ports along the length and breadth of the Mediterranean. Super!

The *Devonshire Magazine* became the home for my cartoons, while my personal journal slowly filled with fuzzy snapshots and watercolour sketches.

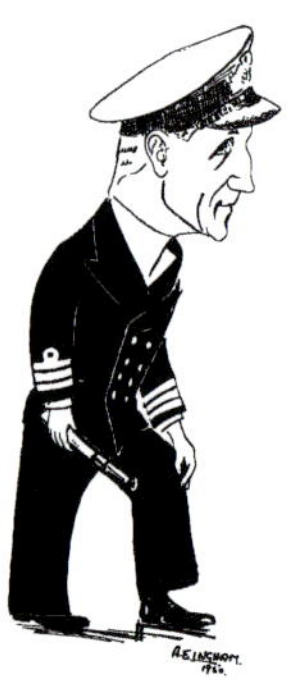
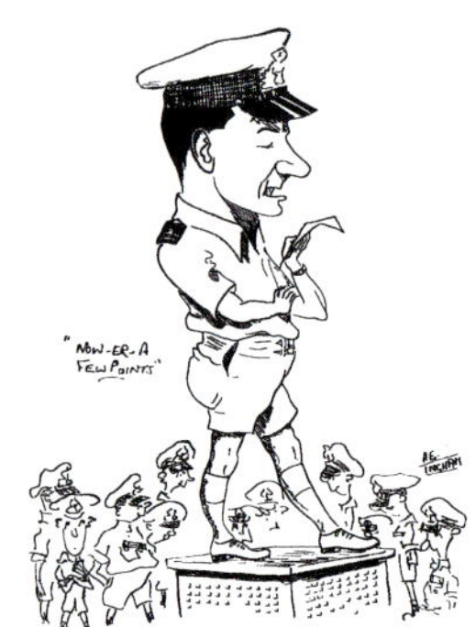

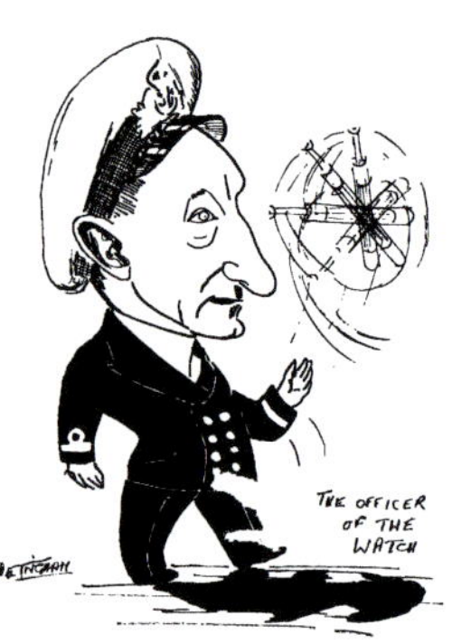

HMS *Devonshire* personalities, 1950
The Commander, The Cadet Training Officer, The Boswain.

In January, 1951, as is the way in most of life's progress, senior cadet fell off the top of one ladder to start at the bottom of another as junior midshipman. I was appointed to the aircraft carrier HMS *Indomitable*, flagship of Admiral Sir Philip Vian, Commander-in-Chief, Home Fleet. Heady stuff for this young man at a time when the Navy's ships were numbered in hundreds!

Under Admiralty Instructions, Midshipmen were required to keep an illustrated journal to ensure their attention to activities on board from day to day. My artistic interests were thus given official backing, and my output reached a pinnacle, providing a large archive of my work at that time.

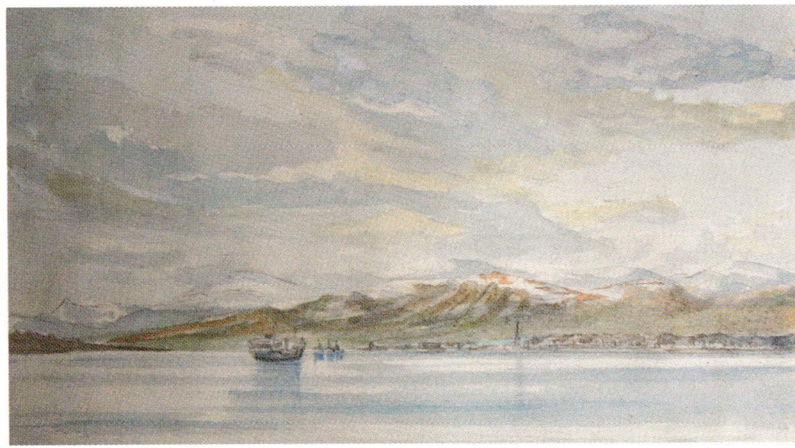

Invergordon, Watercolour, 1951.
From my Midshipman's Journal, 1951.

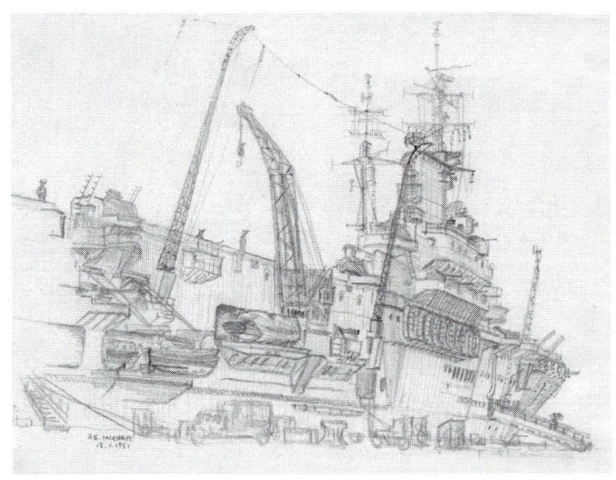

HMS *Indomitable* at Pitch House Jetty, Portsmouth Dockyard. Pencil.
I was overawed by the mammoth size of the carrier when I boarded in early January, and within a week, while the ship's company were embarking stores ready for departure, I had completed the first sketch for my journal (and my largest still-life subject ever).

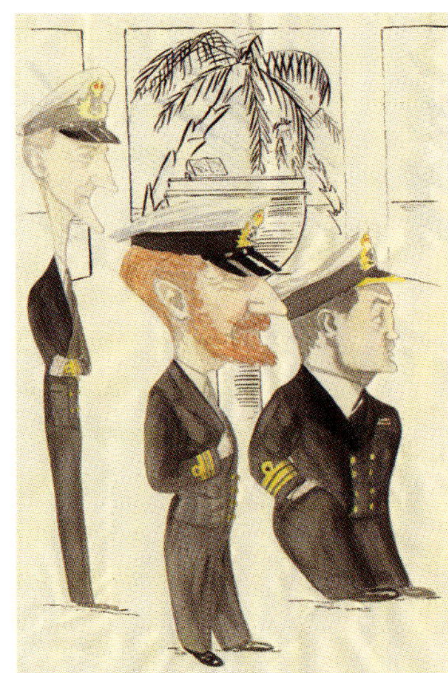

Navigators Three. Pen, Ink and Wash.
The Fleet Flagship warranted not one but three navigators to ensure safe passage – the Fleet Navigating Officer, the ship's Navigating Officer and his assistant. This was my attempt to lampoon the situation en route to Stockholm. It was one of my earlier lead balloons!

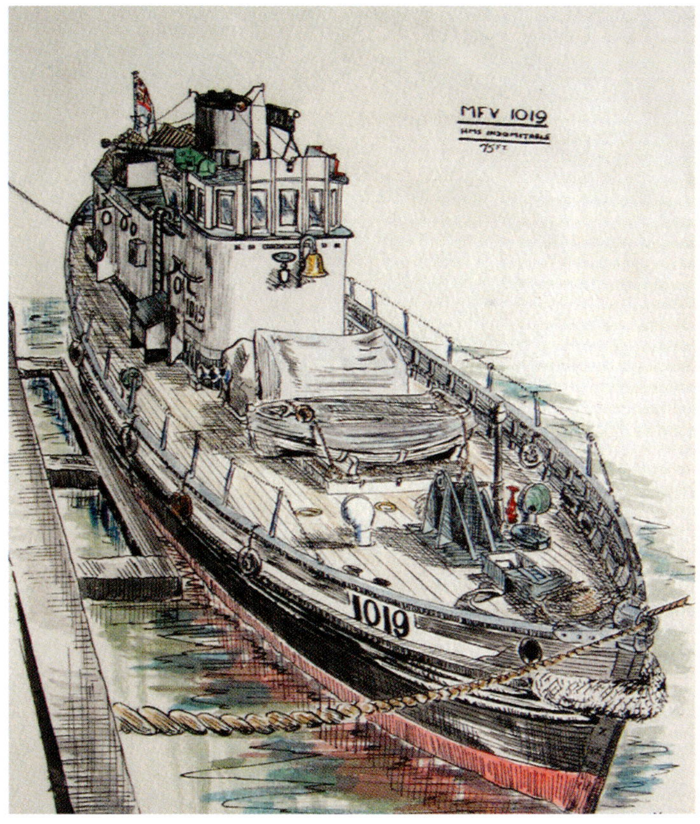

Motor Fishing Vessel 1019. Pen, Ink and Wash.

MFVs were commonly used when the fleet was at anchor, to convey personnel to and from the shore, to take on stores and generally wait upon the ship's requirements. I and a more senior officer were dispatched from Chatham to rendezvous with the fleet at Invergordon during a break in a massive NATO exercise in the North Sea. However, because of a series of incidents chiefly to do with the aged engine of the MFV, the fleet had long gone by the time we arrived. Our new orders were to proceed through the Caledonian and Crinin canals and arrive in the Clyde ahead of the fleet on the completion of the exercise. Once again, we were late, this time because the vessel grounded in the Crinin canal. Never mind it was all a marvellous experience for this budding landscape artist.

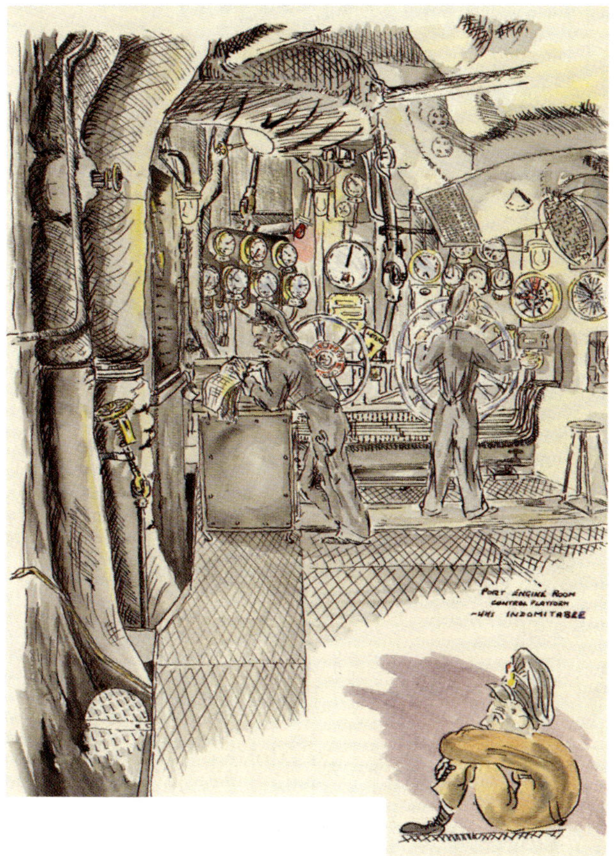

Engine Room Woes. Pen, Ink and Wash.

Regardless of one's field of specialisation, all midshipmen were assigned to engine-room duties for a few weeks. We were a necessary nuisance to the watch keepers and left more-or-less to our devices, and the hours passed exceedingly slowly

Comeback Time

From the end of my naval training to my retirement from the Navy in 1965 and beyond, there was little time to spare for hobbies. For a budding artist it could be said they were twenty lost years – though not entirely, as will be made evident.

Specialising as a hydrographic surveyor took me away from the fleet into a world of relatively strange people, who earned their keep mainly in remote parts of the globe, in ships which were unarmed, painted overall in white, with a buff funnel, and operated entirely alone. Yet this was still a branch of the Royal Navy, and the white ensign flew proudly from the mast.

Surveyors tended to work long hours, gathering the survey data during daylight hours and (before computers) during the evening inking-in the details on the collector sheet which, in due course, would be copied to the fair sheet: all a part of the process of producing the navigational chart familiar to mariners throughout the world. This was excellent for developing a keen eye for the lie of the land, and the steady hand needed to plot the survey work, and which led directly to my detailed style as an artist, with landscape subjects as my speciality.

Later, it was all I could do to keep head above water as a lecturer in hydrographic surveying for the offshore oil industry at the North East London Polytechnic, where I learned that teaching is *not* a sinecure, students *are* demanding, and there *was* a textbook to write, since the subject was hitherto covered only by the naval manual.

The time for sketching and painting was severely limited, but by 1972 things had simmered down somewhat, and it was at Rose's suggestion that I enroled for classes at the local technical college. This proved to be exactly what I needed. I was able to refresh my drawing abilities and try my hand at the various painting media before deciding to concentrate on watercolour exclusively.

Catching up with my past...

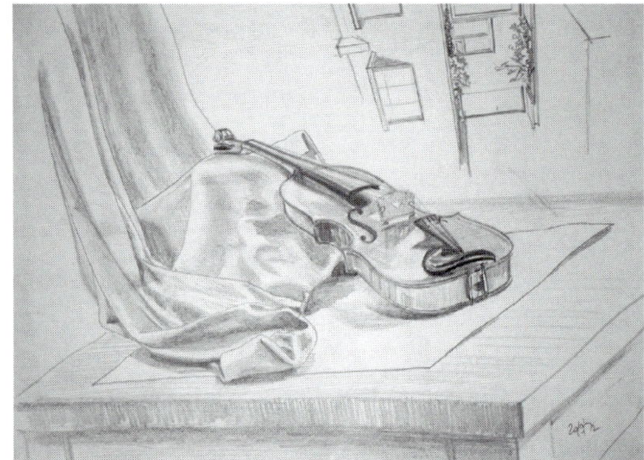

Still Life. Pencil, 1972

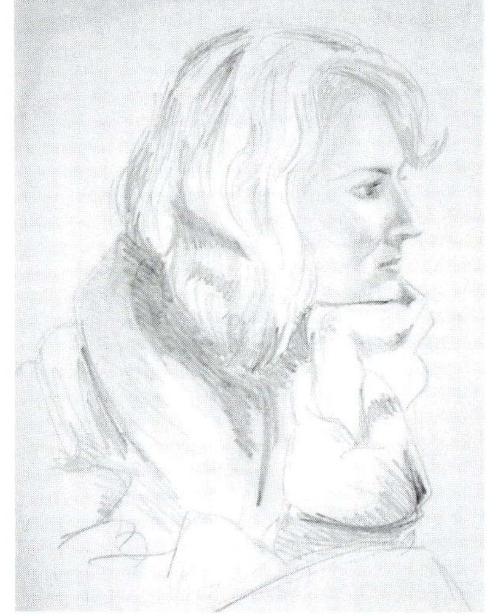

Portrait. Pencils, 1972.

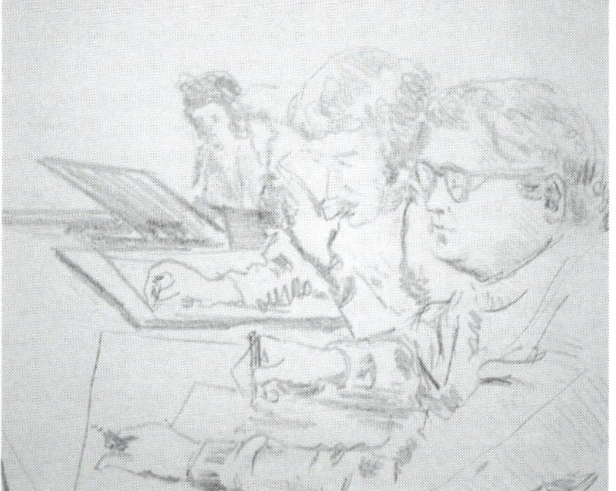

Classmates. Pencil, 1972.

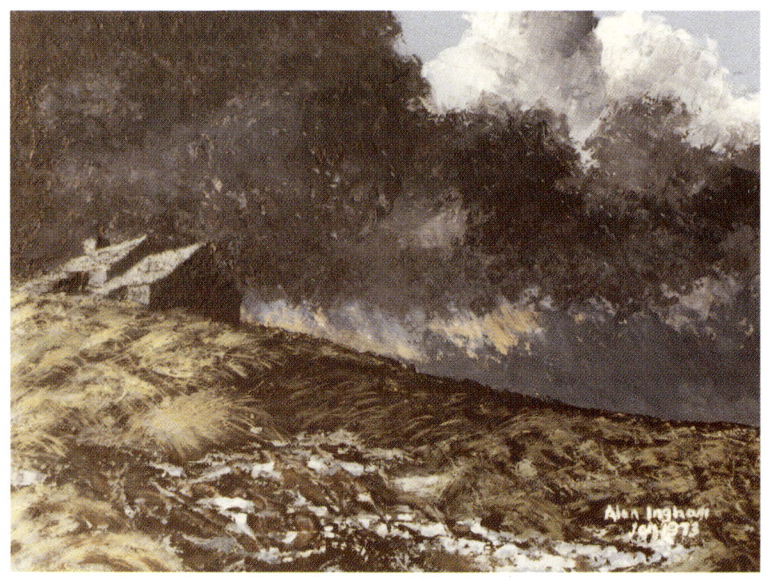

Top Withens. Acrylic, 1973.
One of my tentative sorties into media other than watercolour. The theme is after a photograph by the eminent Bill Brandt.

And still, the caricatures and sketches kept on coming...

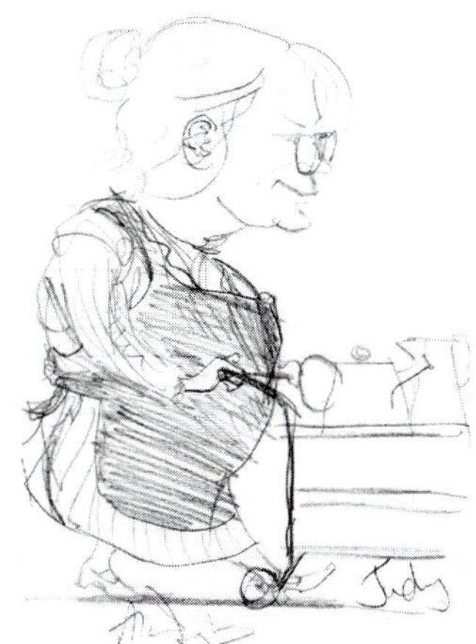

Judy the Tea Lady. Biro, 1996.
Sketch done after my heart operation. One of our favourites at the John Radcliffe Hospital in Oxford – always cheerful and with a heart of gold.

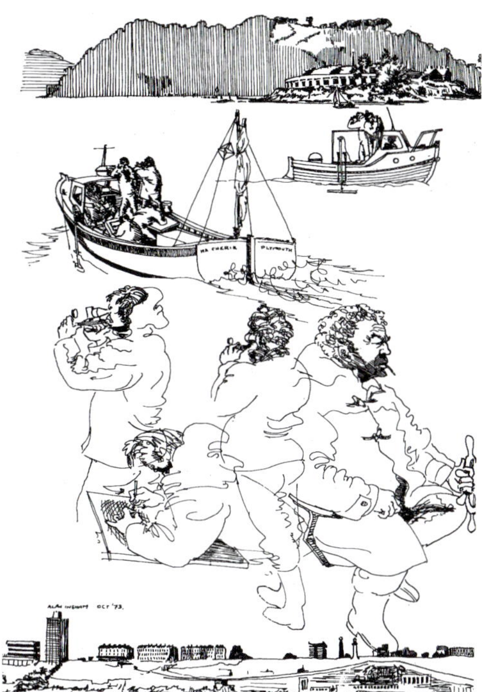

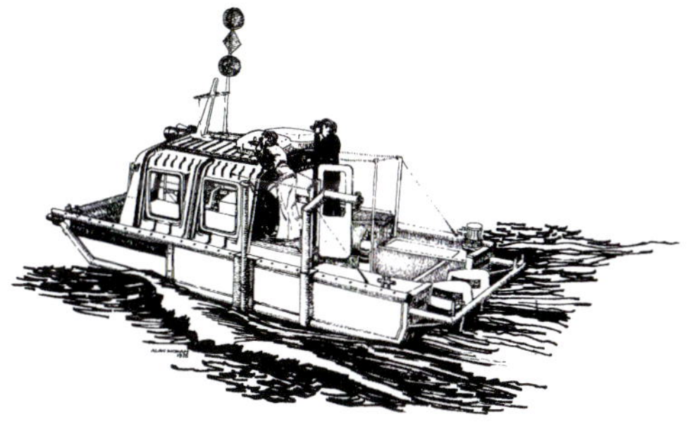

Surveying Training, Plymouth. Pen and Ink, 1973-1975.
Thumbnail sketches made during boatwork in Plymouth Sound for the courses in hydrography at the North East London Polytechnic. The Hydrographic Journal *(which I founded).*

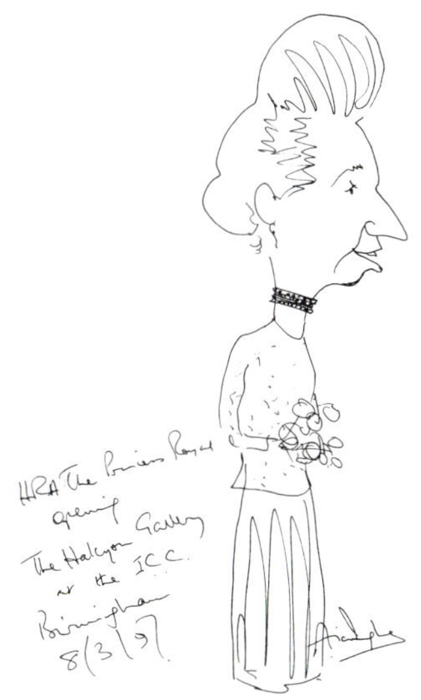

HRH the Princess Royal, Halcyon Gallery. Biro, 1997.
Her Royal Highness officially opened the Halcyon Gallery at the new International Convention Centre, Birmingham, before attending a dinner as President of the Save the Children Fund.

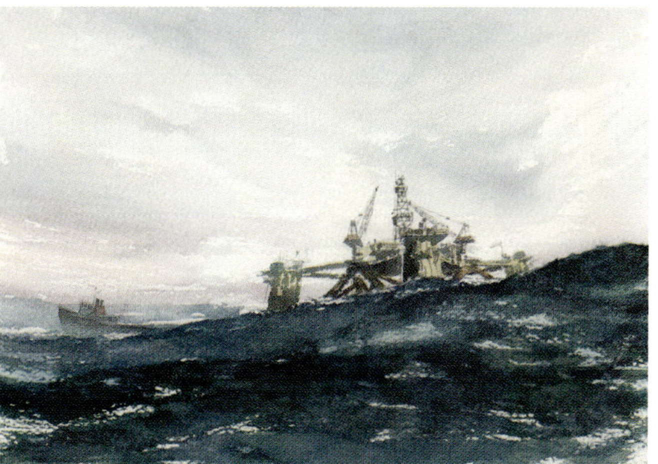

Offshore Oil Rig. Watercolour sketch, 1978.
The offshore hydrocarbons industry was burgeoning, and drilling rigs were venturing into ever-deeper waters. My surveying textbook was published and the second was on the stocks. The courses in hydrography were well subscribed. My spare time work – painting – was going well and, as it turned out, about to become much more successful. This little sketch epitomises these times exactly.

The Professional Years

Over time, the comeback years merged into the professional years as income began to accrue from sales of my paintings at summer fêtes, charity fund-raising events and galleries locally.

In the late 1970s I exhibited at the Mall Galleries in Pall Mall (exhibitions of the Royal Institute of Artists in Watercolour and the Royal Society of British Artists), and one of my paintings was accepted for publication in the prestigious Laing Calendar for 1978.

Came the 1980s, and I found Royle Publications (whose Art Director happened to be Rowland Hilder, the source of my artistic inspiration), and the Granby Gallery found me. Royles began to publish my work on cards, calendars and prints, while the Granby sold my originals. Both promoted my career beyond my most optimistic expectations.

By 1984 I was able to turn to painting full time. Rose and I moved to Gloucestershire and were captivated by the beauty of the Cotswold villages and farms, which were immediately included, along with the north country lakes, dales and peaks, among my favourite hunting grounds for painting subjects.

Further exhibitions, promotions and publishing activity followed in 1989 when I approached the Halcyon Gallery and its associated publishing company Washington Green in Birmingham.

My first limited edition prints *Easter Miracle* and *November Skies* were published in 1990, and my book *Under A Watercolour Sky* in 1996.

Less happily in 1996, and again in 2001-2, my enjoyable lifestyle was jolted by the need for surgery. As ever, such setbacks are also opportunities, in my case to take stock of life as an artist, husband, father and grandfather, and see things in perspective. The notes given when leaving hospital to recover at home urged one to 'take life easy... have a nap or take a stroll... *paint a picture*.' Right on!

I was then in my late sixties. Throughout my life I had been driven to succeed and prosper, but now I found myself amenable to this new situation. I was eager to experiment (tentatively) instead of sticking to 'safe' subjects and a style that would win ready sales, and to take my time. The pursuit of perfection should not be hurried!

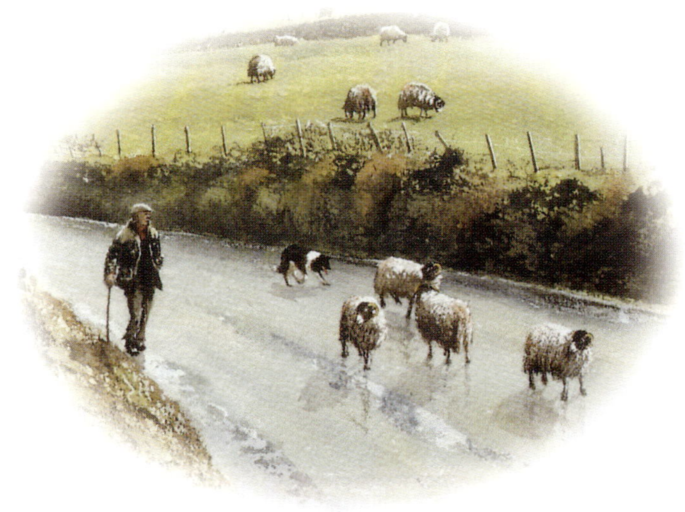

Selection from my Calendar Collection

1979–1988

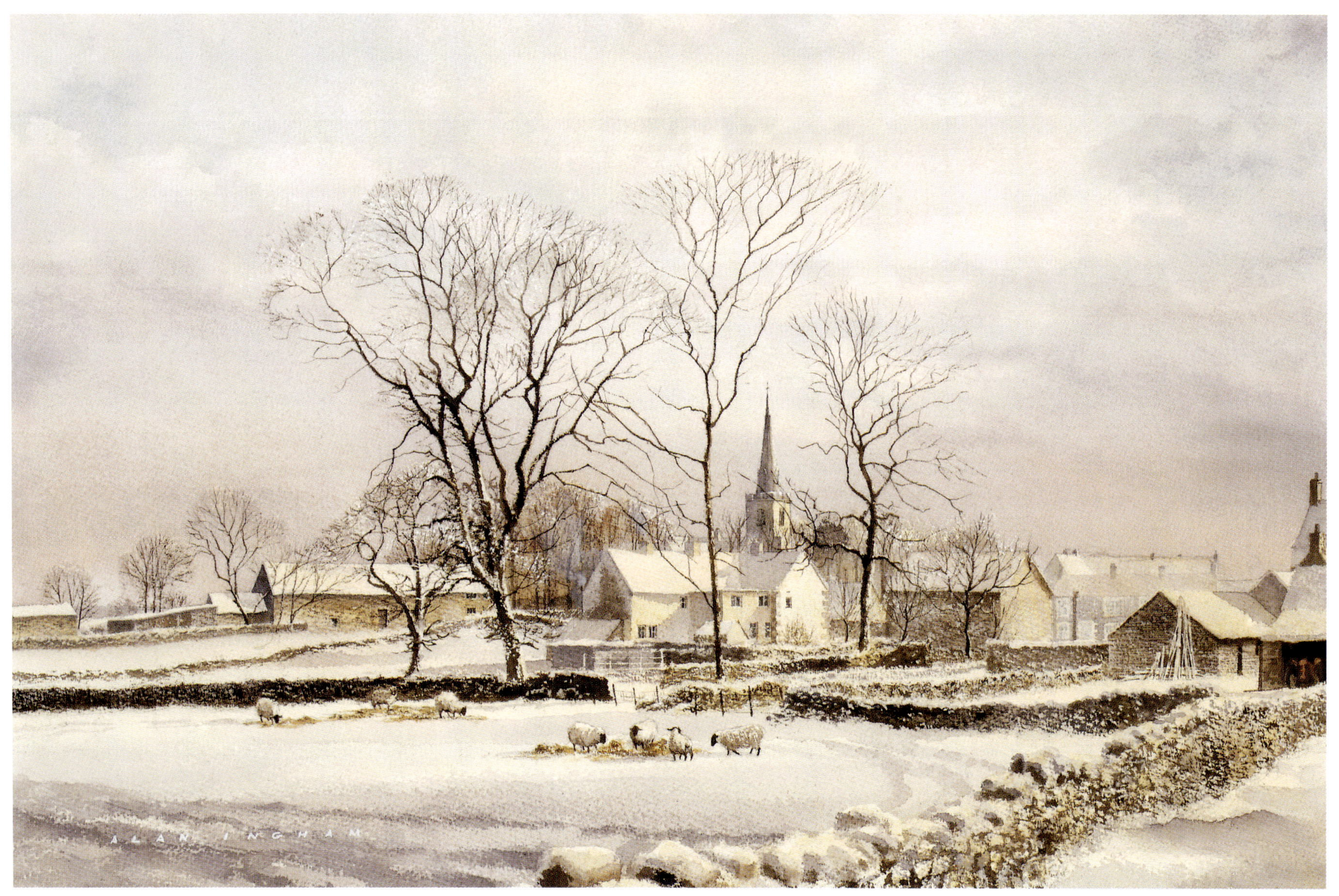

Winter Sunshine, Monyash, Derbyshire, 1986.

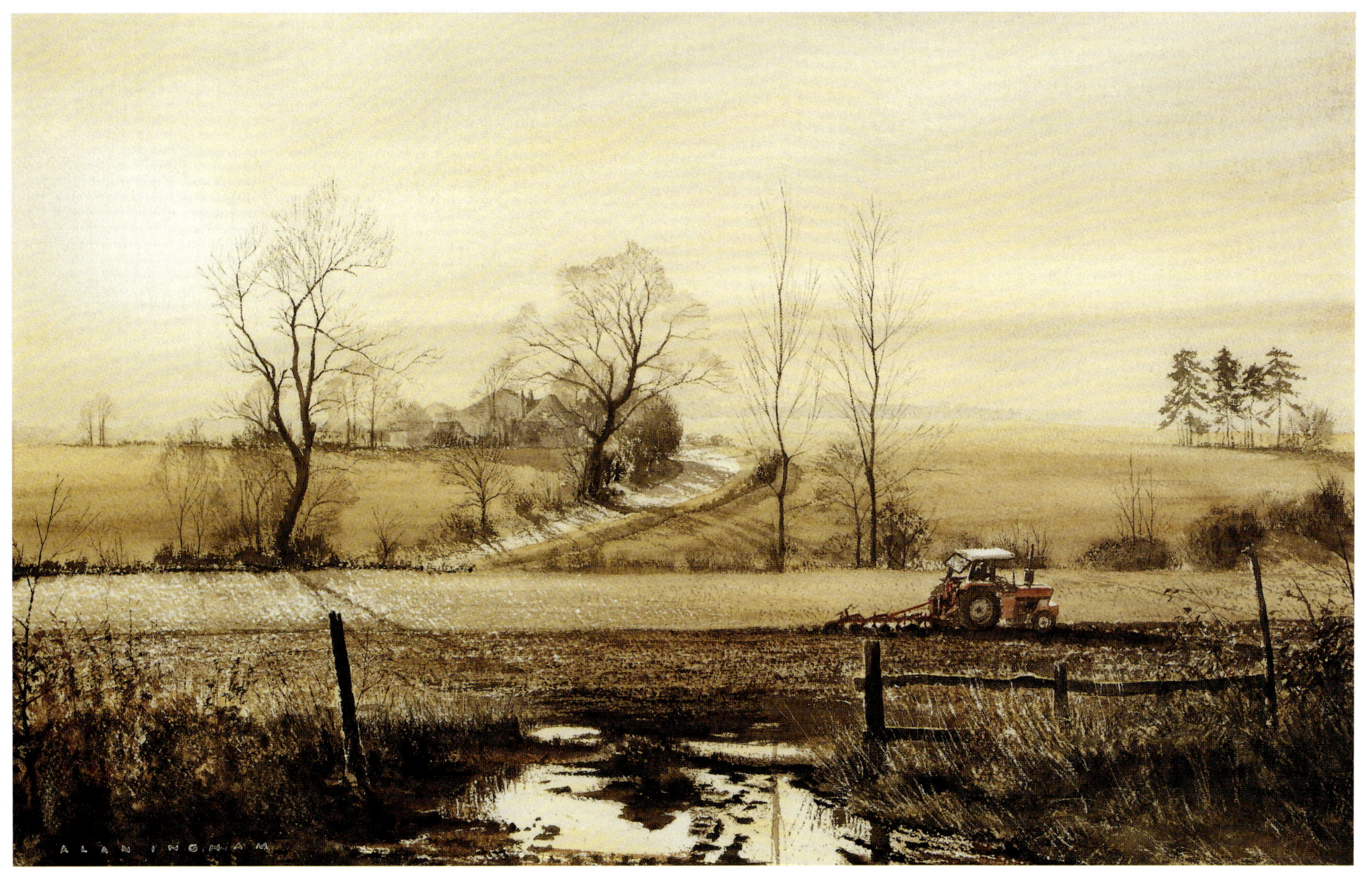

Wenlocks Lane, Essex, 1989.

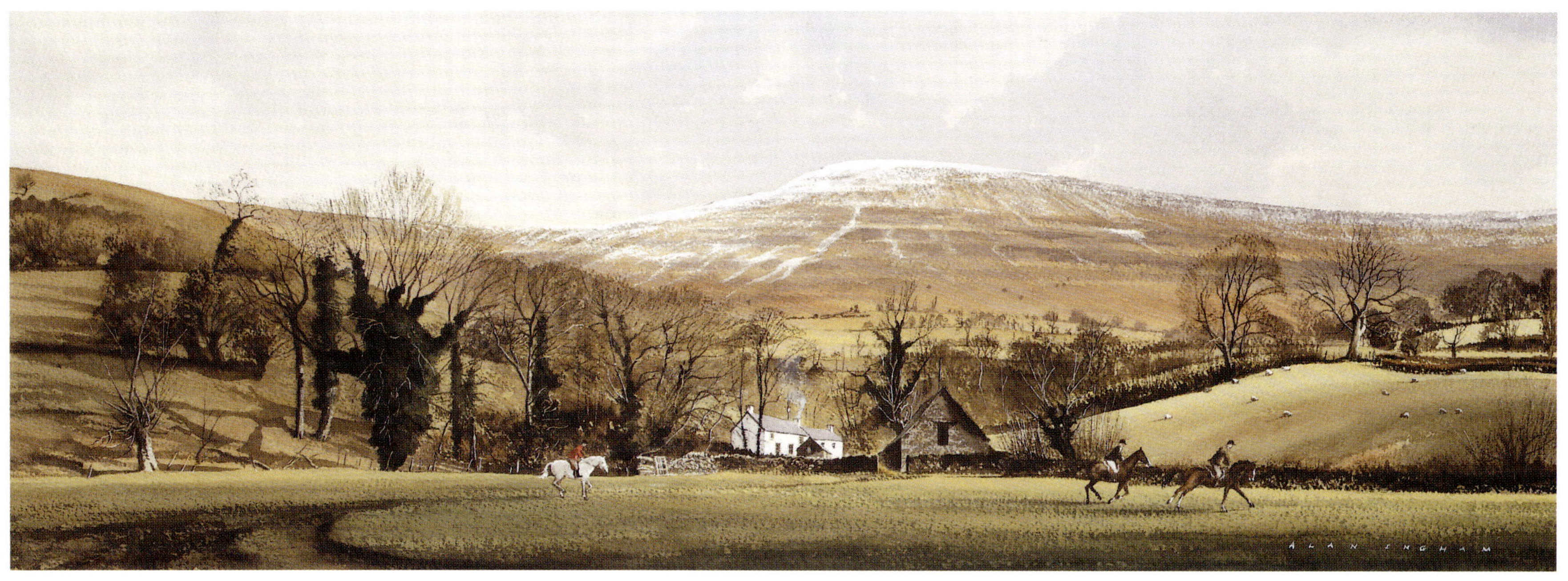

With the Sun on their Backs, Powys, Wales, 1990.

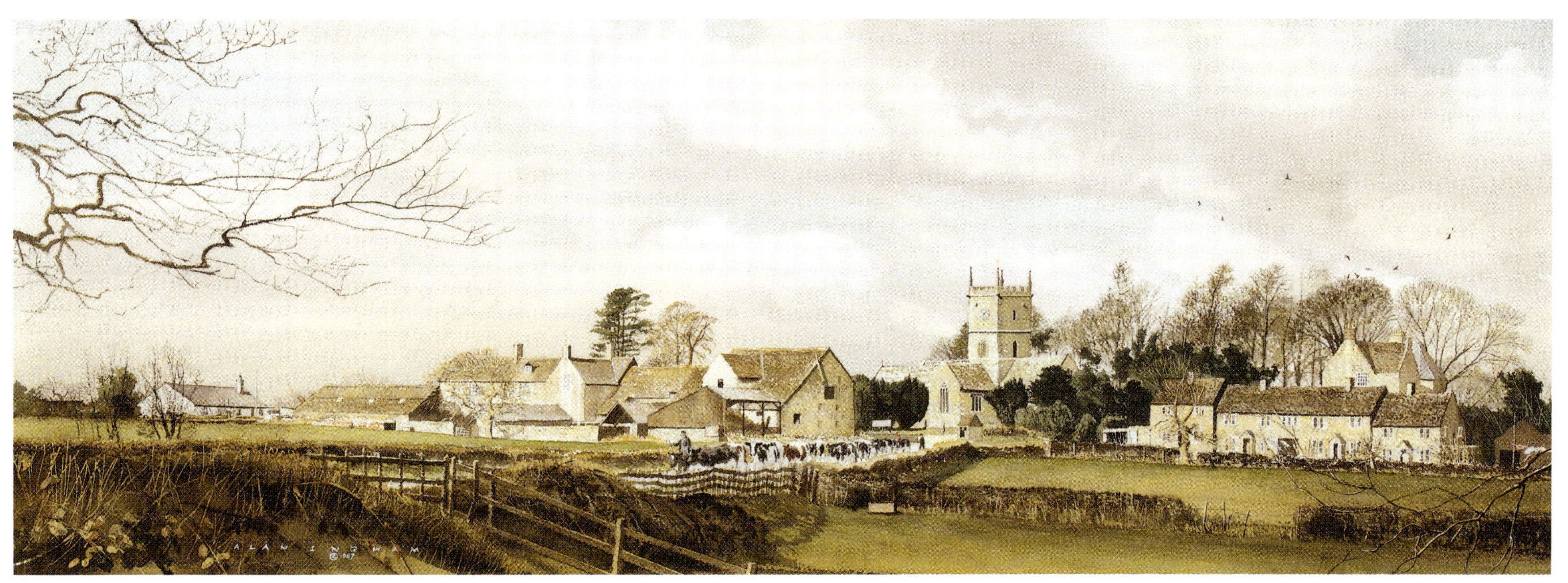

Staunton, Gloucestershire, 1991.

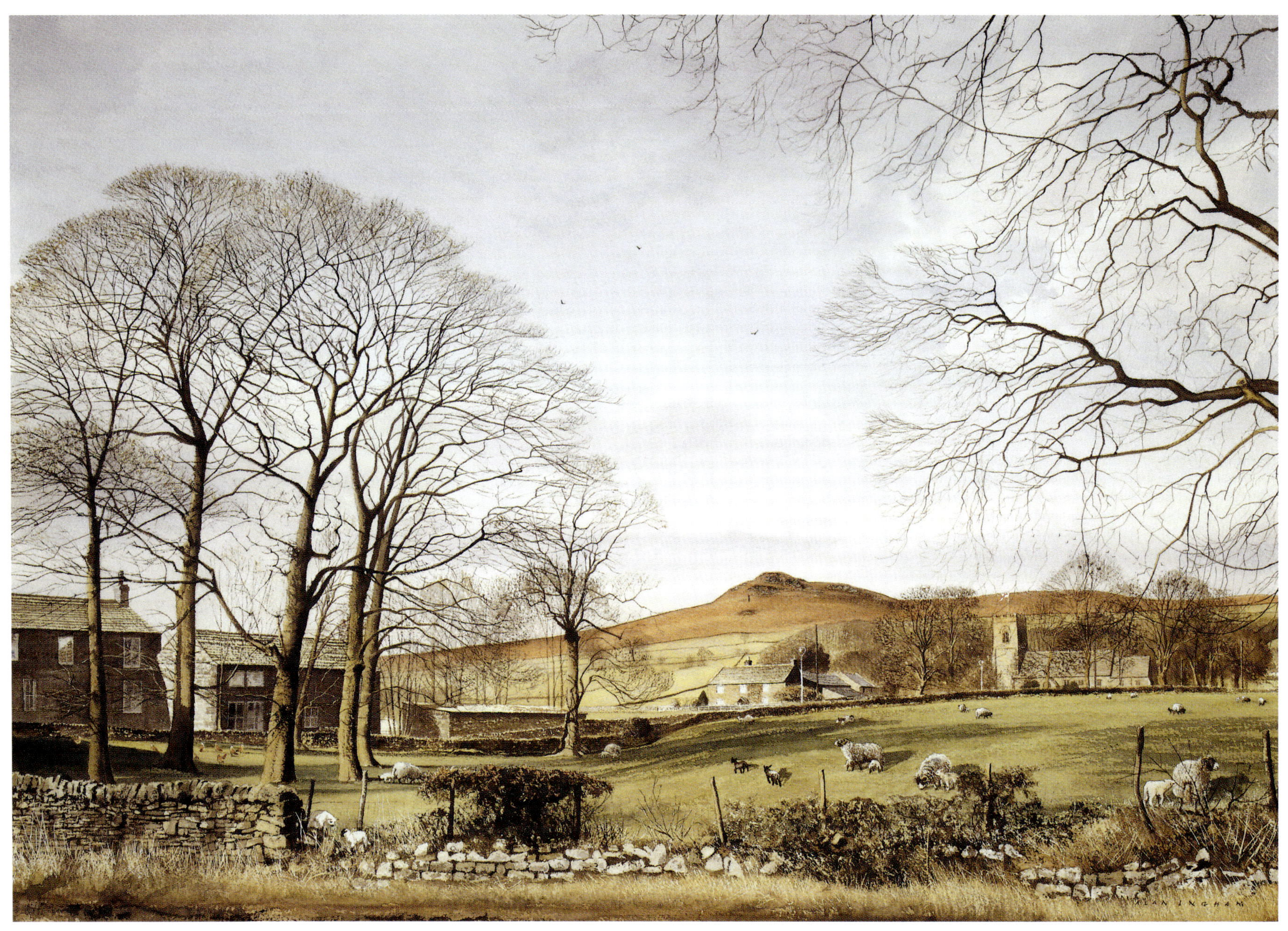

Embsay Crag, North Yorkshire, 1992.

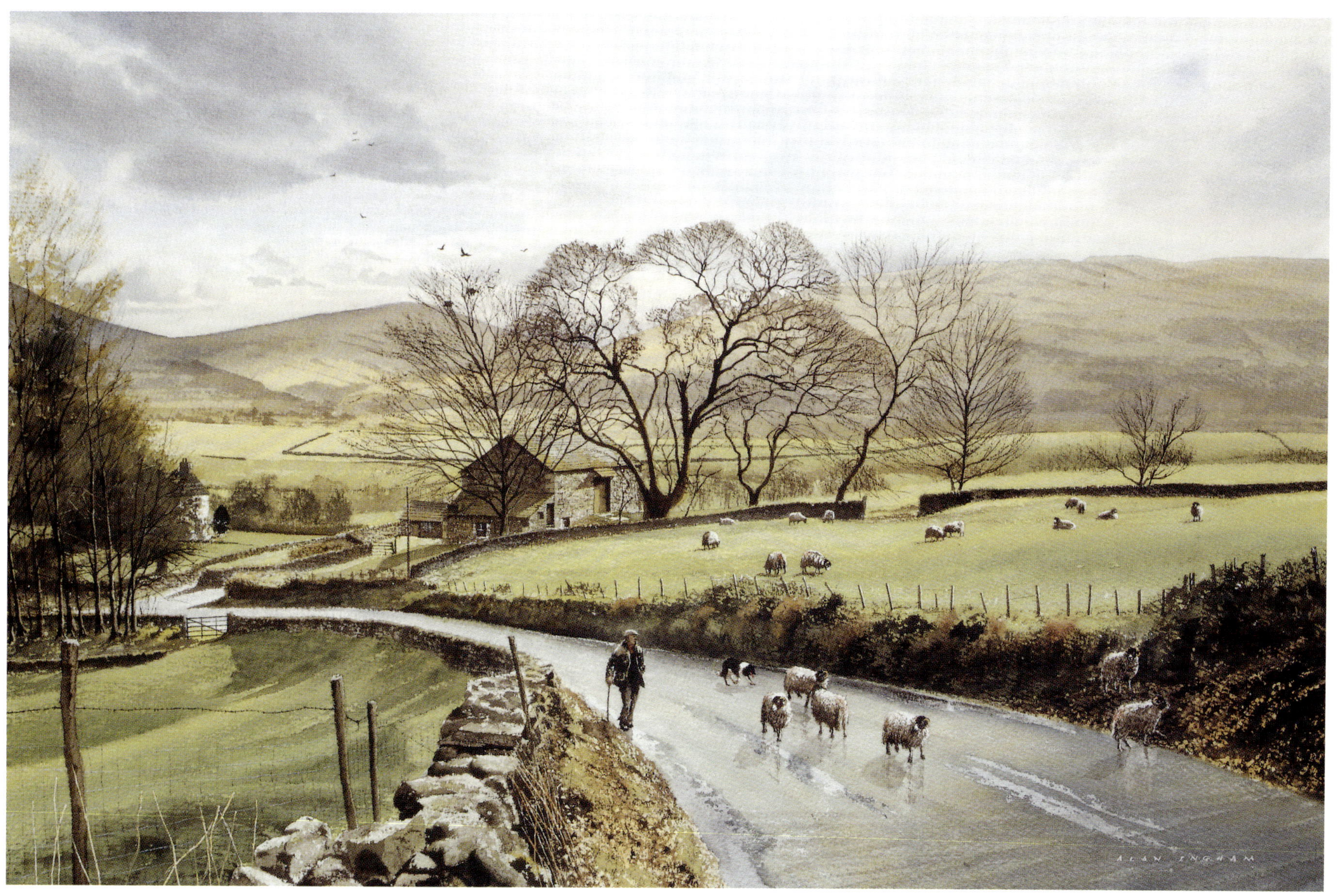

Rounding up the Strays, Whitehall Farm, near Sedburgh, Cumbria, 1994.

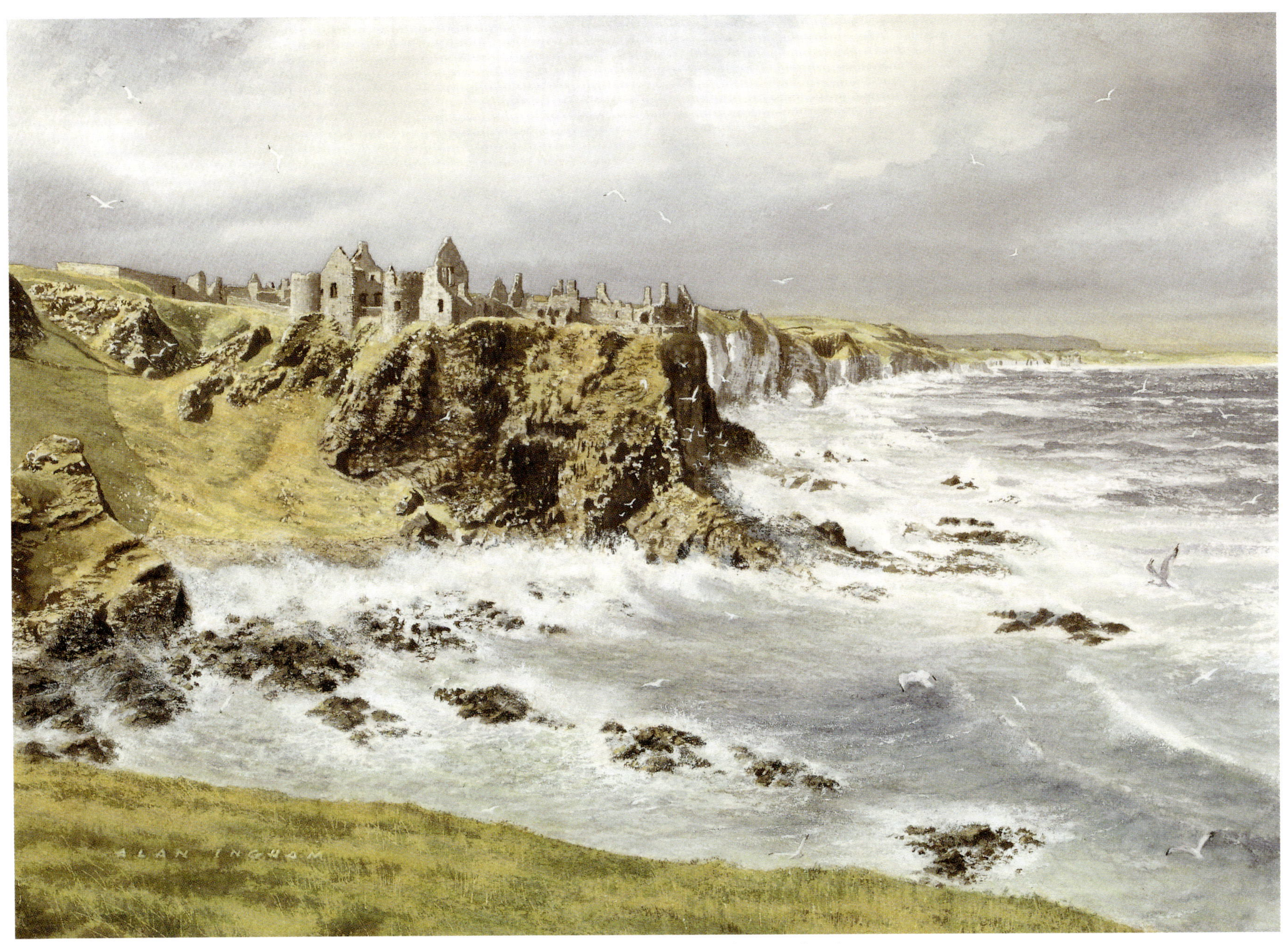

Dunluce Castle, County Antrim, Northern Ireland, 1993.

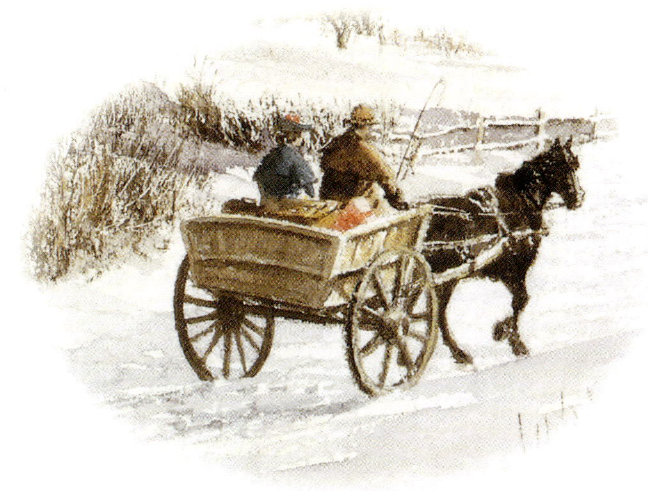

Selection from my Card Collection

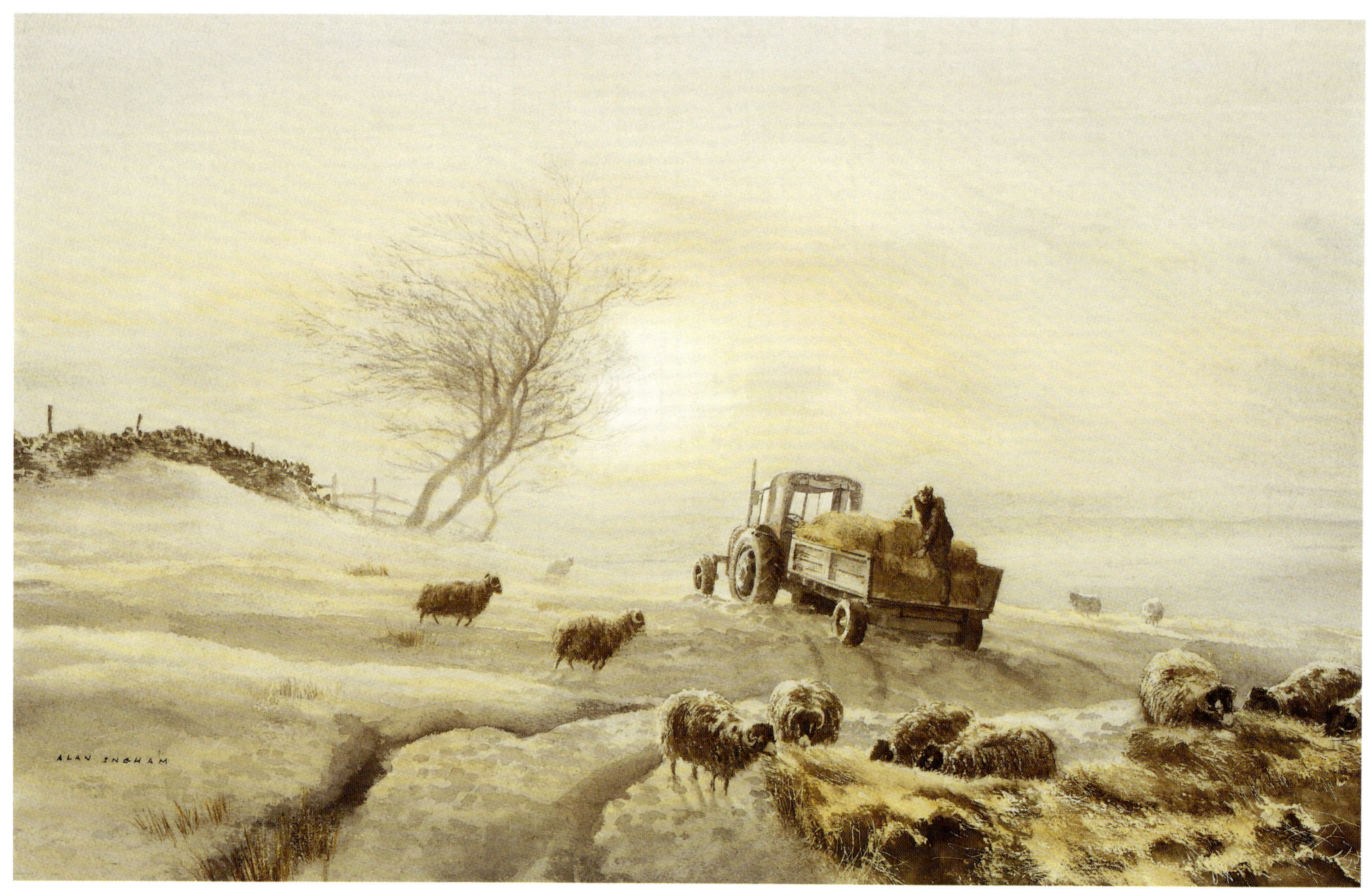

Moorland Feast, North Yorkshire, 1979.

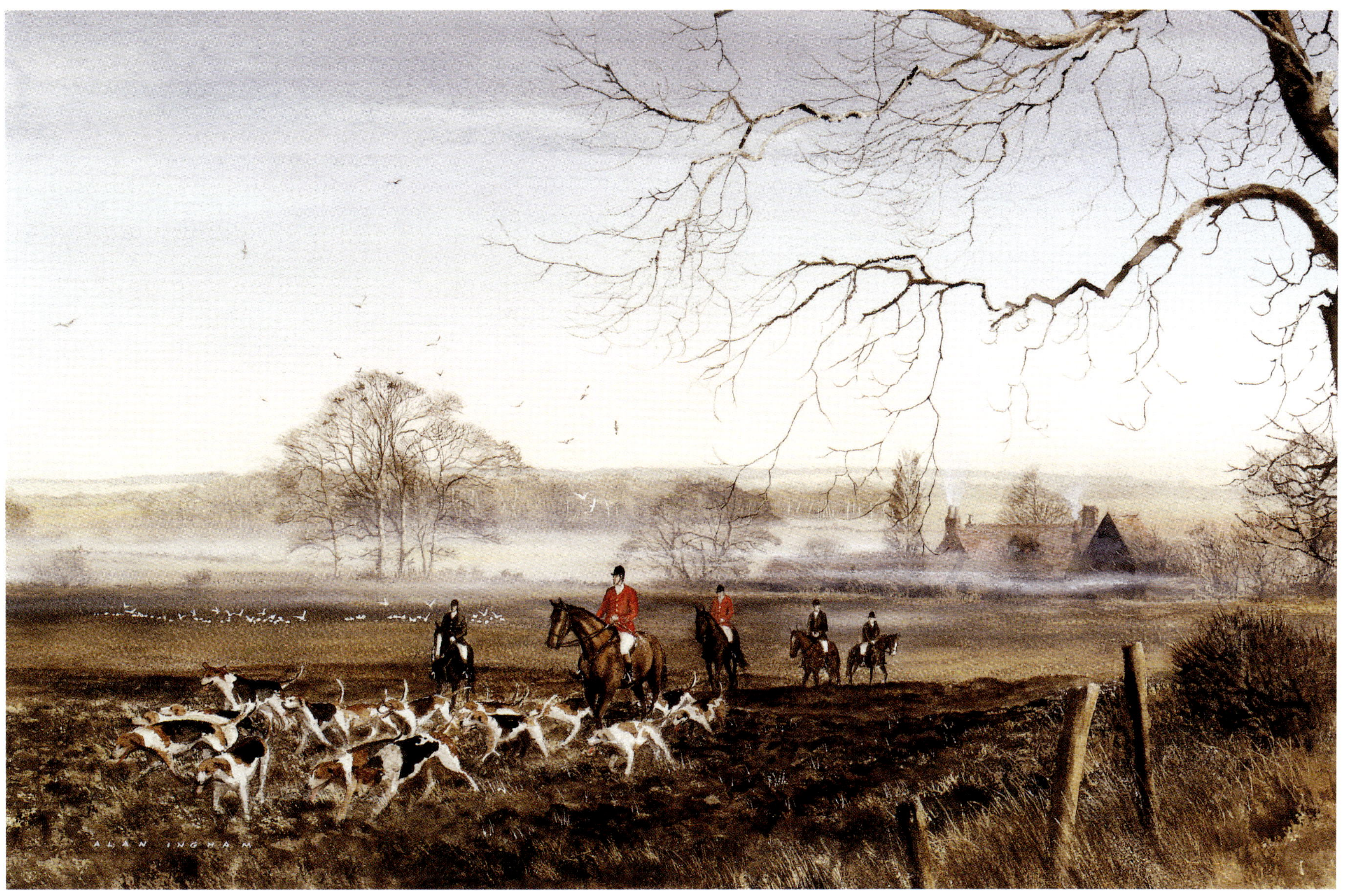

The Scent is Lost, Roding Valley, Essex, 1980.

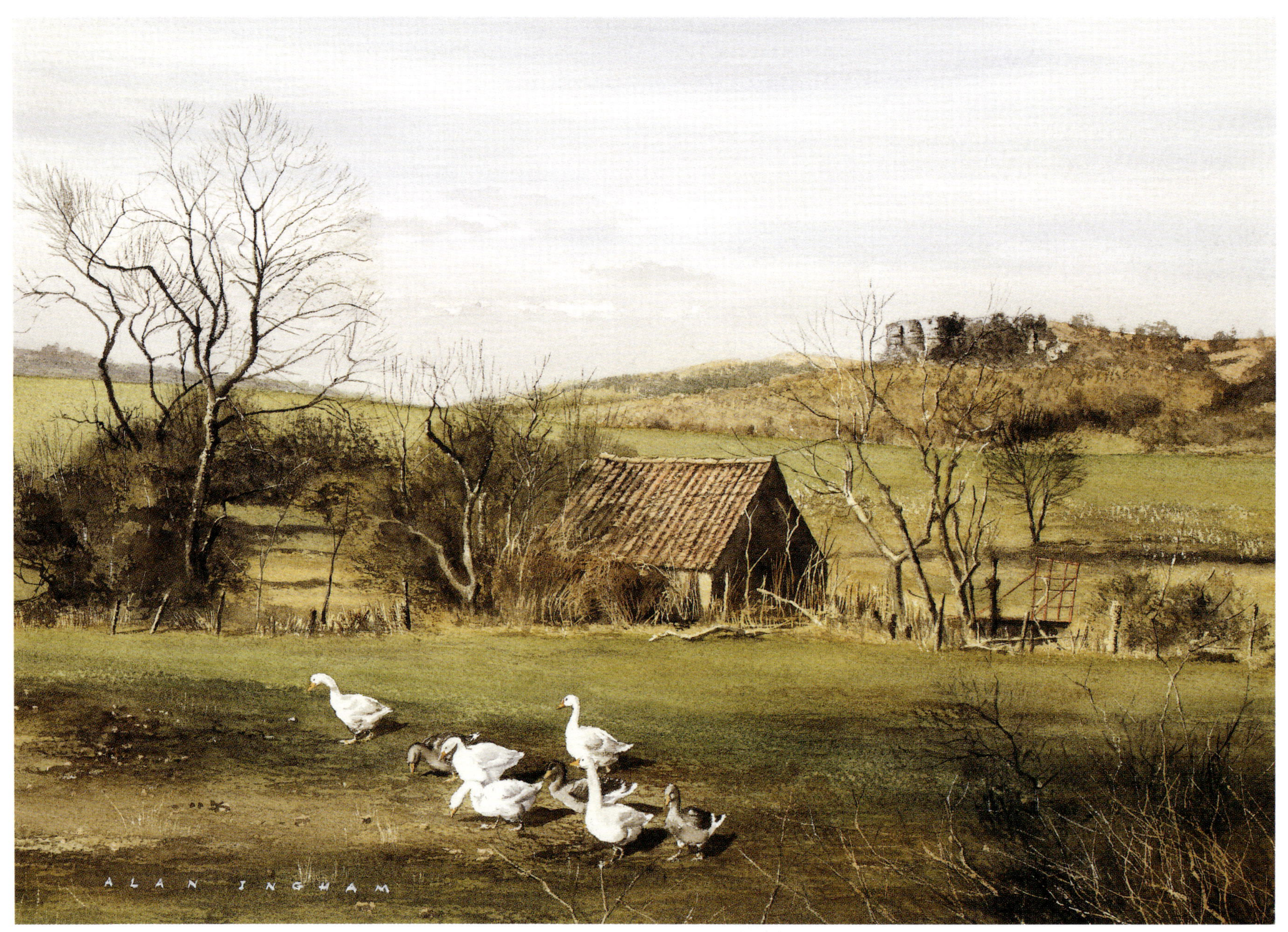

Eagle Tor, Derbyshire, 1984.

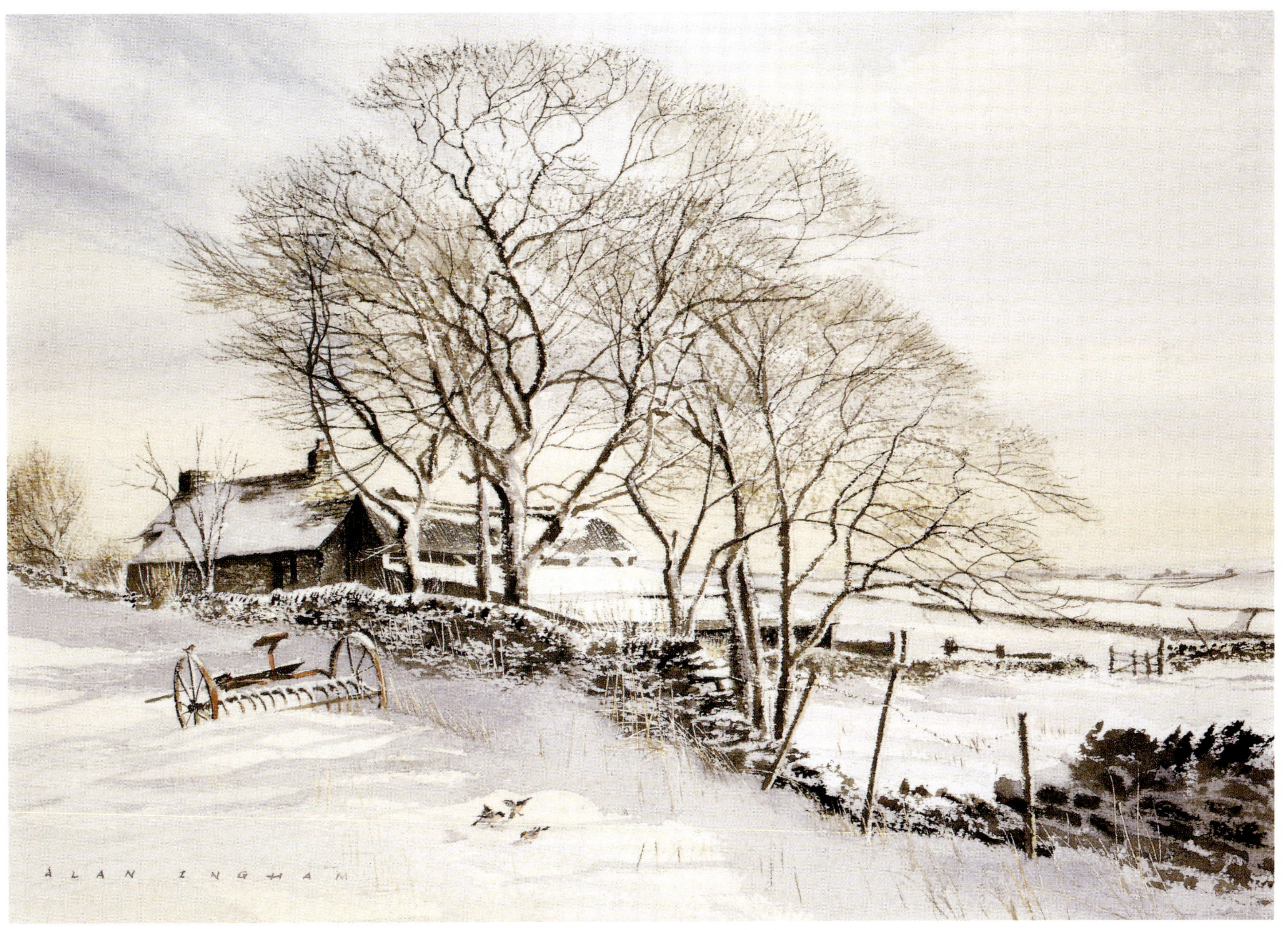

Stonelow Flat Farm, Eastmore, Derbyshire, 1984

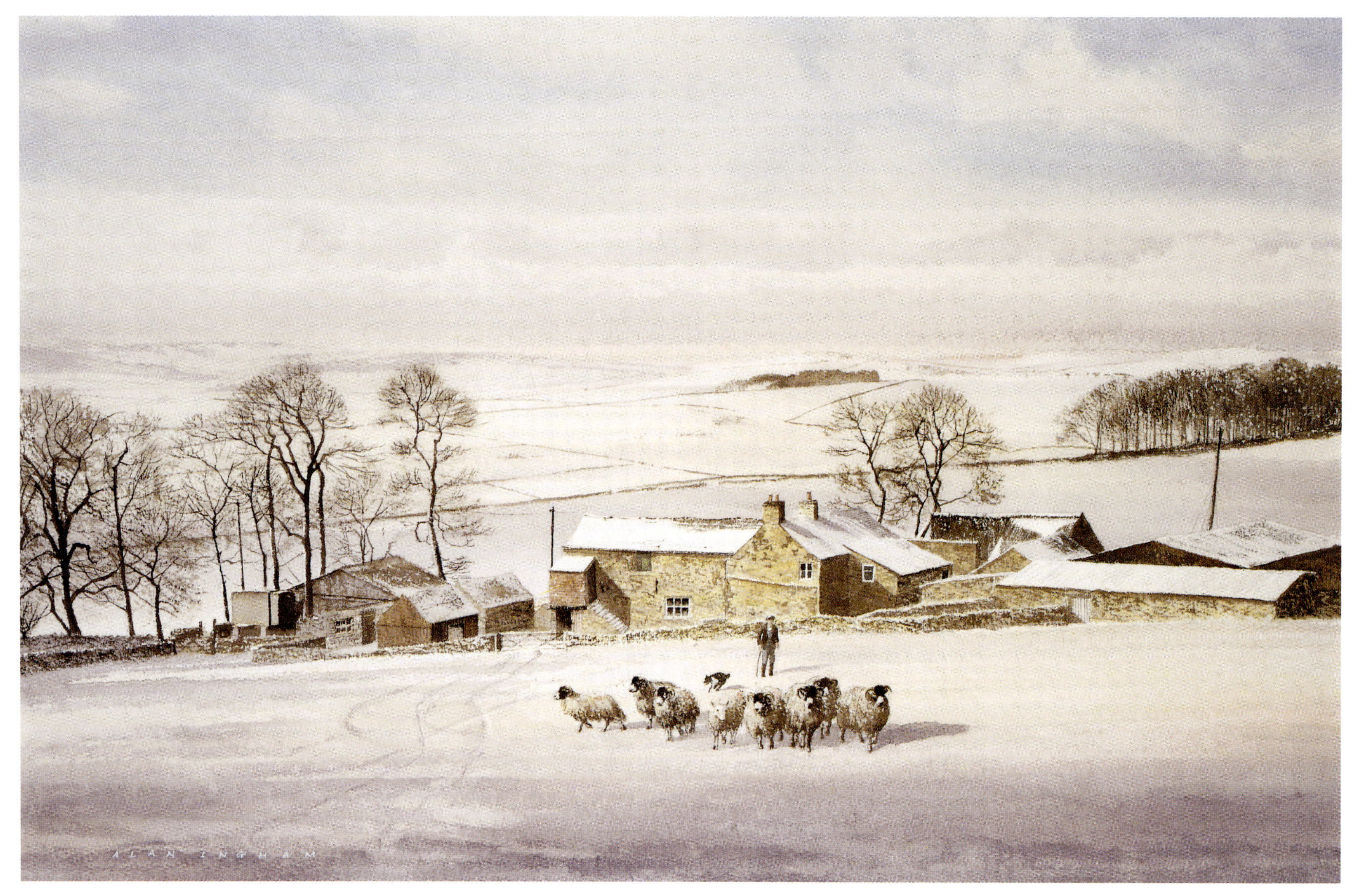

Moscar Farm, Parsley Hay, Derbyshire, 1984.

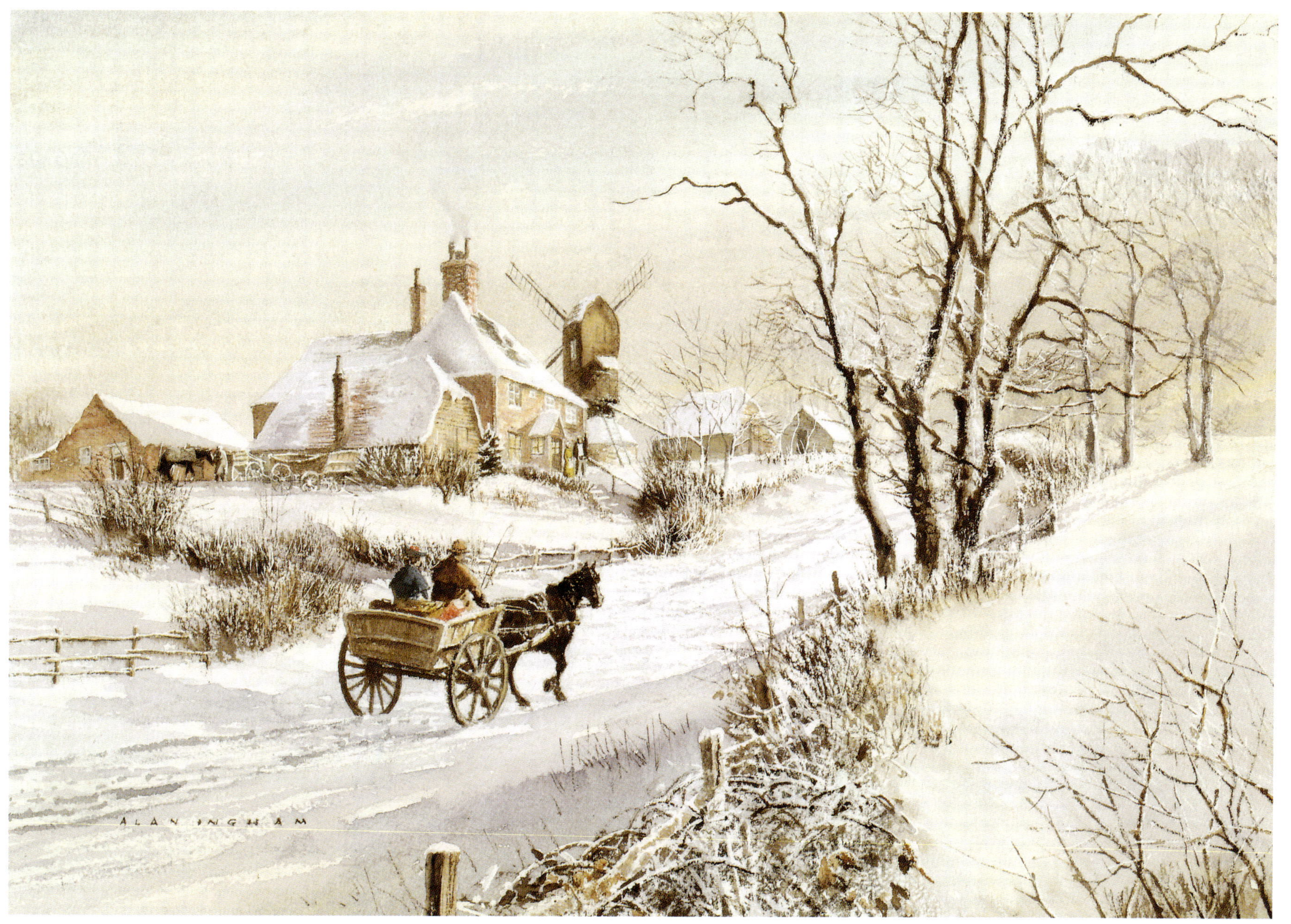

Snow Scene with Pony and Trap, Essex, 1984.

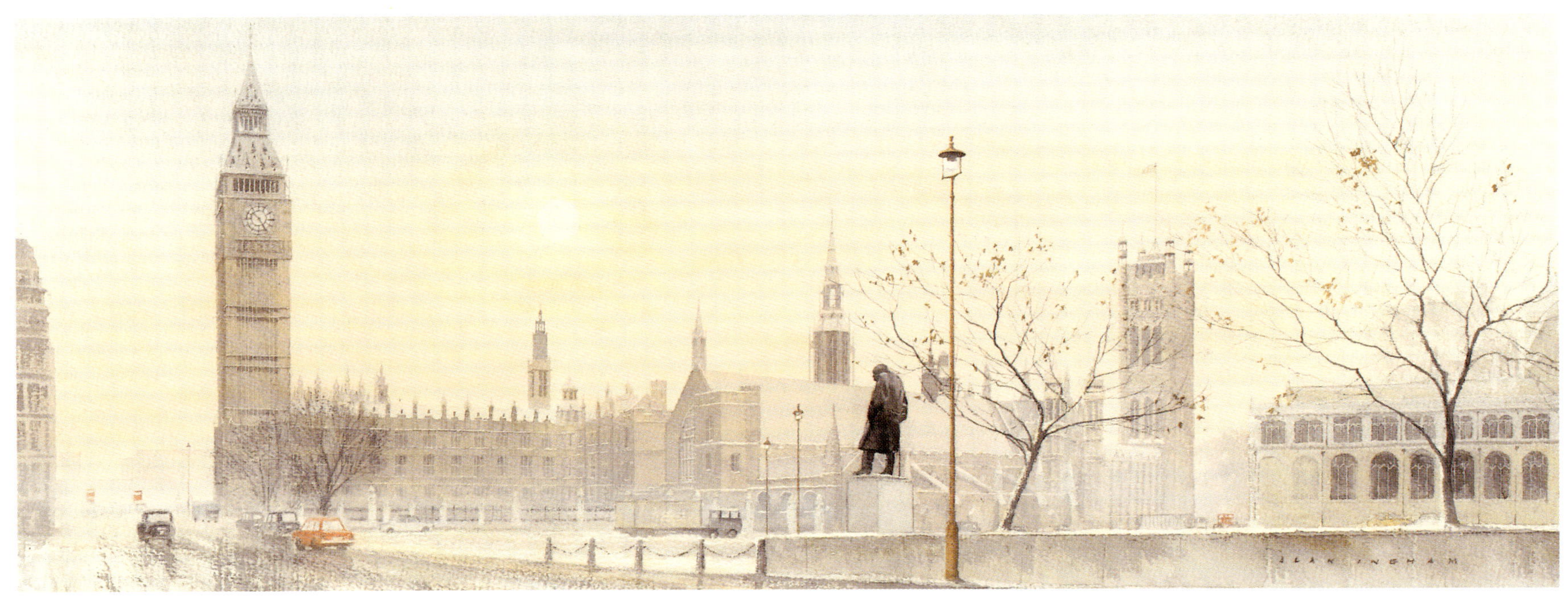

'Churchill', Parliament Square, London, 1985.

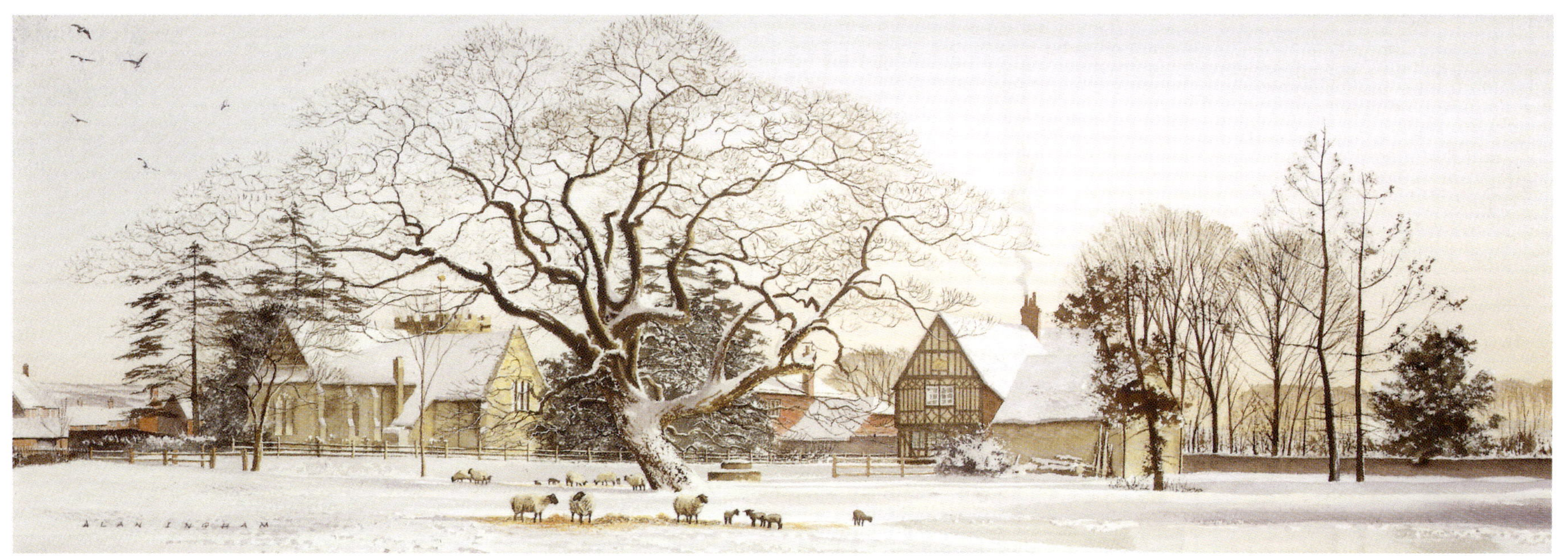

The Old Walnut Tree, Staverton, 1985.

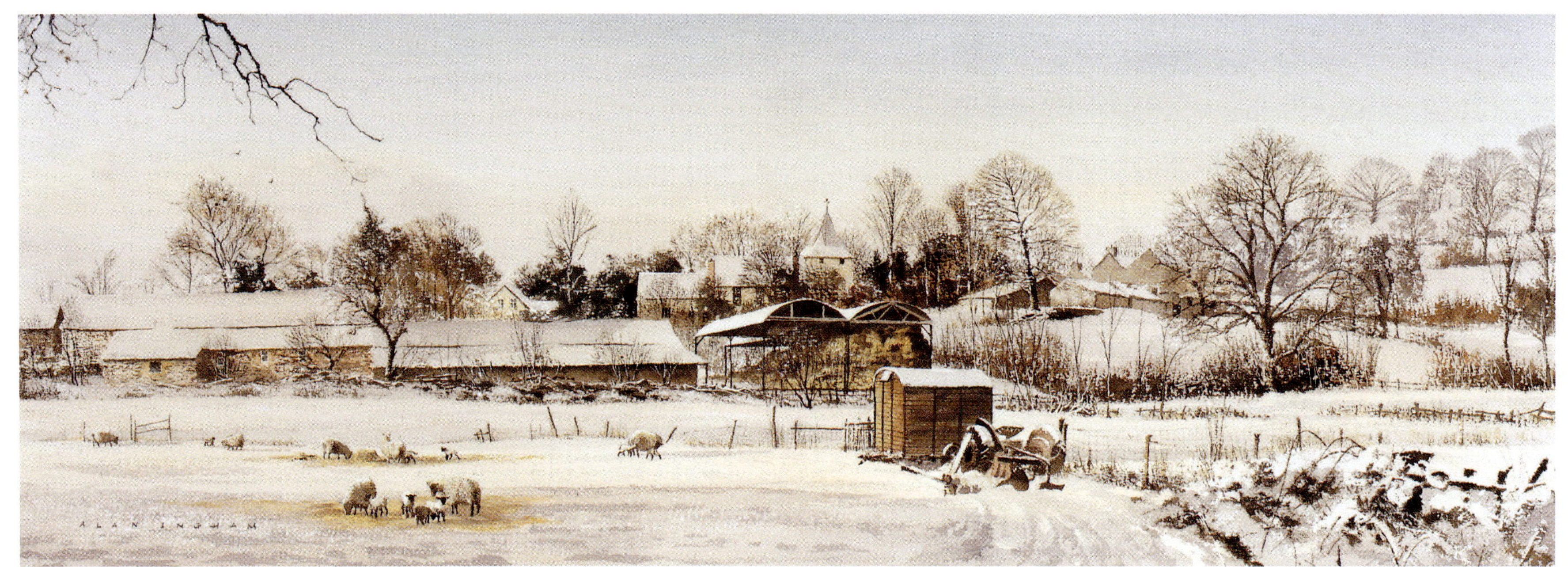

Christmas Lambs, Llanfilo, Powys, 1985.

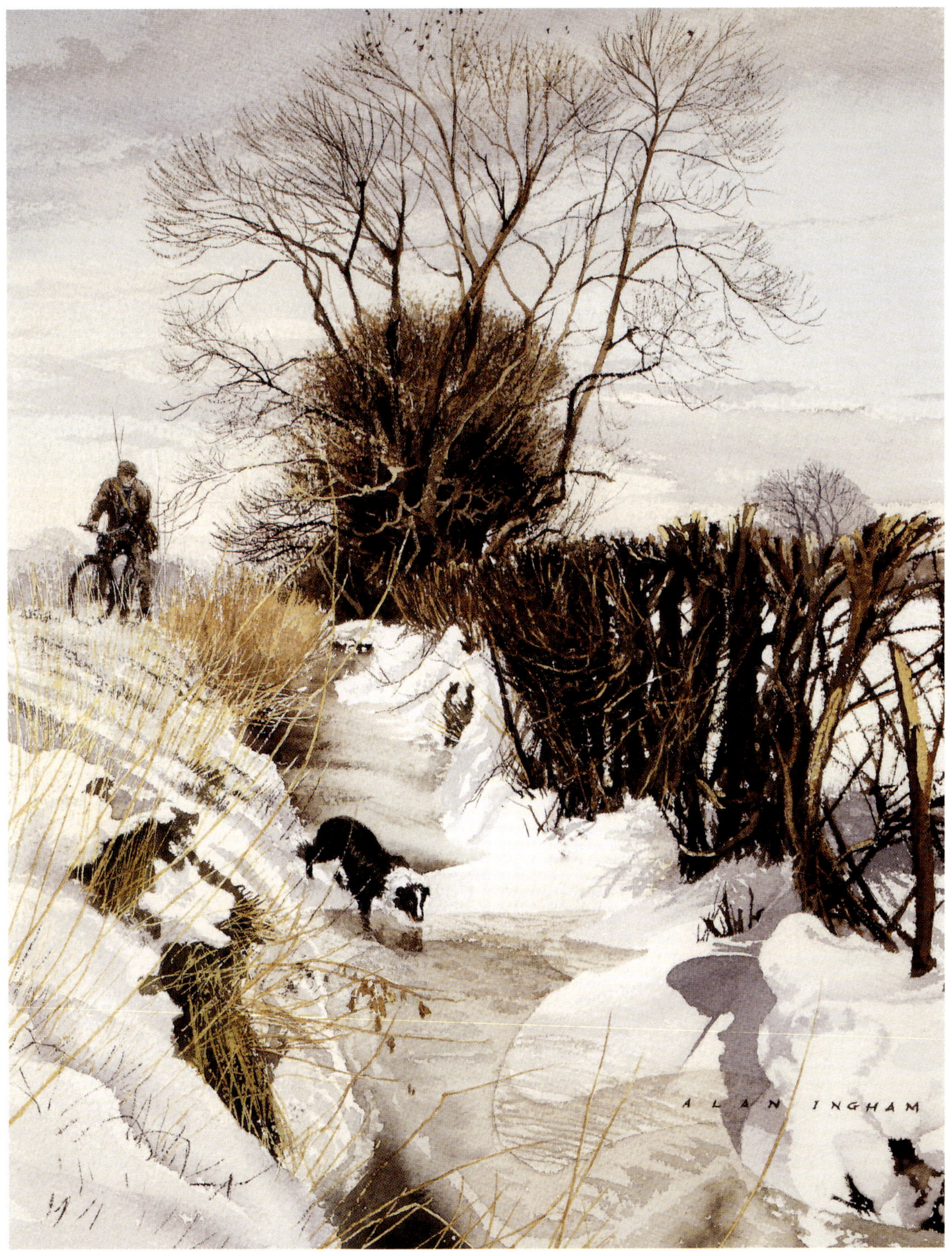

A Quick Drink on the Way Home, 1985.

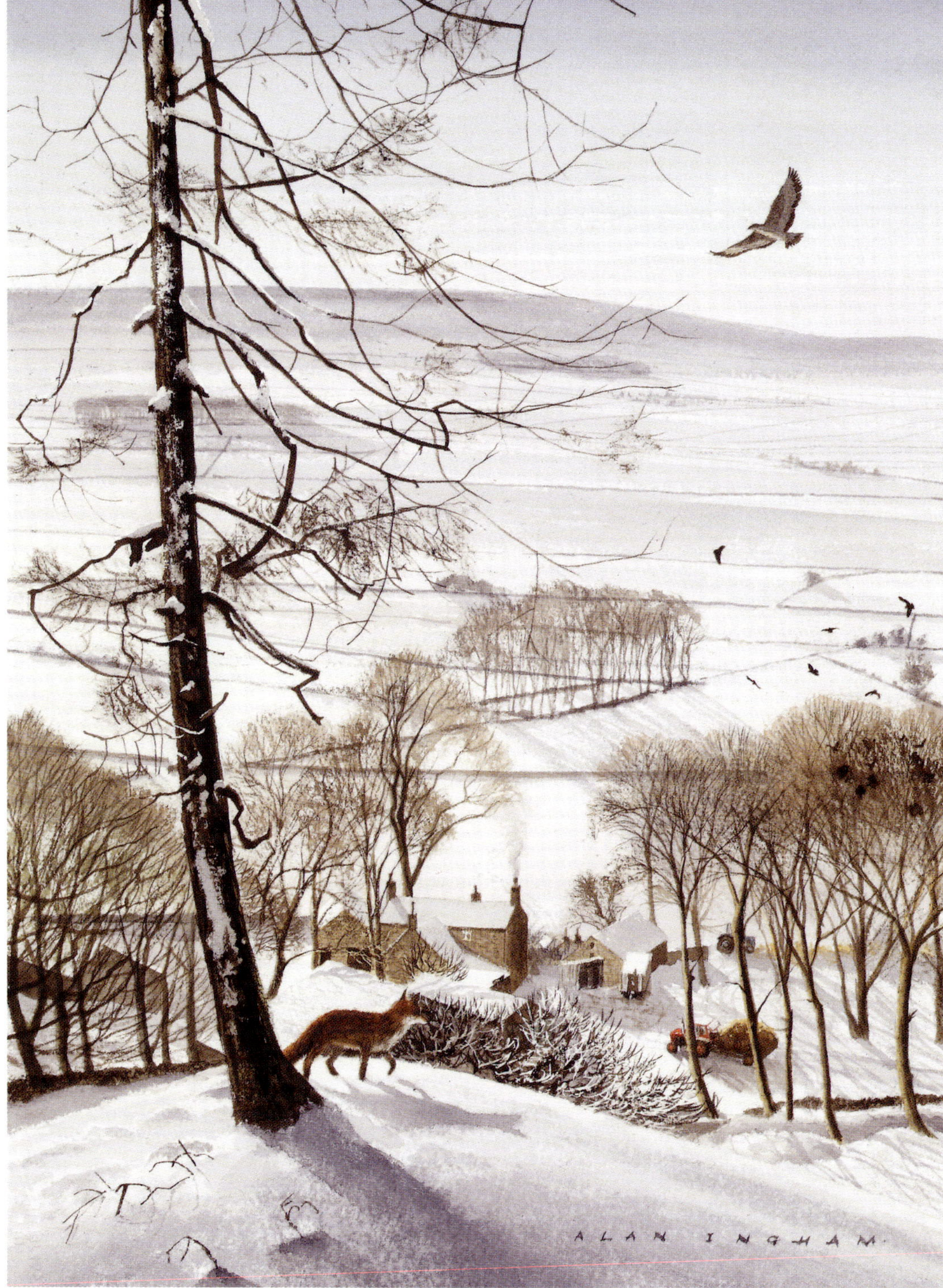

Shepherd's Park Farm, Foolow, Derbyshire, 1987.

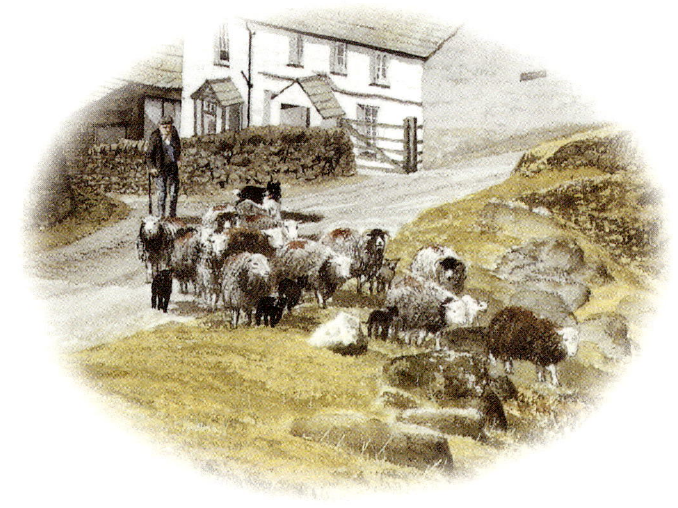

The Print Collection, Royles Publisher

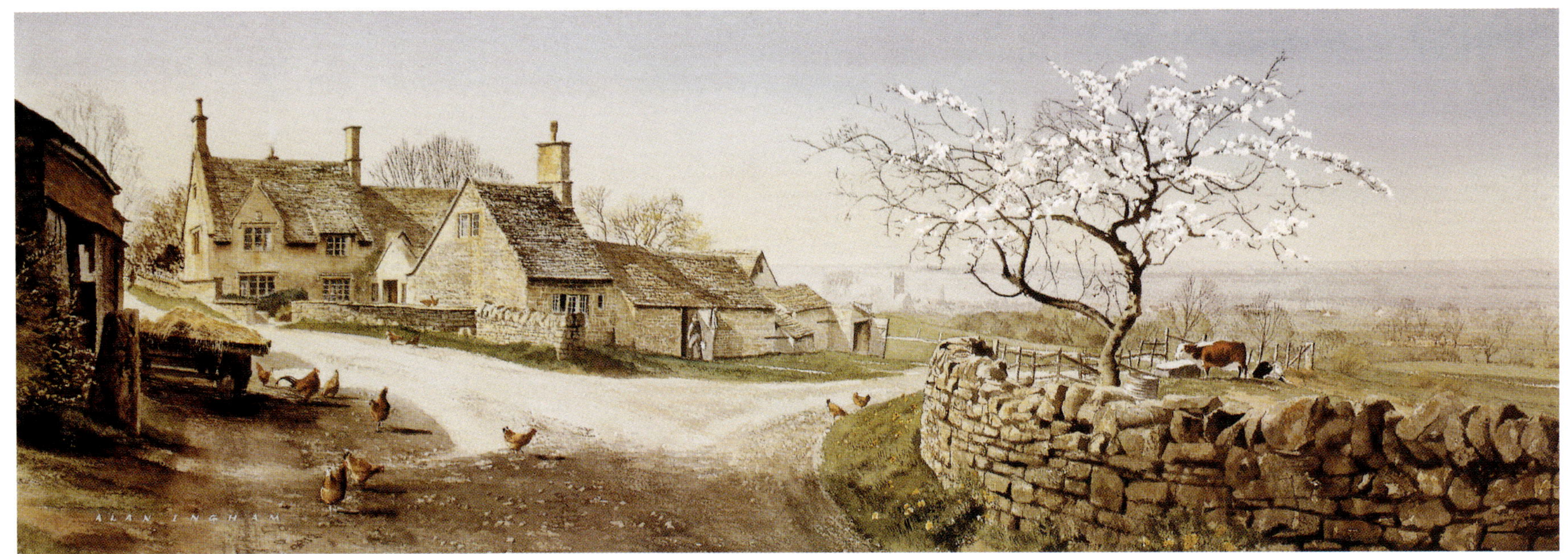

Upper Wall Farm, Saintbury, Gloucestershire, 1985.

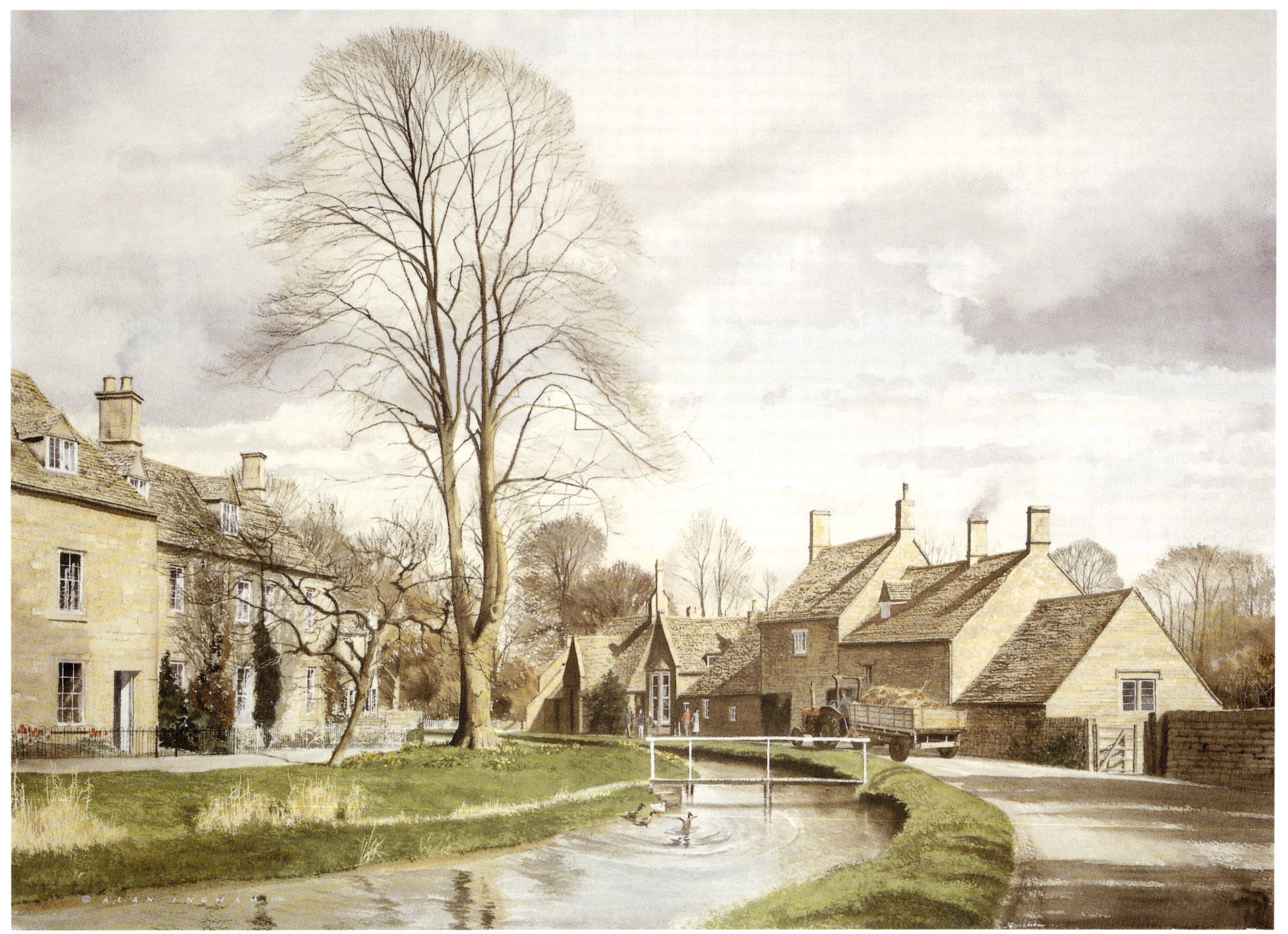

Cotswold Spring, Lower Slaughter, Gloucestershire, 1985.

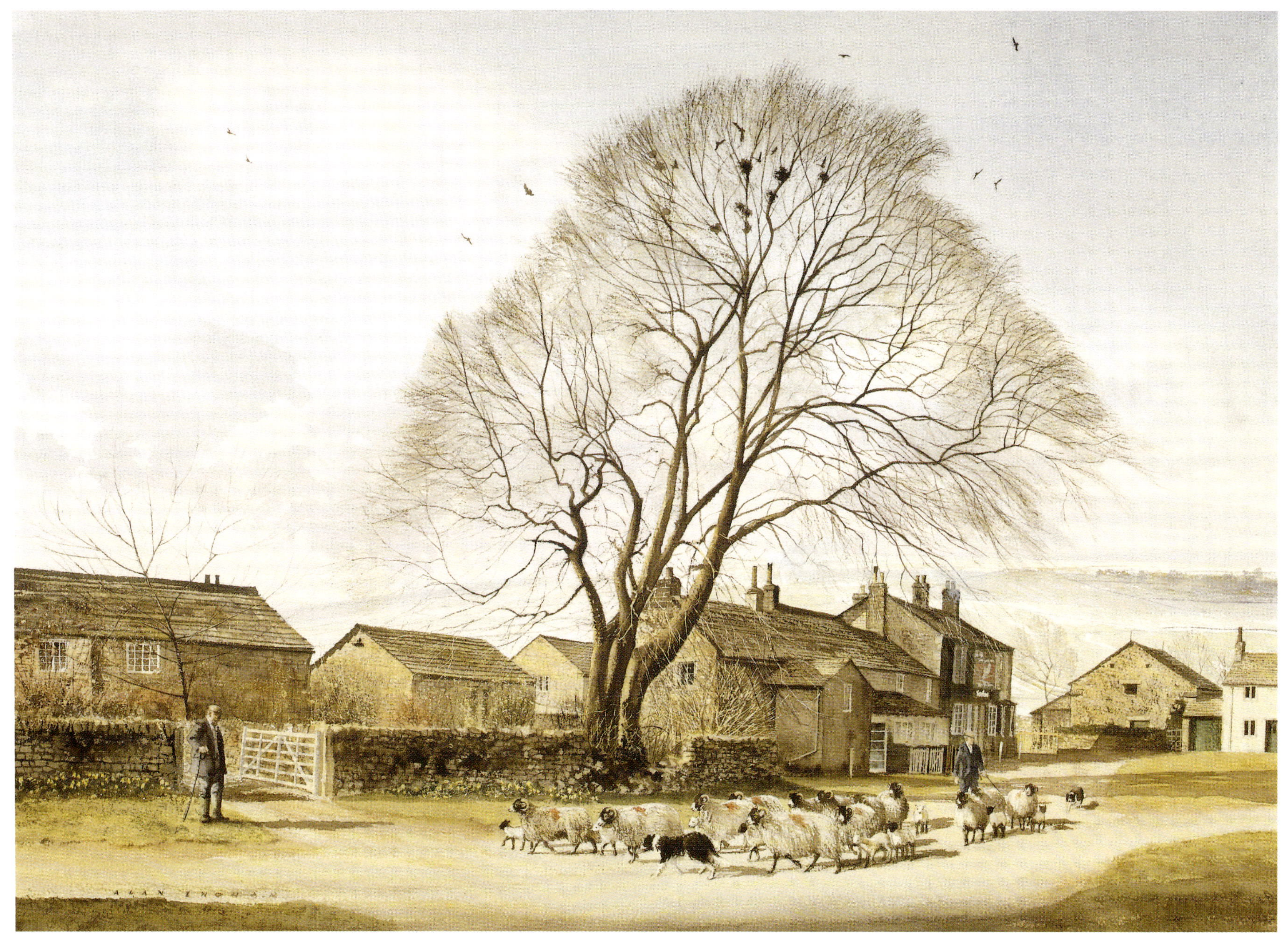

Spring in the Dales, Arncliffe, North Yorkshire, 1987.

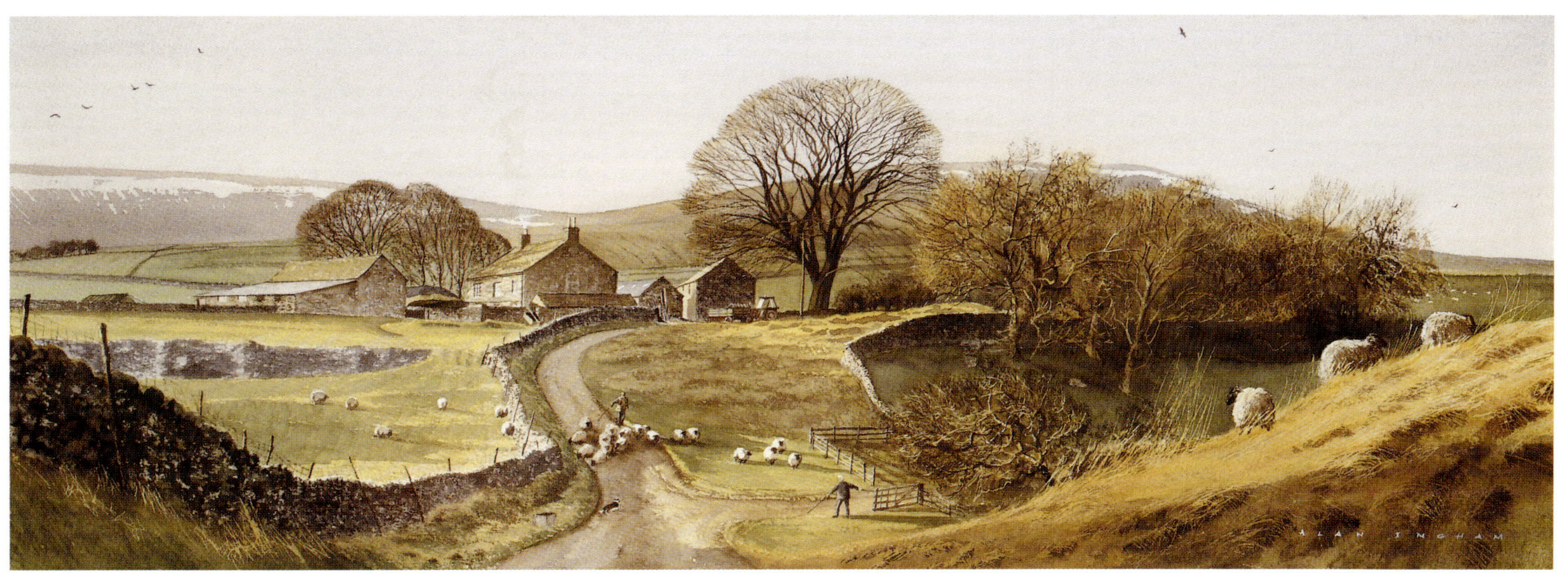

Evening's Last Light, Selside, North Yorkshire, 1988.

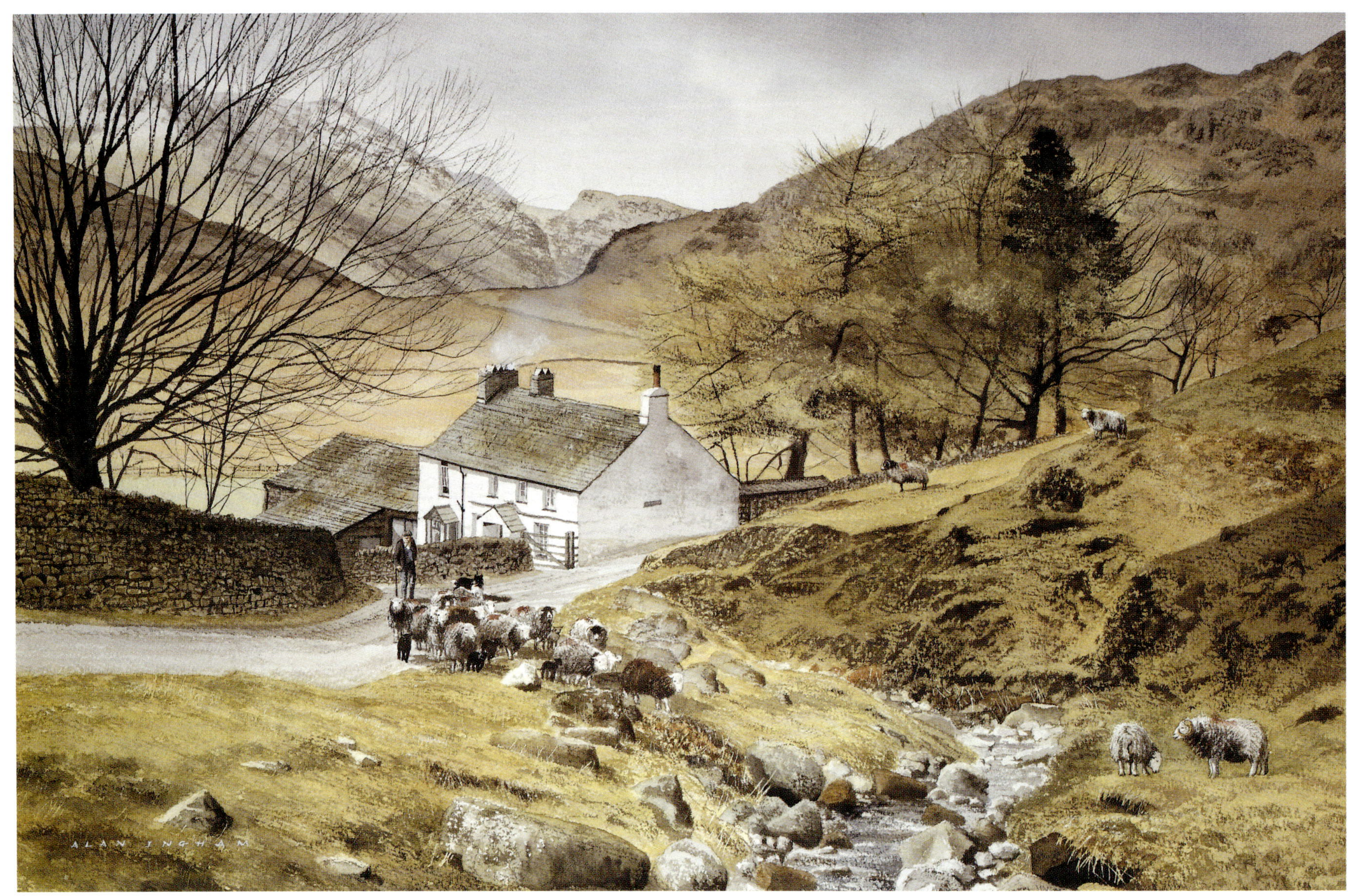

To Pastures New, Blea Tarn, Cumbria, 1989.

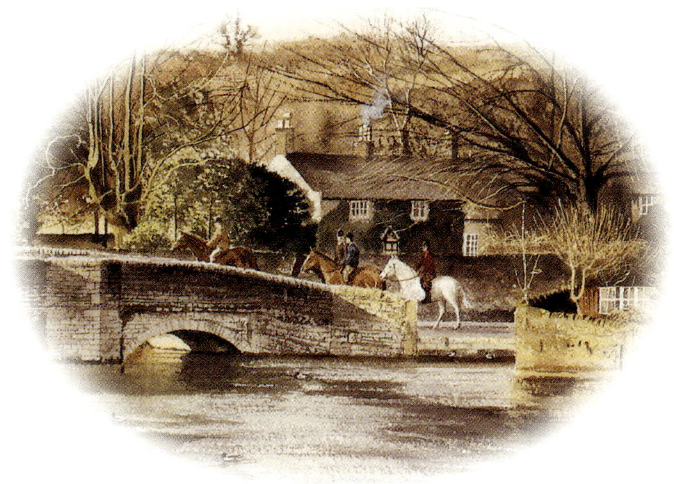

1980s

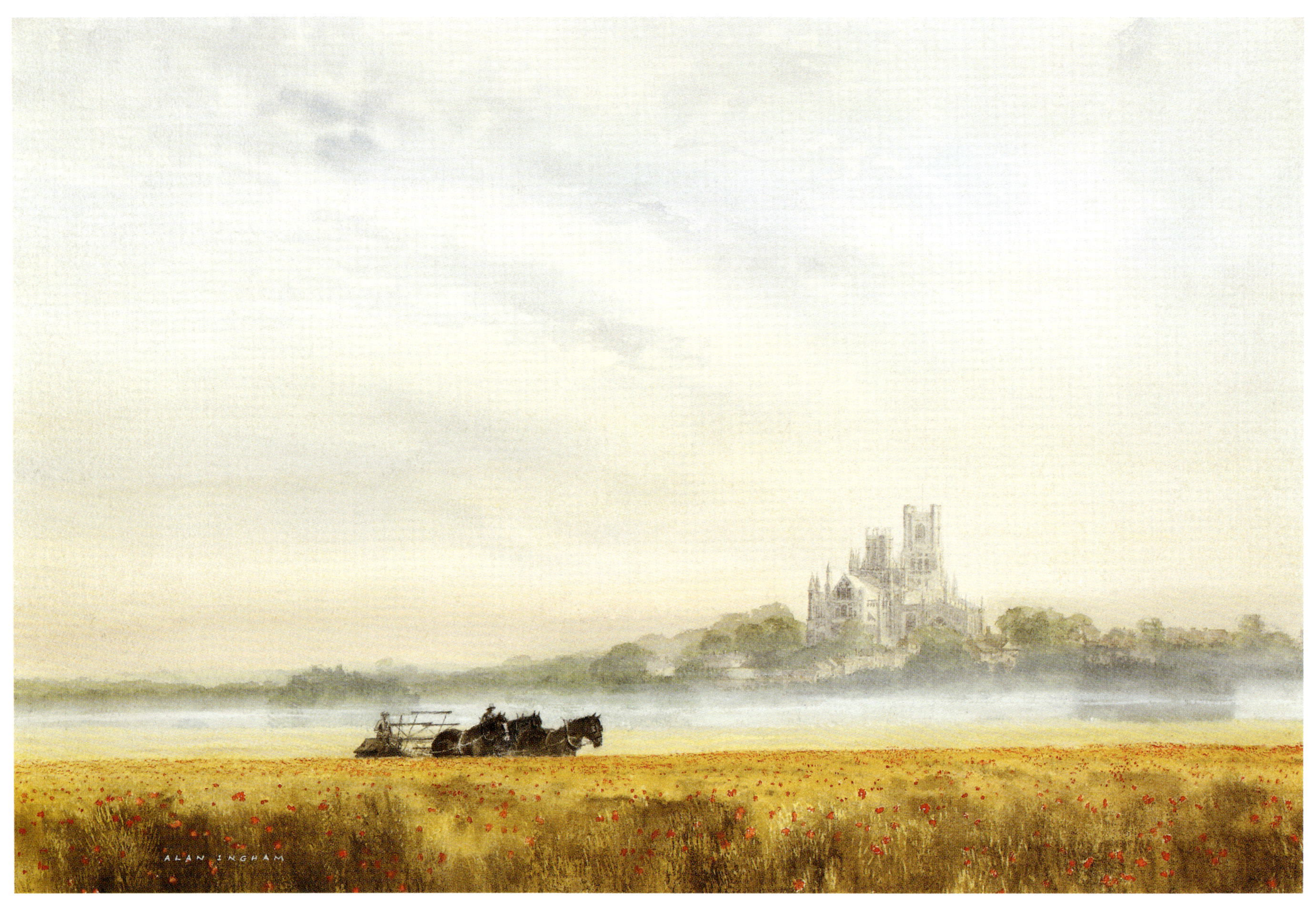

Ely Cathedral, Cambridgeshire, 1981.

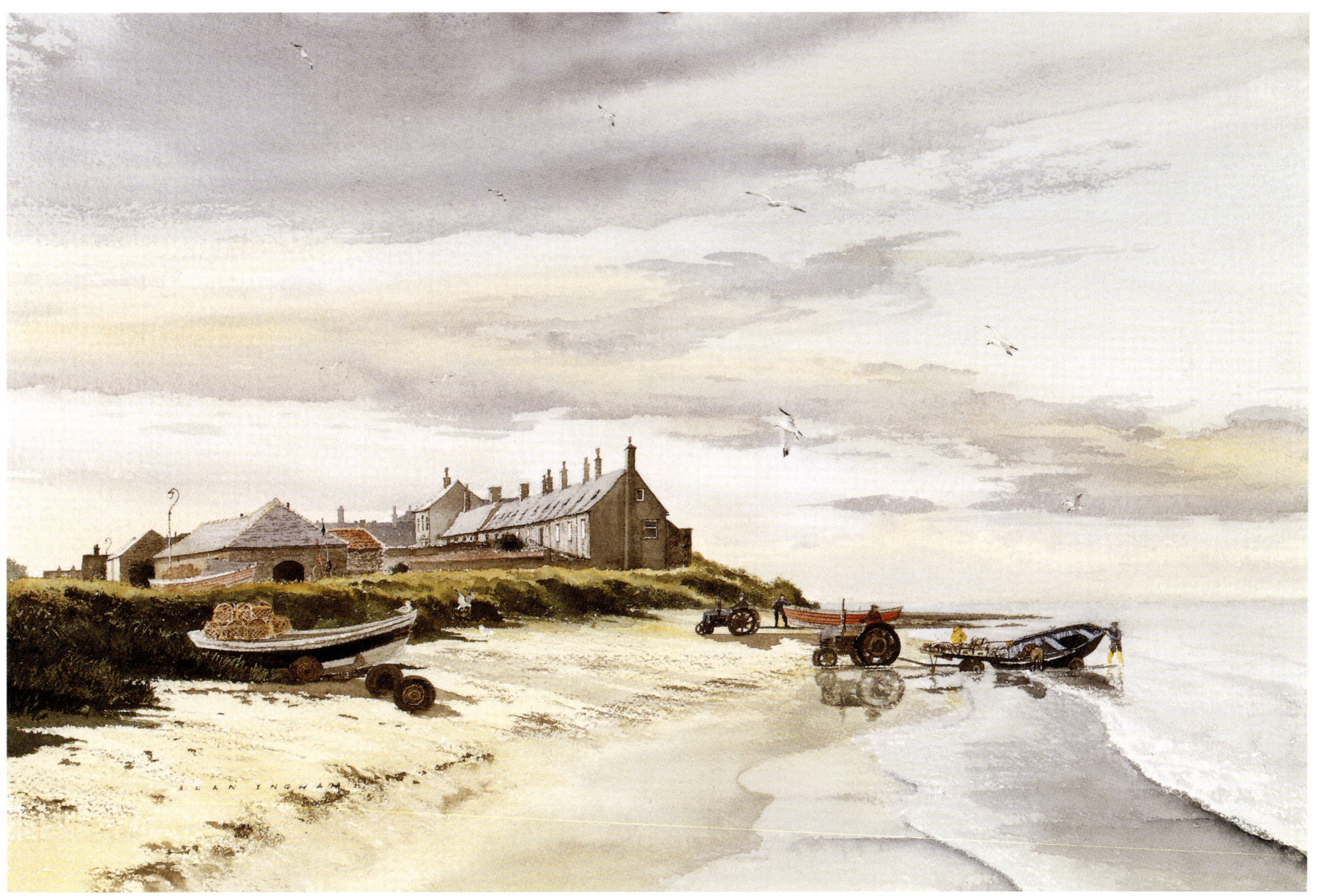

Fishermen's Cottages, Boulmer, Northumbria, 1982.

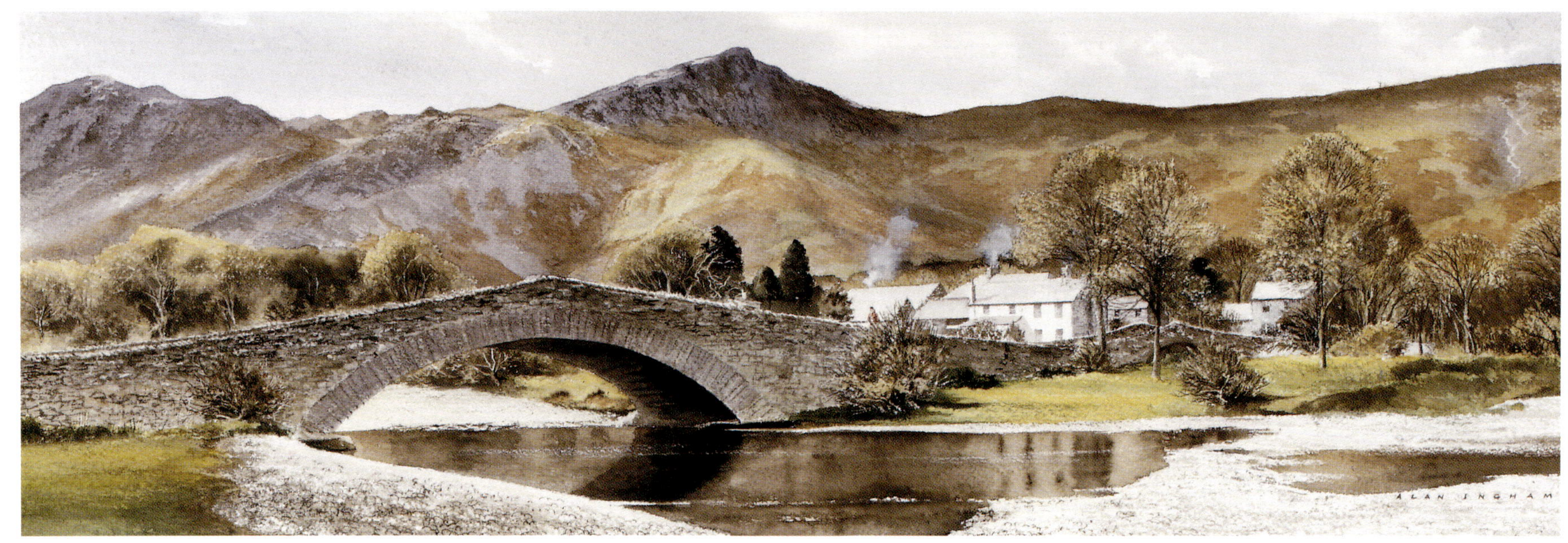

The Jaws of Borrowdale, Grange, Cumbria, 1983.

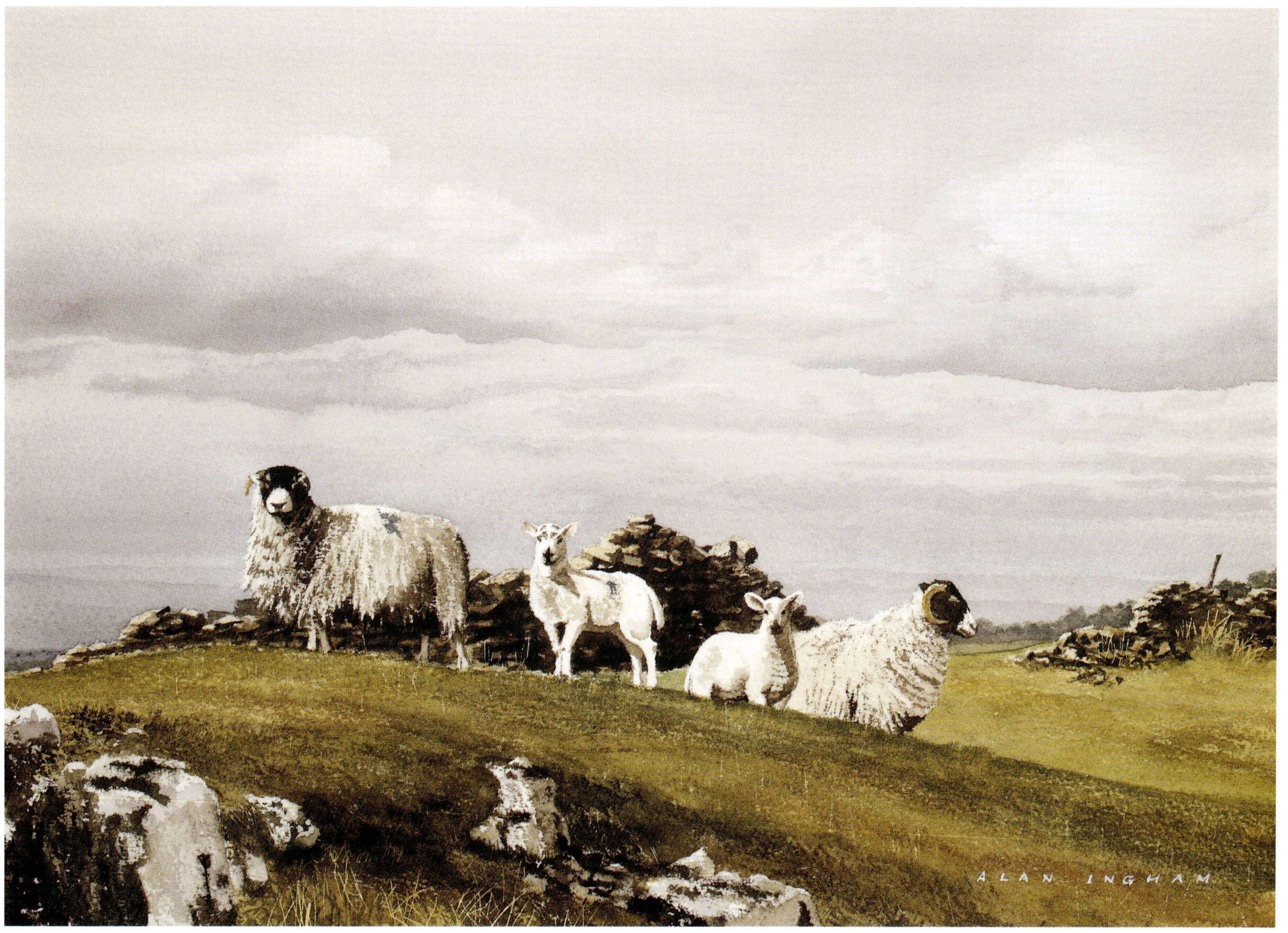

I Spy Strangers, Pendleside, Lancashire, 1974.

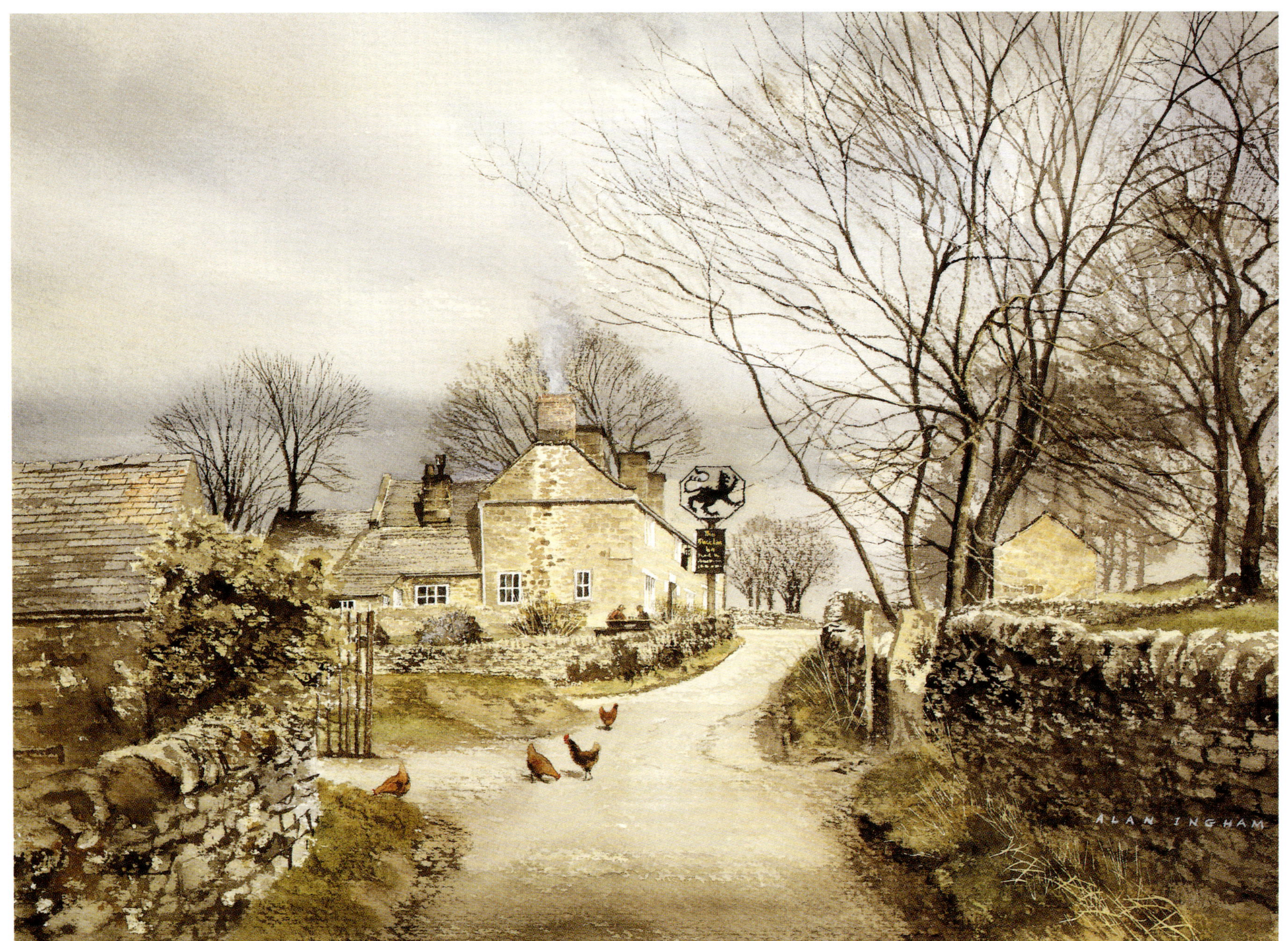

The Black Lion, Butterton, Staffordshire, 1984.

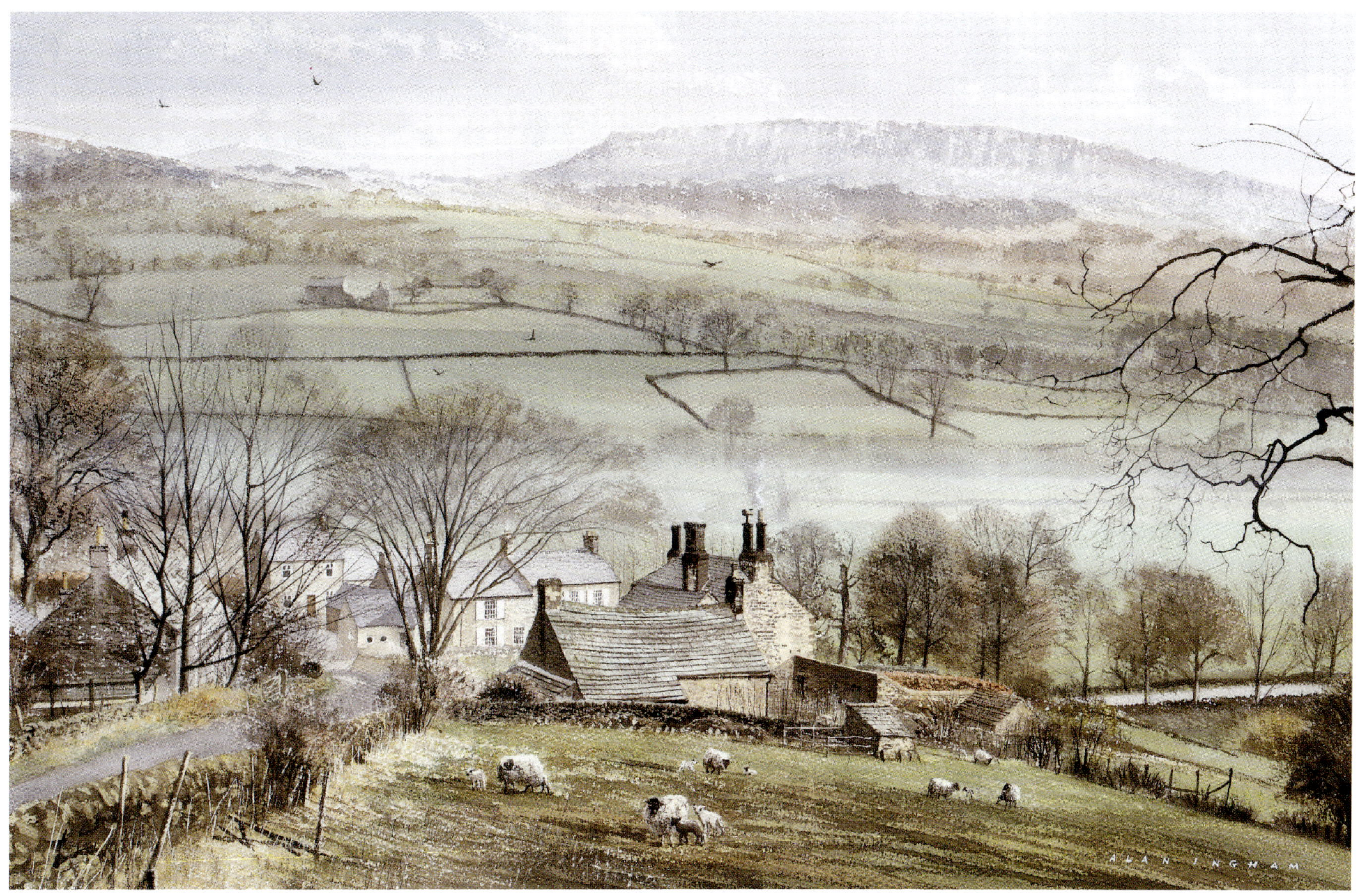

Millstone Edge, from Abney Road, Derbyshire, 1985

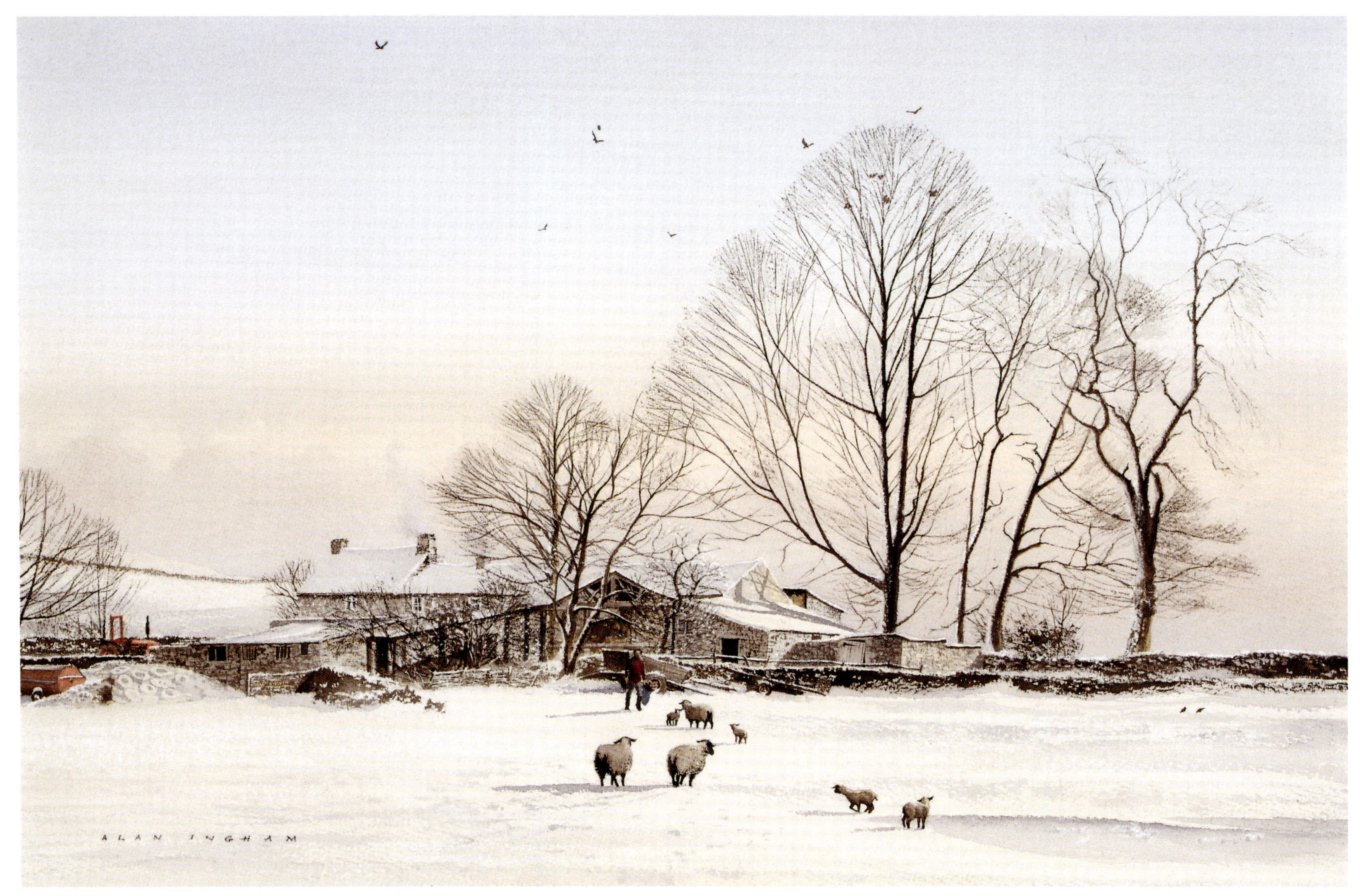

Loads Head Farm, Eastmore, 1985.

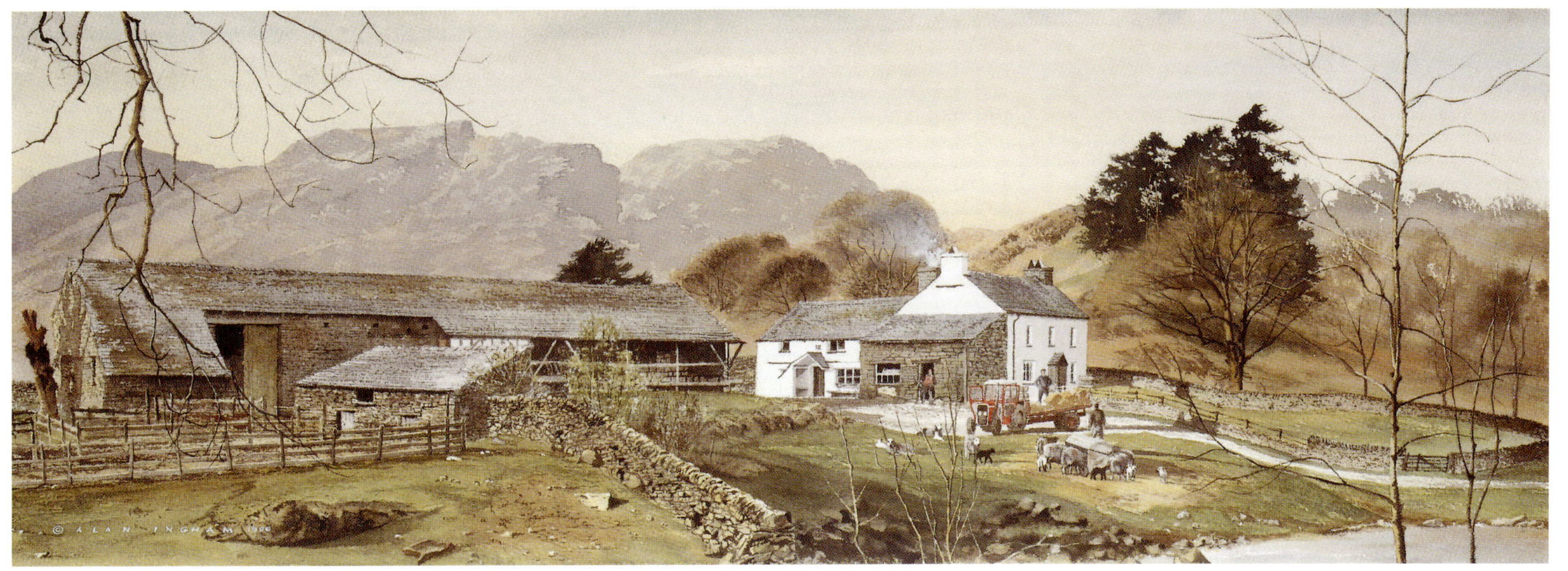

The In-By-Pasture, Yew Tree Farm, Cumbria, 1986.

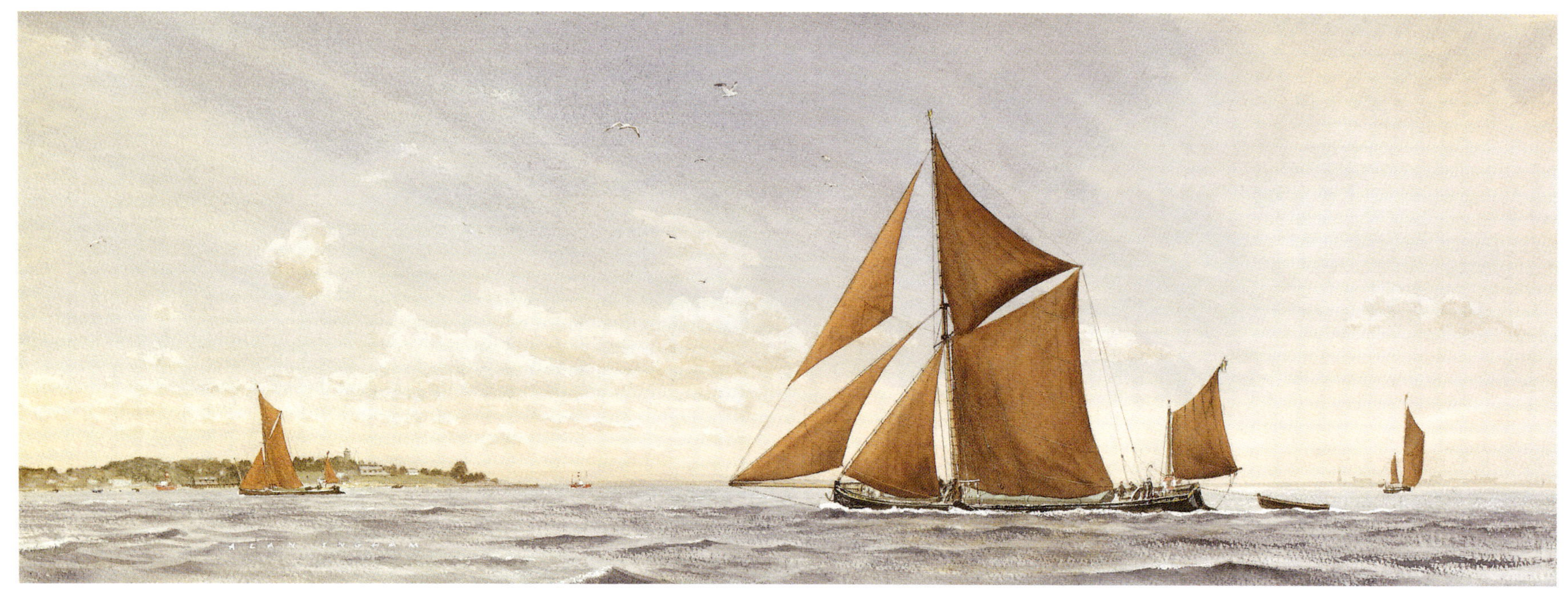

The East Coast Traders, 1987.

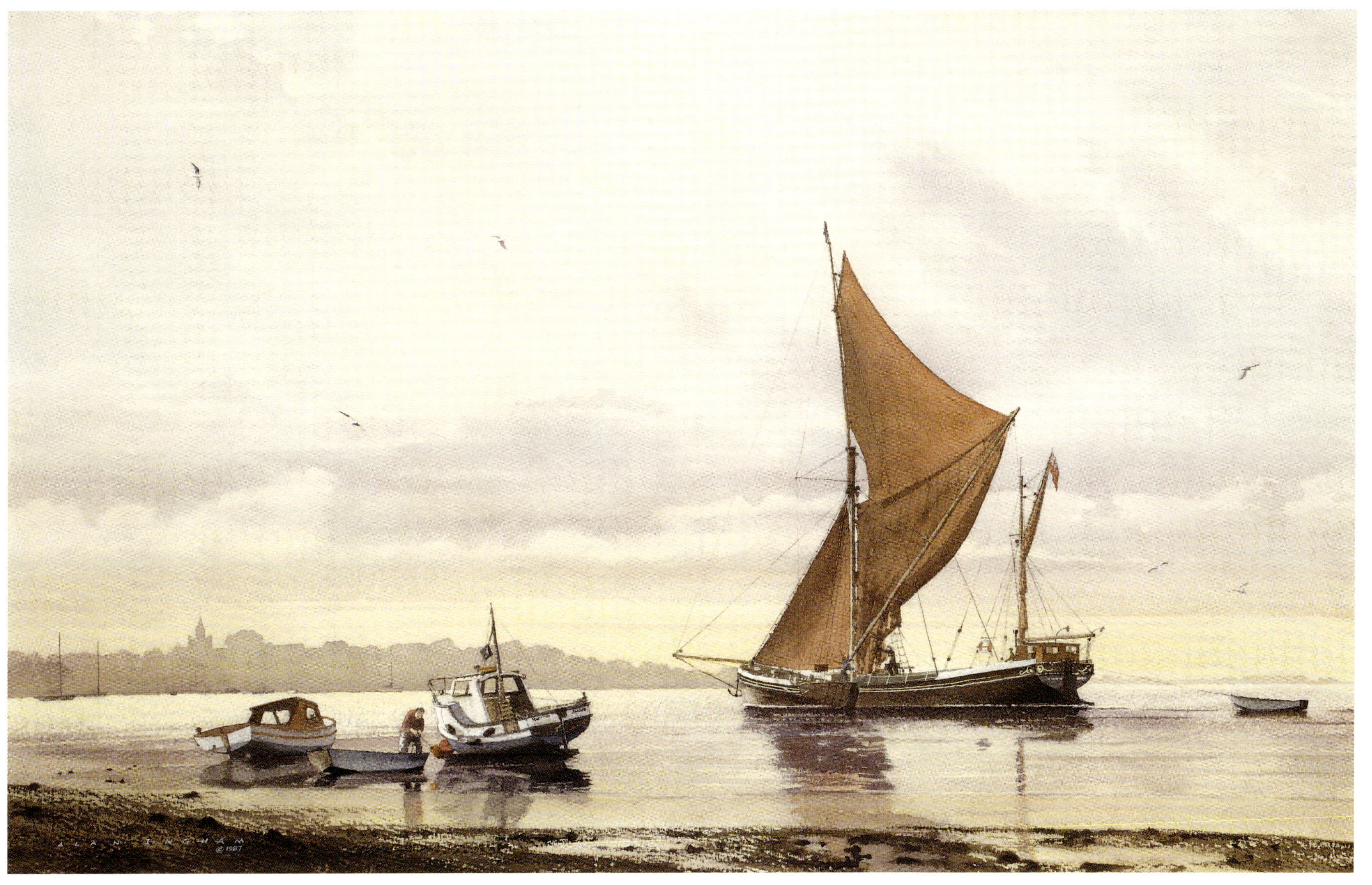

A Beauteous Evening, Thames Barge, Maldon, Essex, 1987.

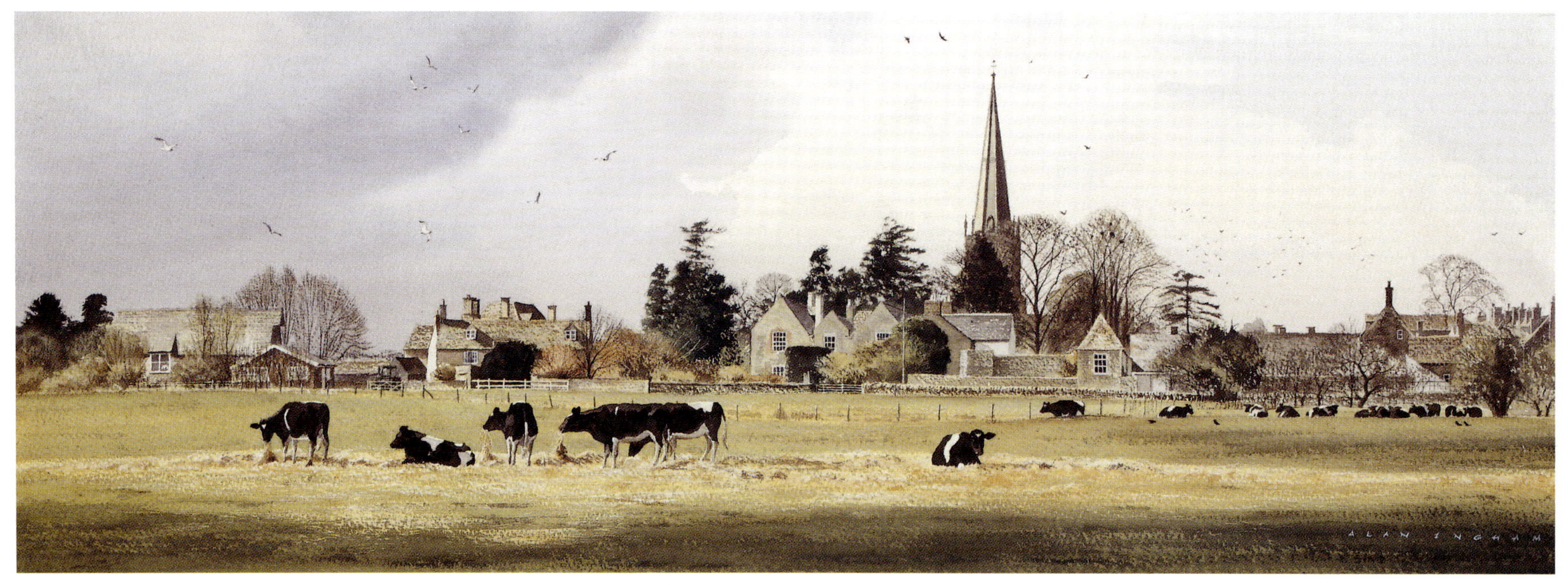

At Peace in the Watermeadows, Lechlade, 1988.

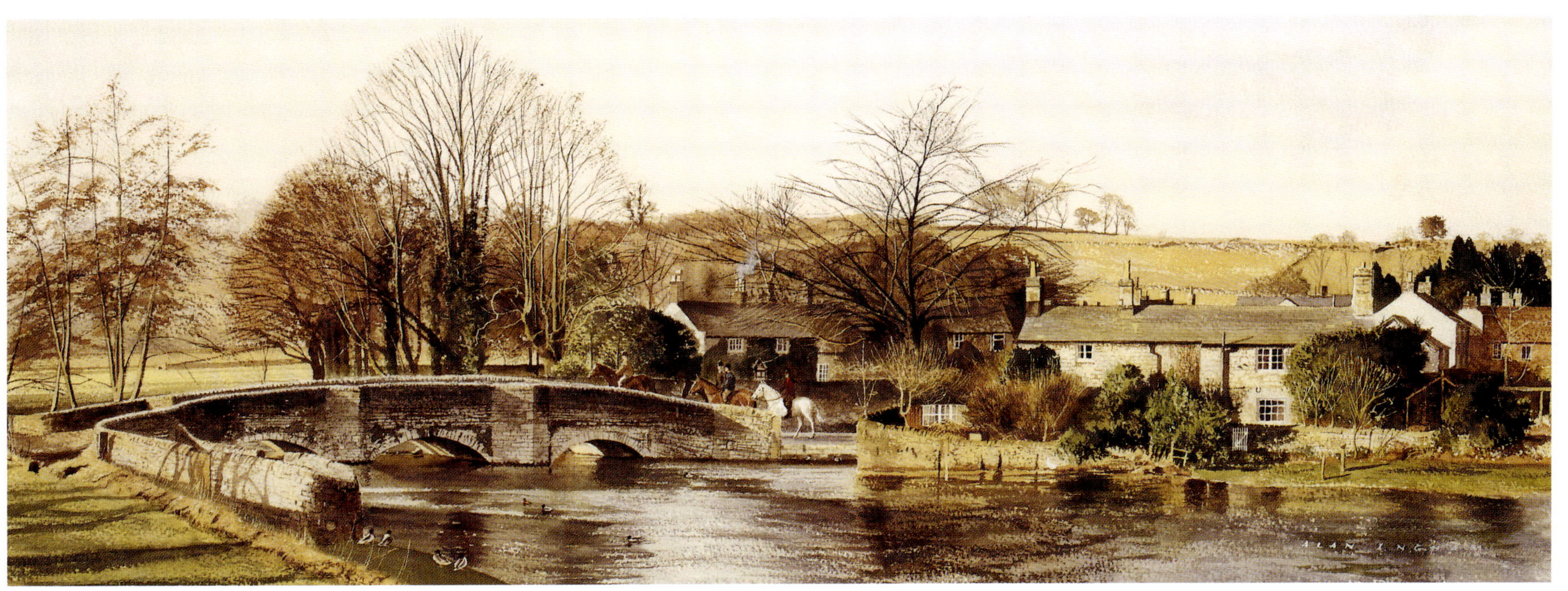

Horseman Riding By, Ashford, Derbyshire, 1988.

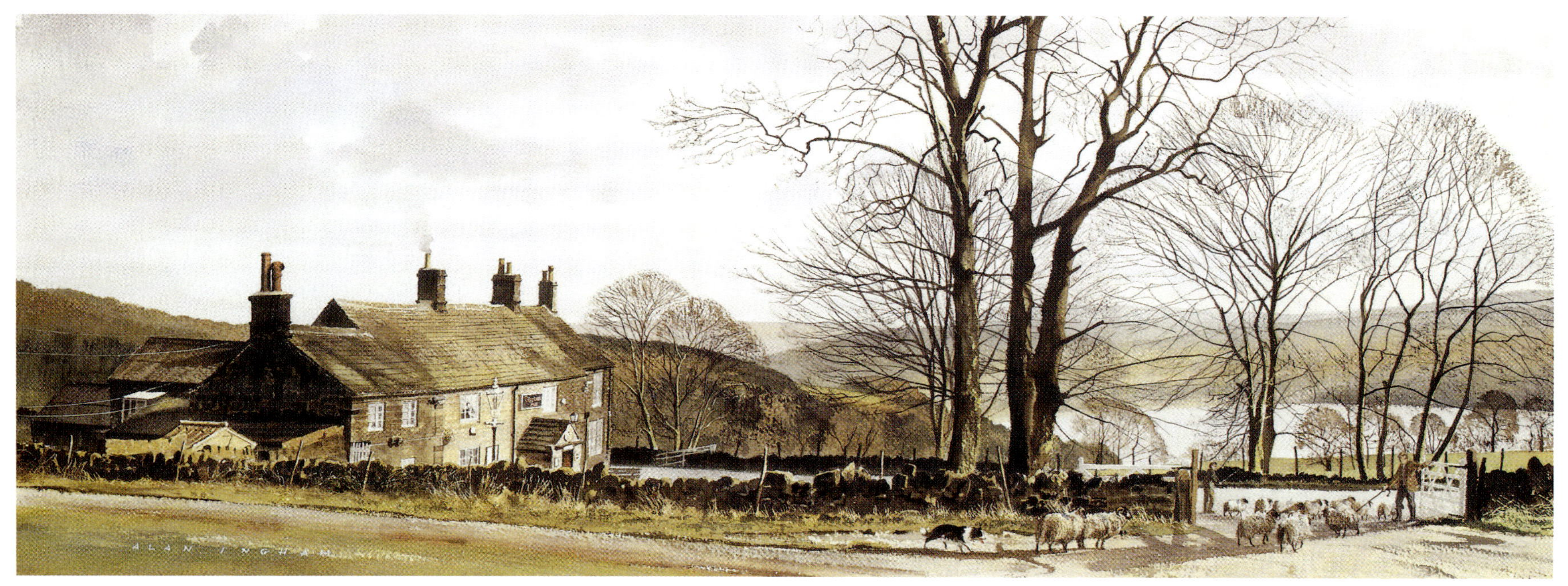

Oasis in the High Peak, The Strines, Derbyshire, 1988.

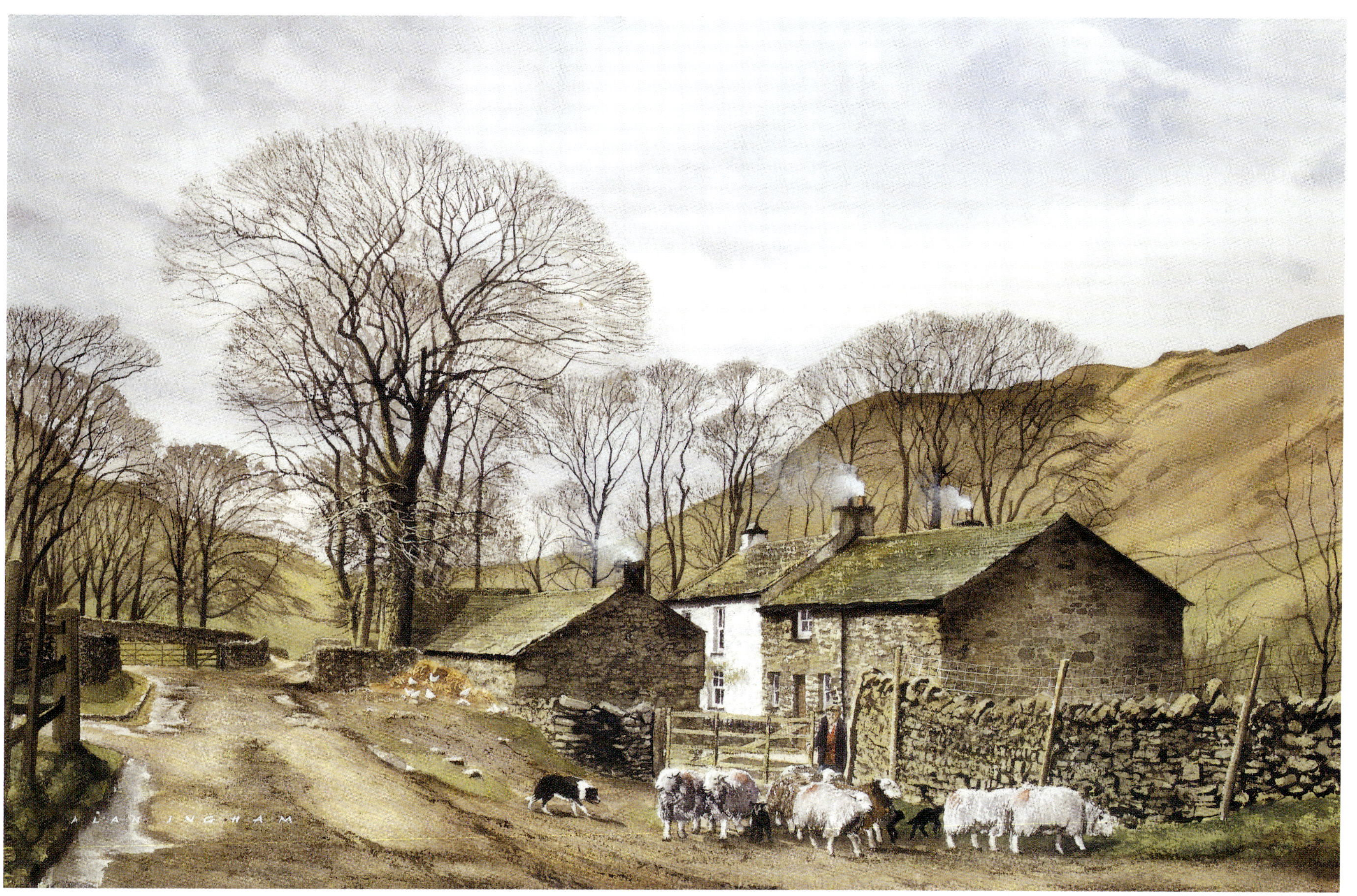

Garth Heads in Boardale, Derbyshire, 1988.

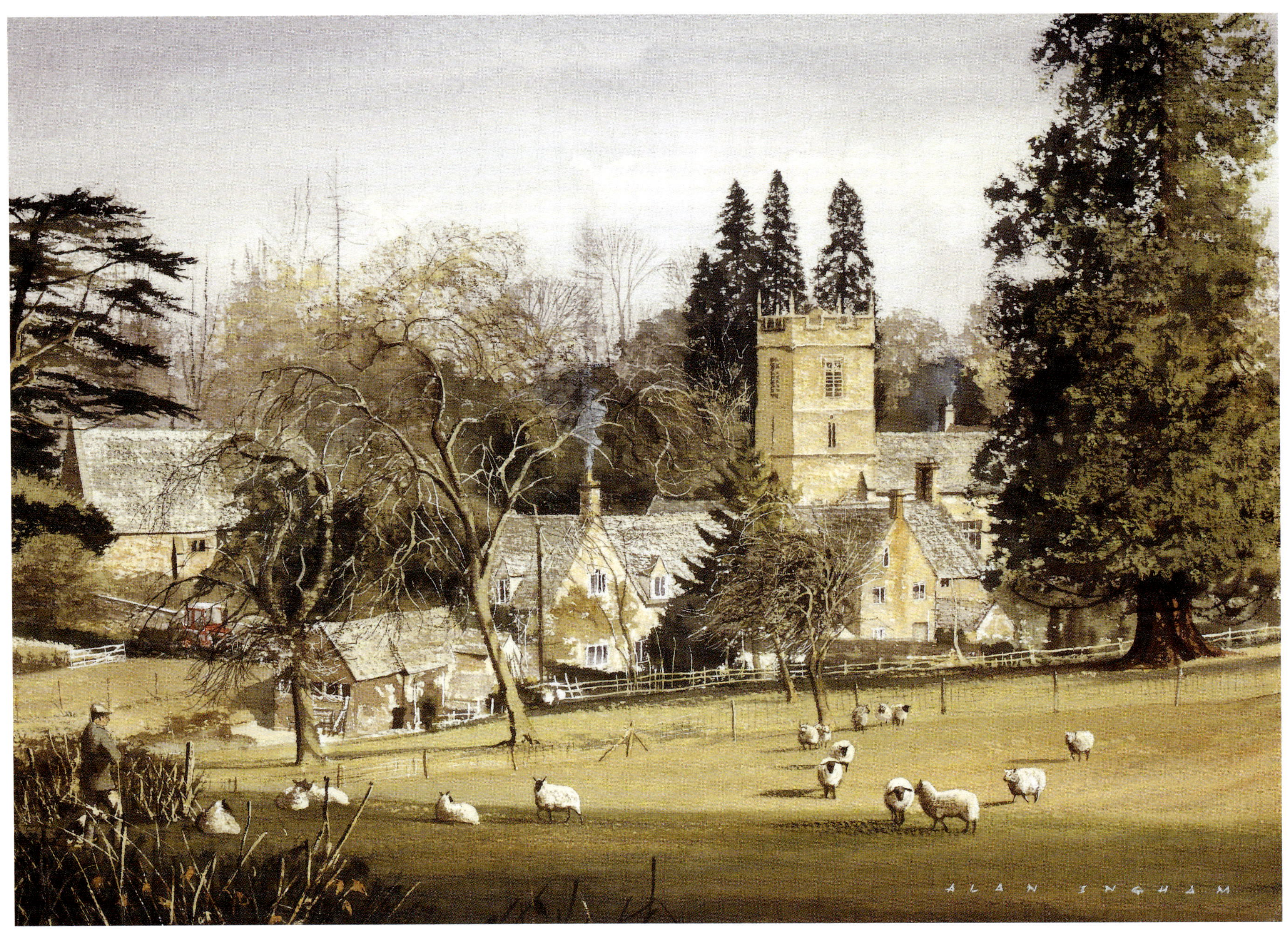

Trapped in the Past, Stanway, Gloucestershire, 1988.

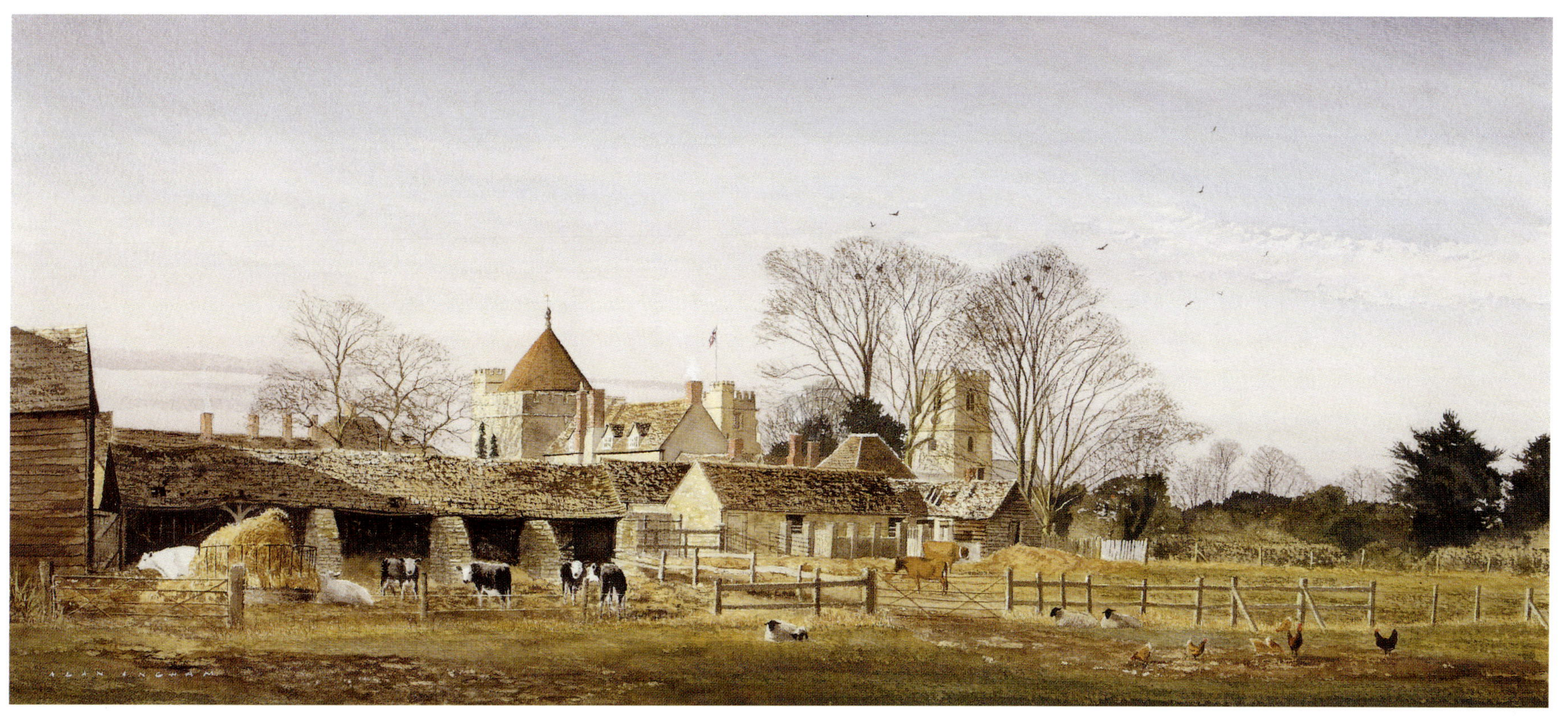

Manor Court Farm, Stanton Harcourt, Gloucestershire, 1988.

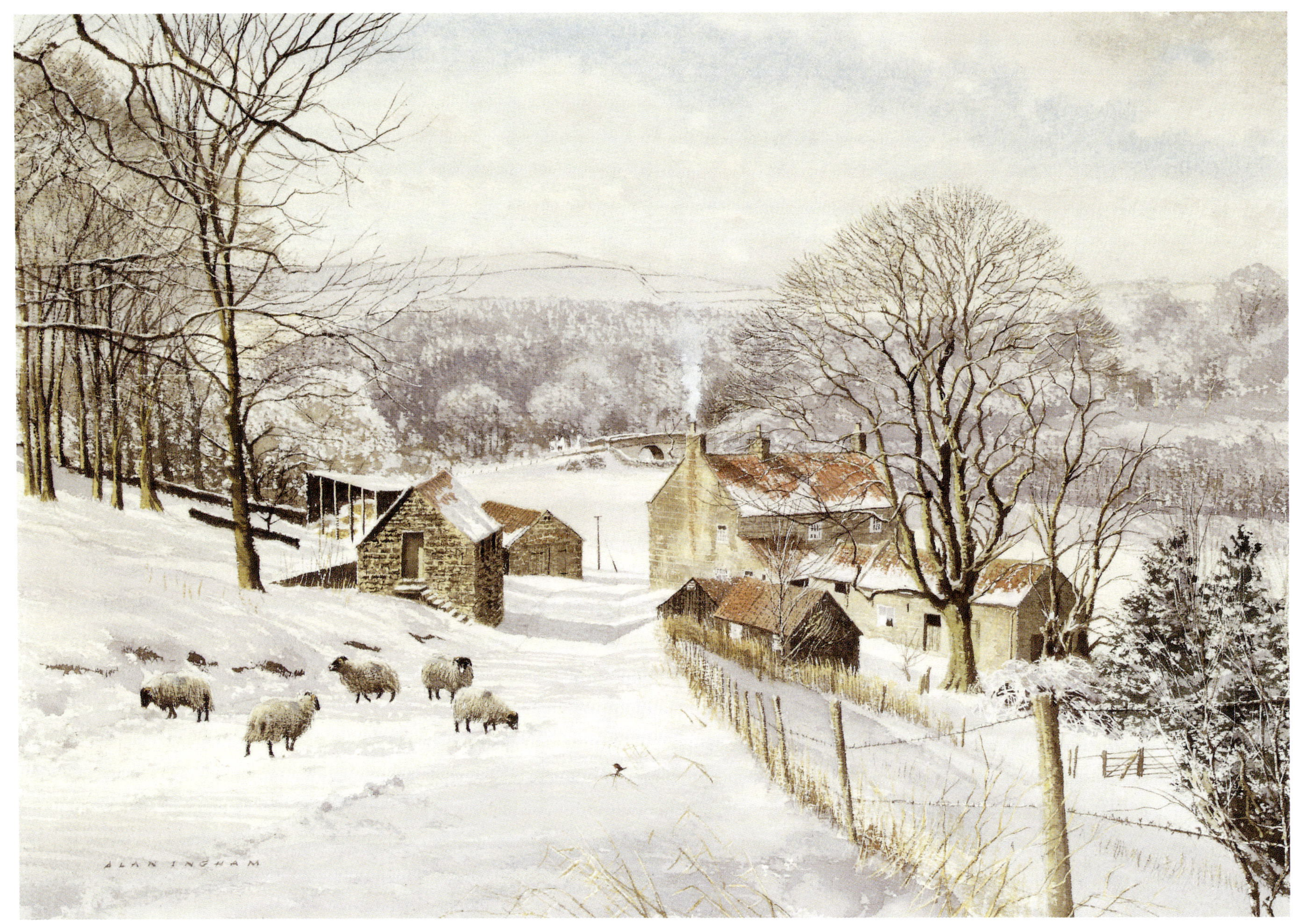

Foragers in the Snow, West Ho, 1988.

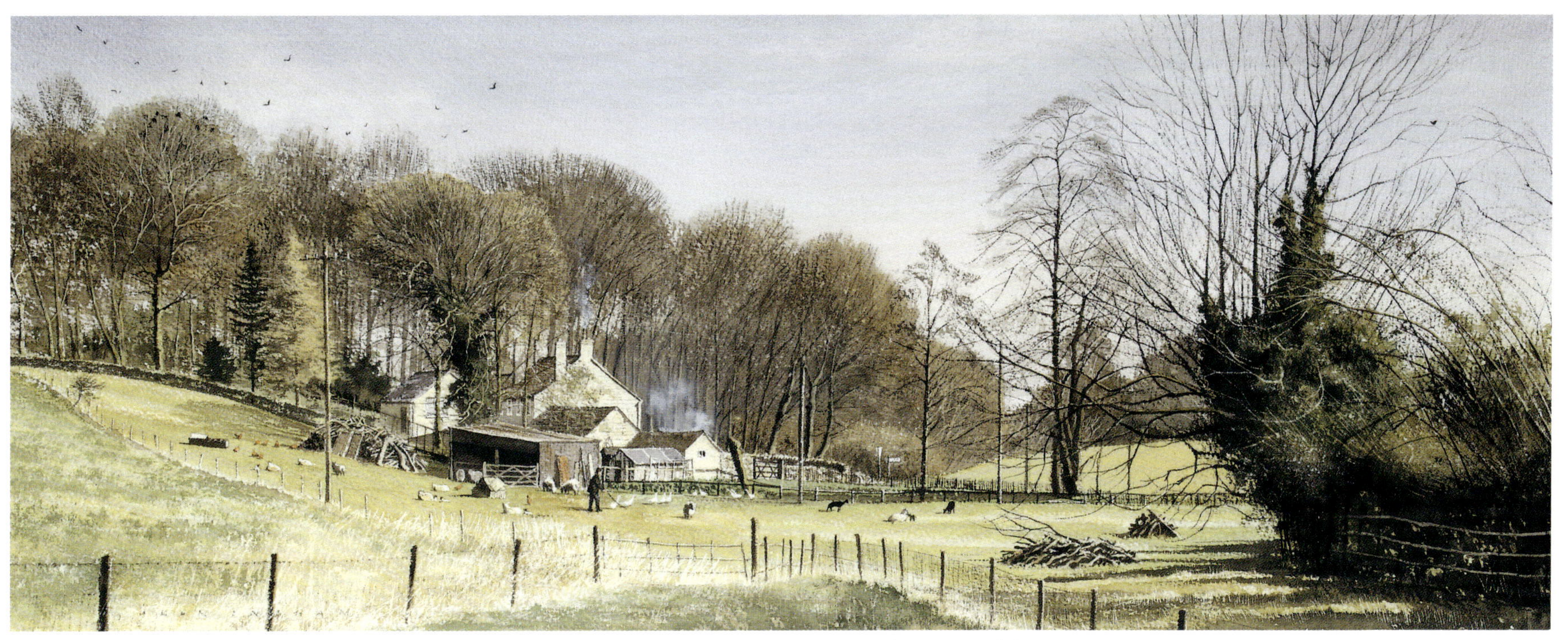

A Small Country Living, Ullenwood, Gloucestershire, 1988.

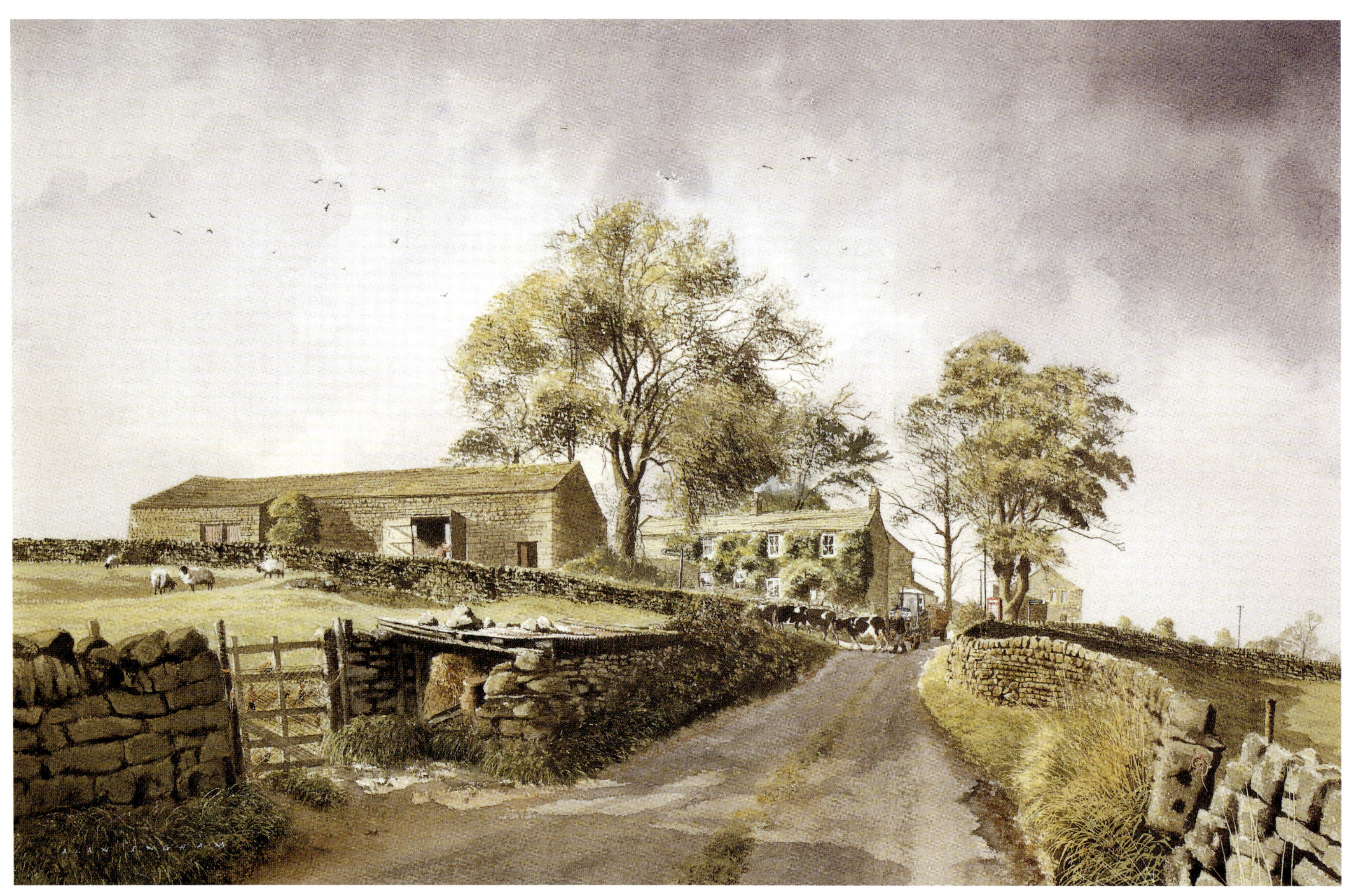

Storm Clouds Passing, Small Banks, North Yorkshire, 1989.

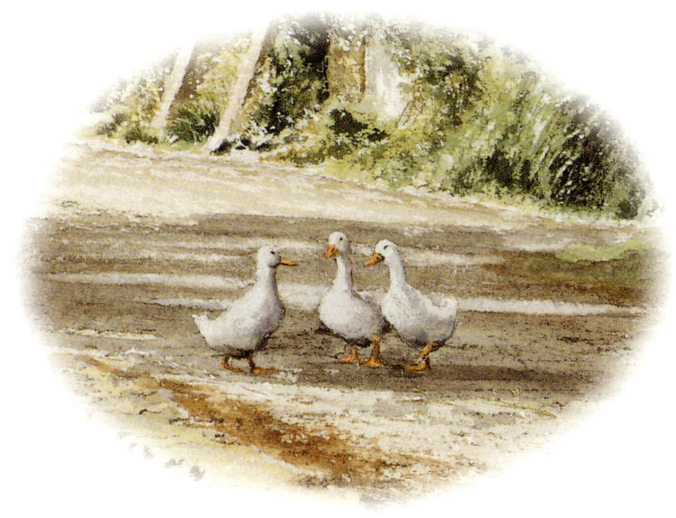

1990s

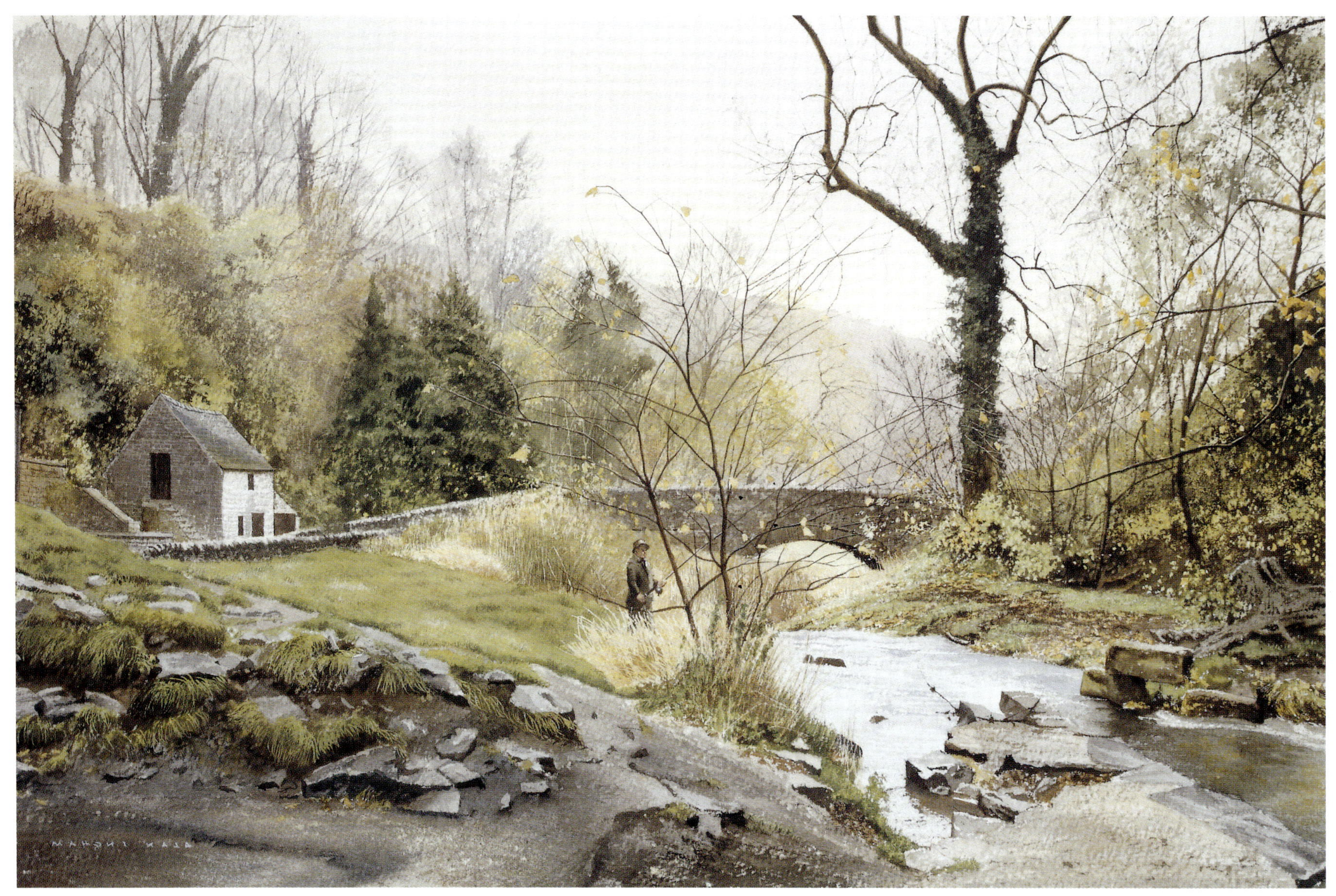

Gone Fishing, Milldale, Derbyshire, 1990.

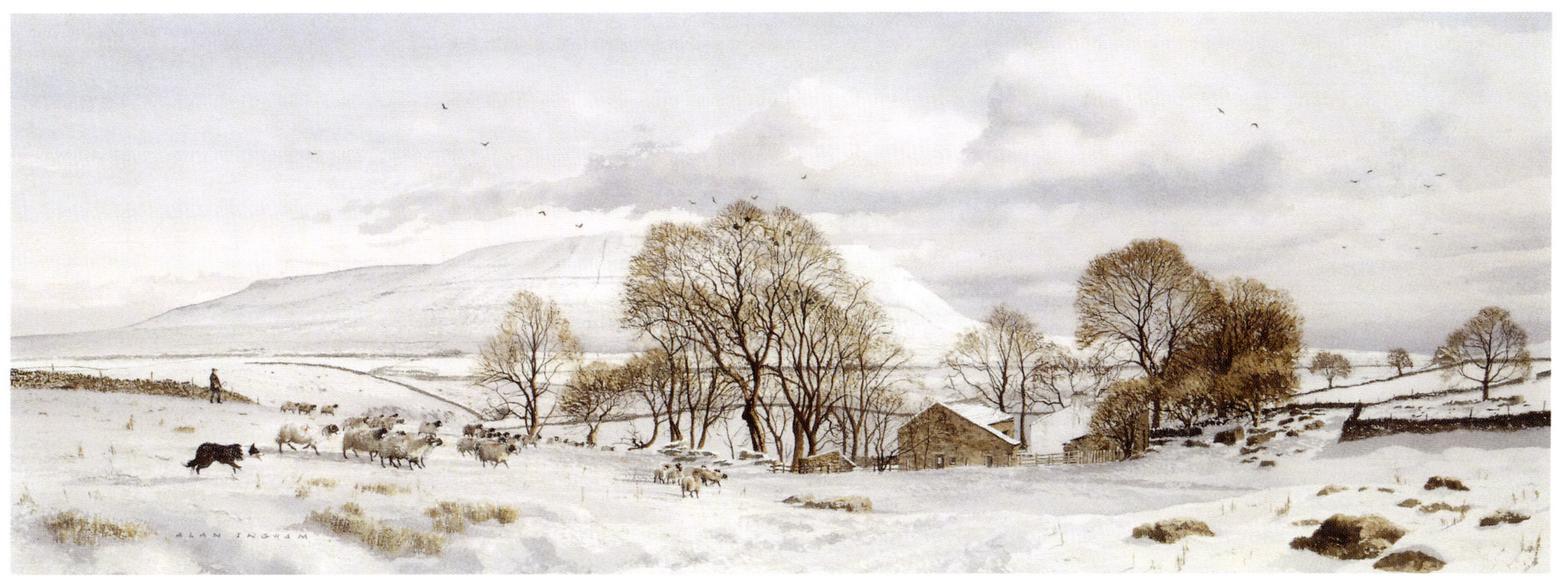

The Winter Gather, Far Gearstones, Derbyshire, 1990.

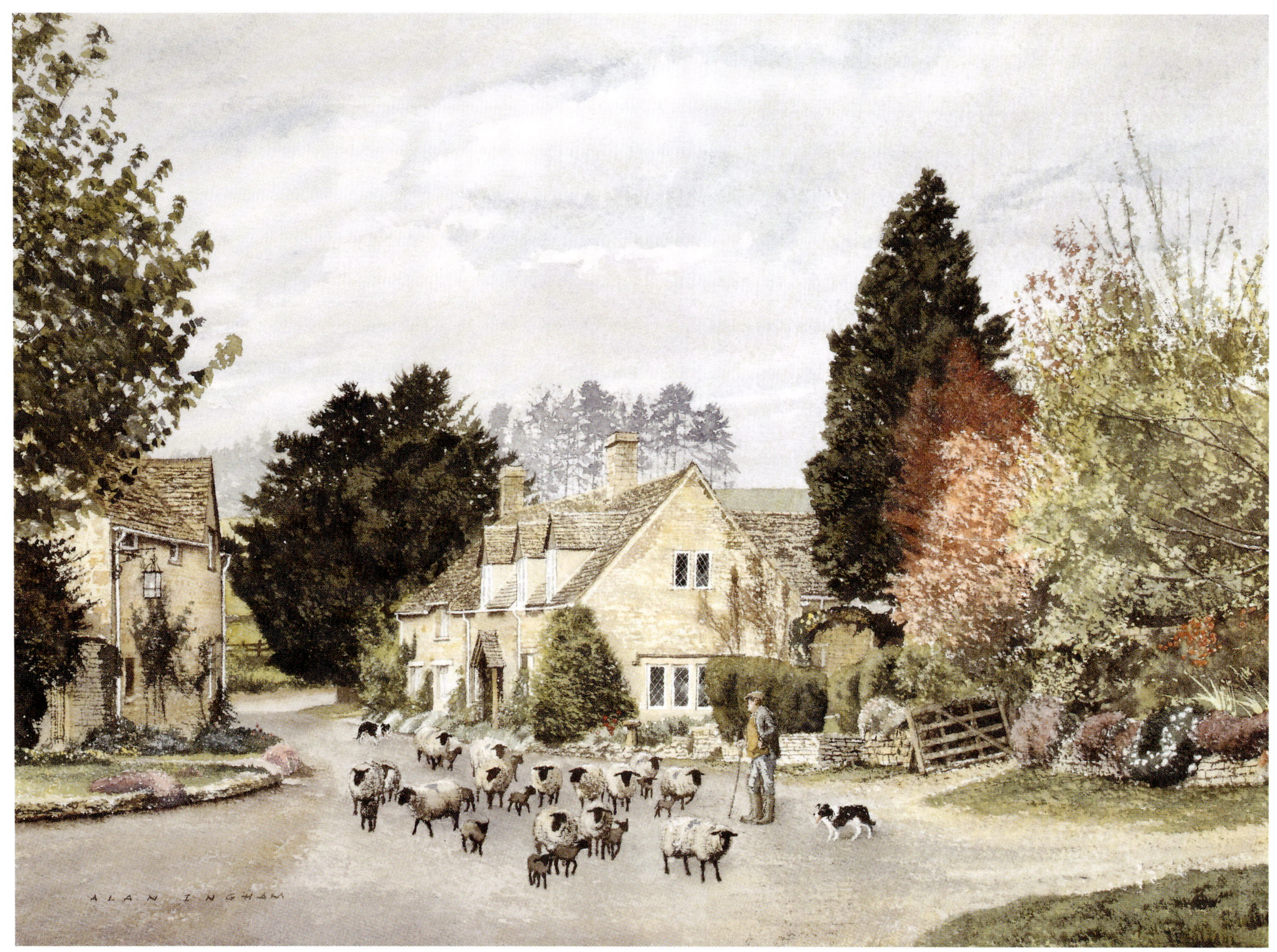

Far From the Madding Crowd, Icombe, Gloucestershire, 1991.

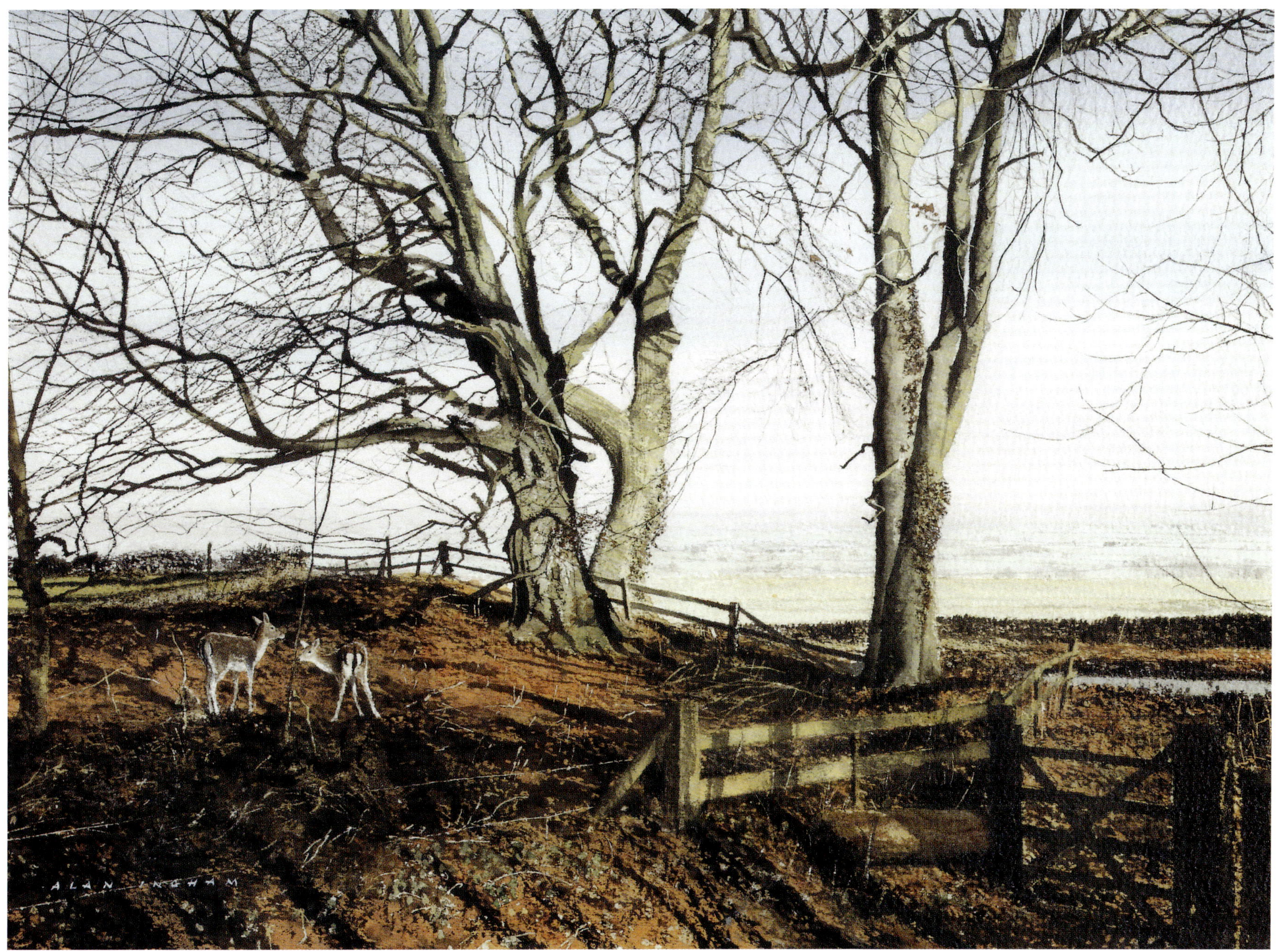

Woodland Vista, Sezincote, Longborough, Gloucestershire, 1991.

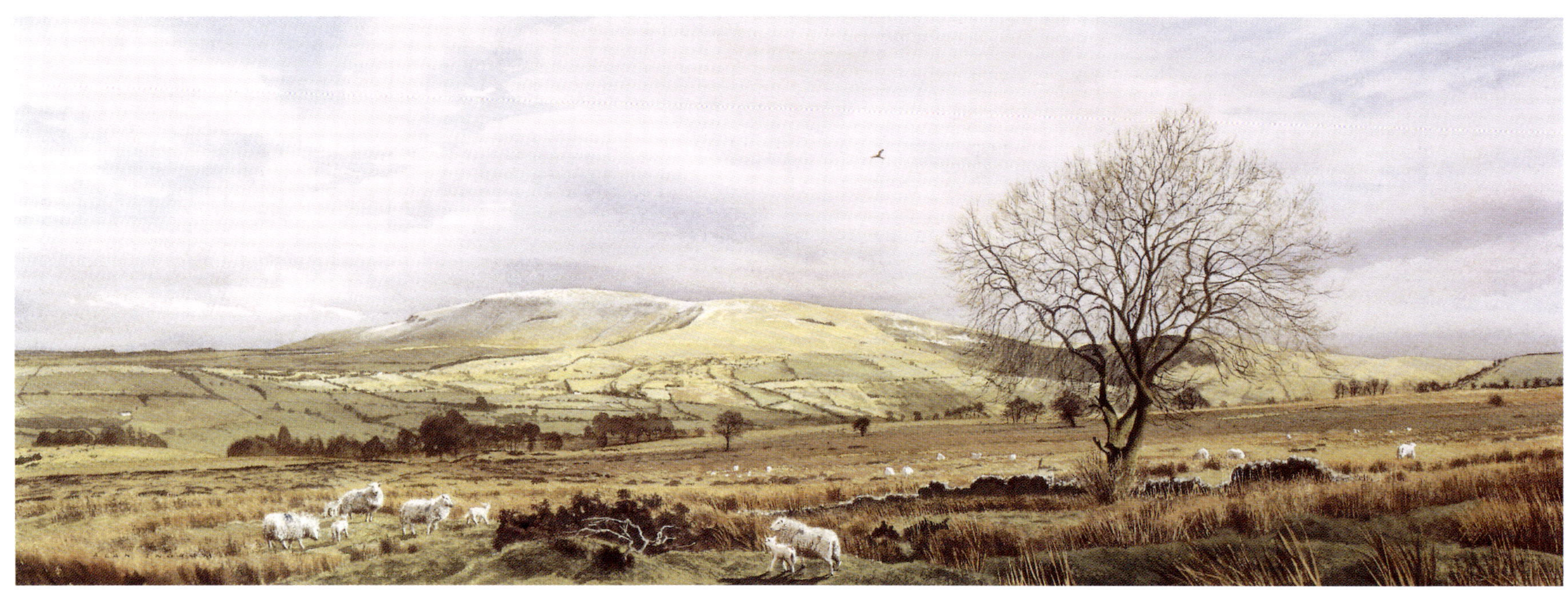

On a Clear Day, Brecon Beacons, Wales, 1991.

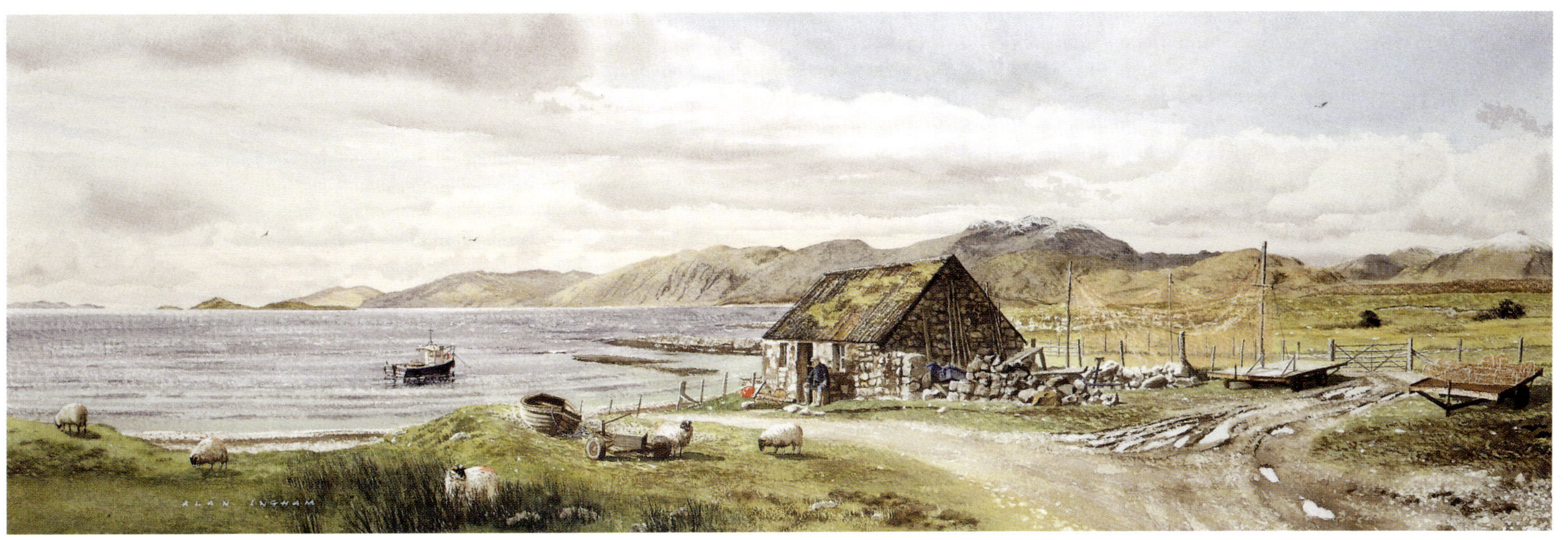

Scottish Idyll, Cuil Bay, Scotland, 1992.

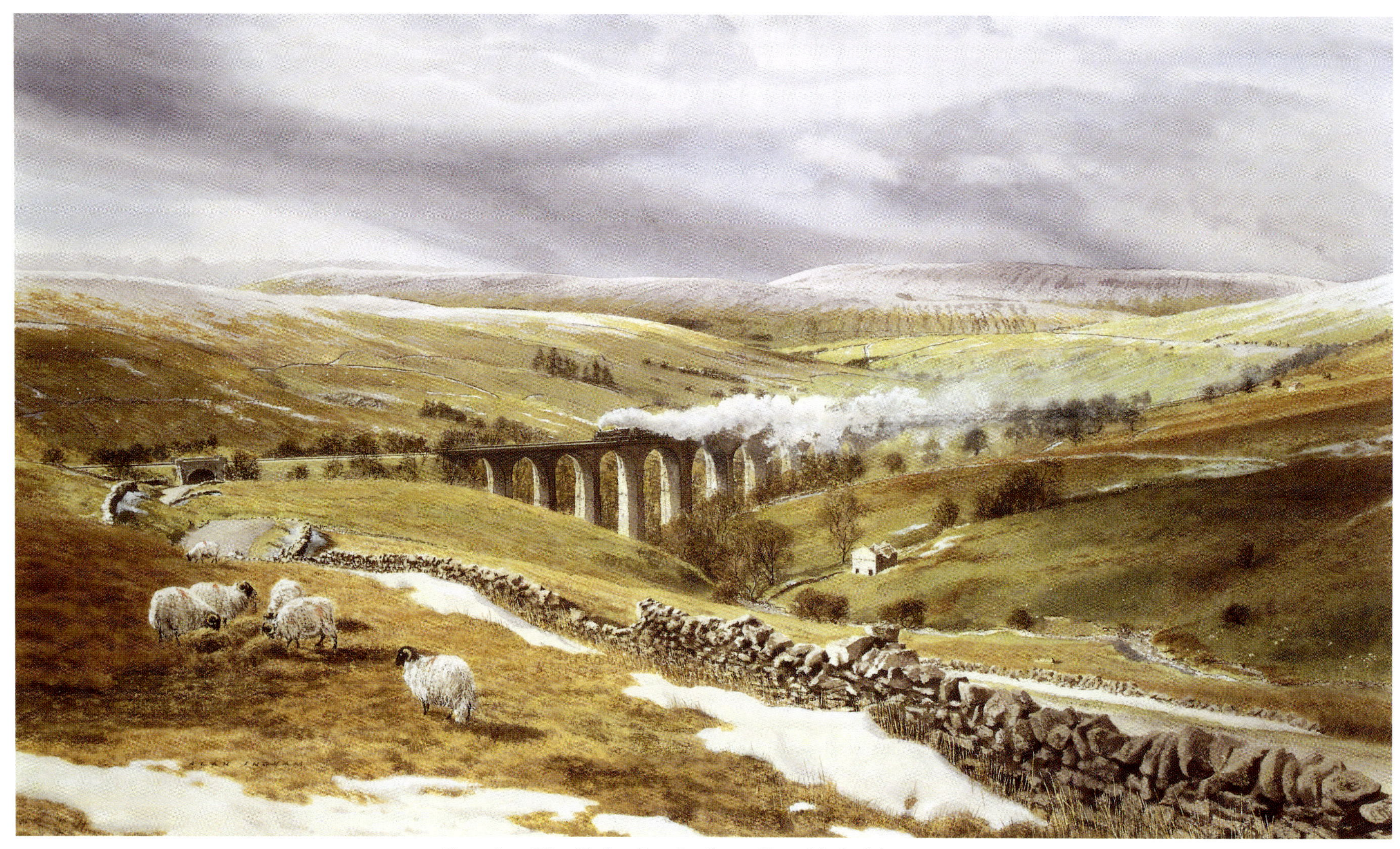

Crossing The Dale, On the Snowline, Yorkshire, 1992.

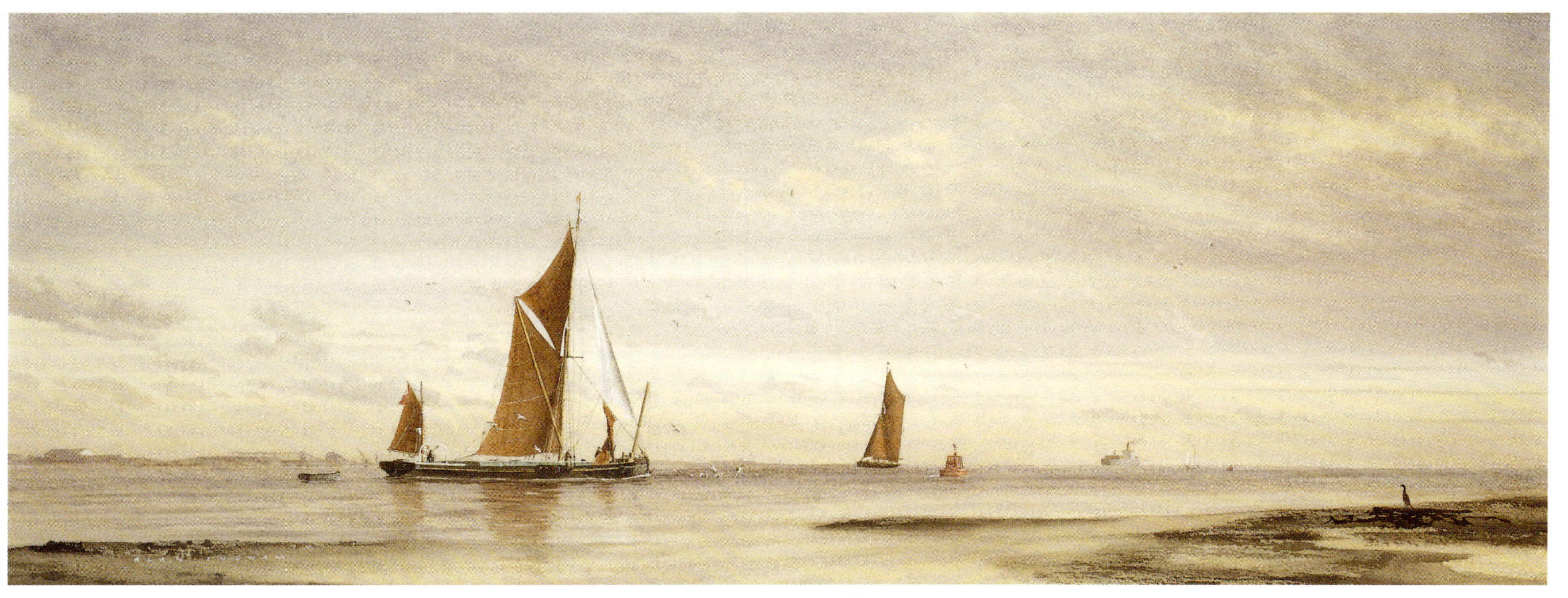

Evening Departure, Harwich, Essex. 1993.

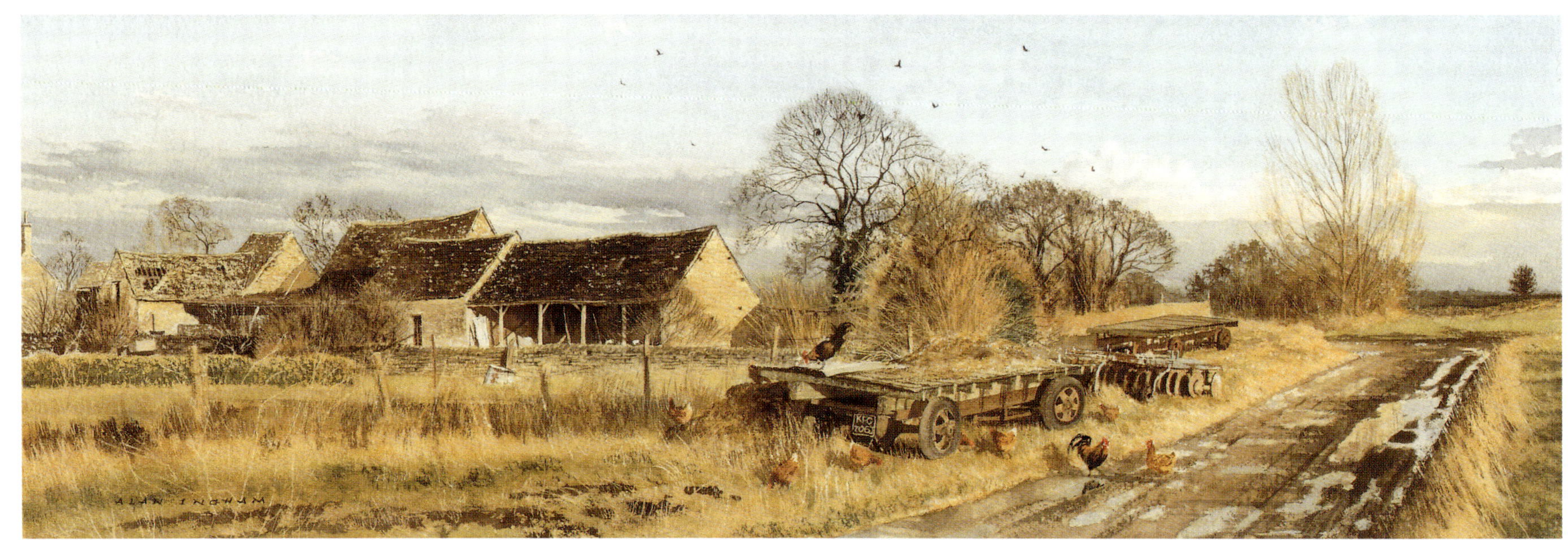

Winter Recess, Brighthampton, Oxfordshire, 1993.

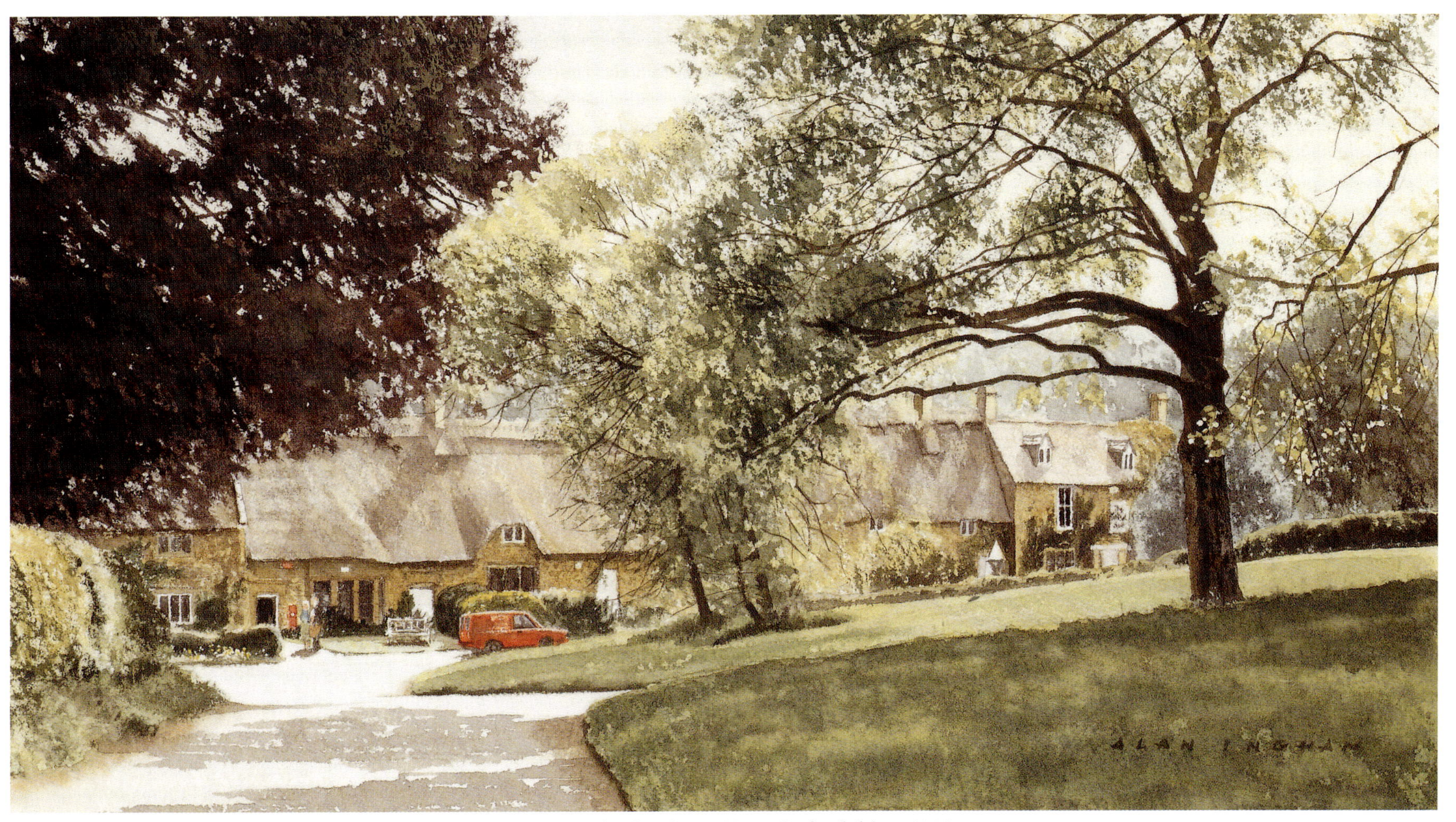

Summer Shade, Great Tew, Oxfordshire, 1993.

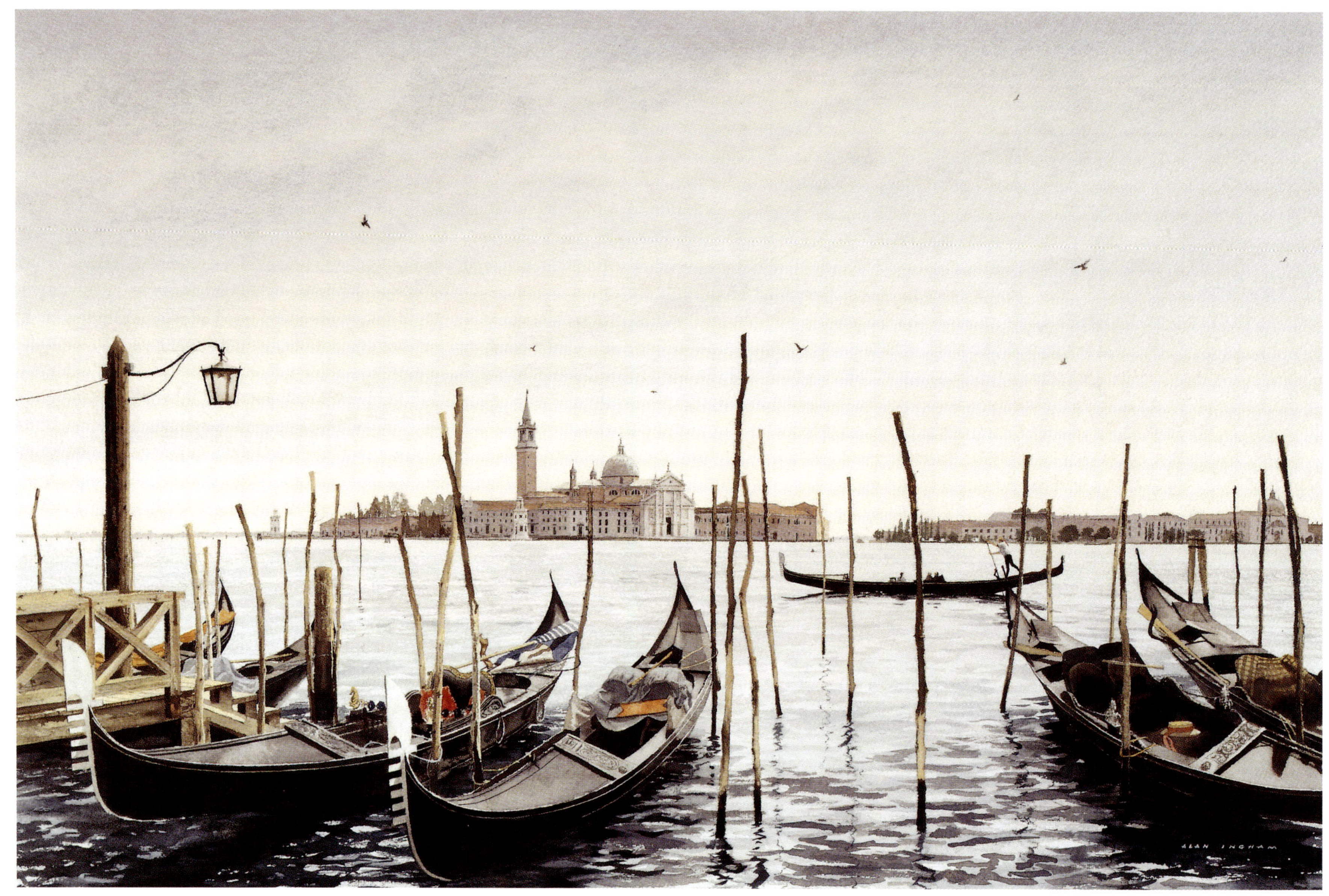

Venetian Lagoon, Venice, 1991.

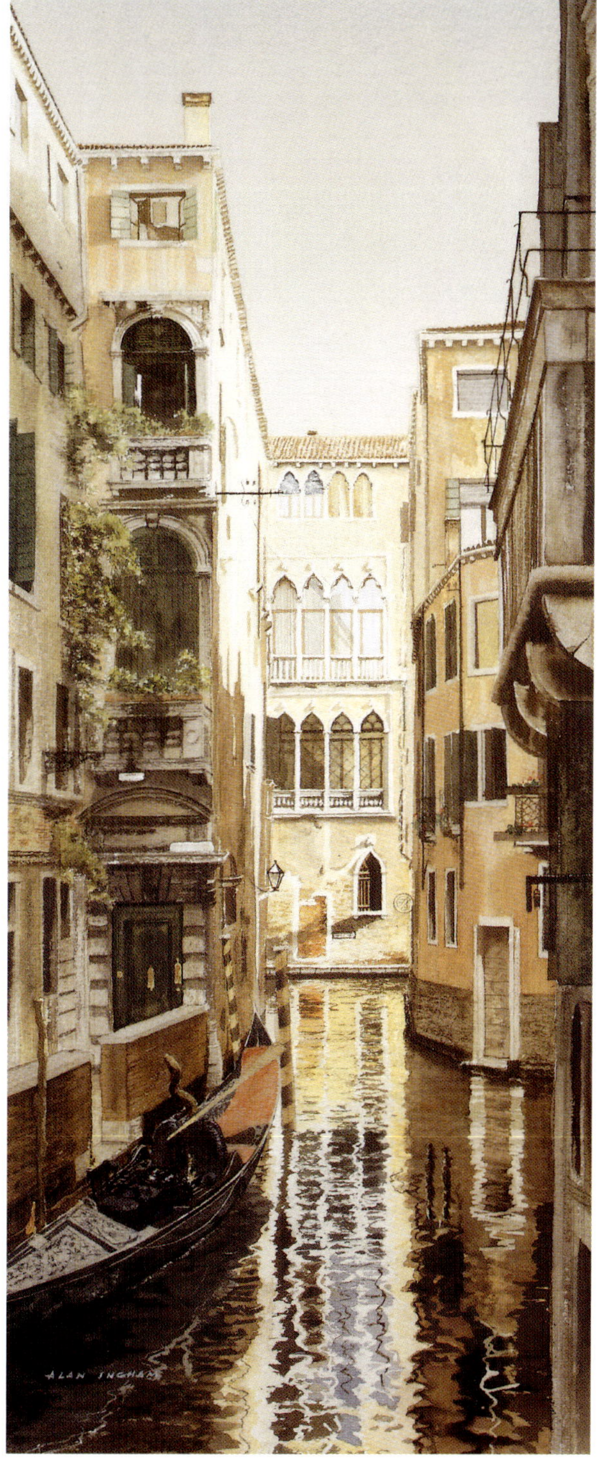

Rio de la Verona, Venice, 1993

Tratoria Sempione, Venice, 1993

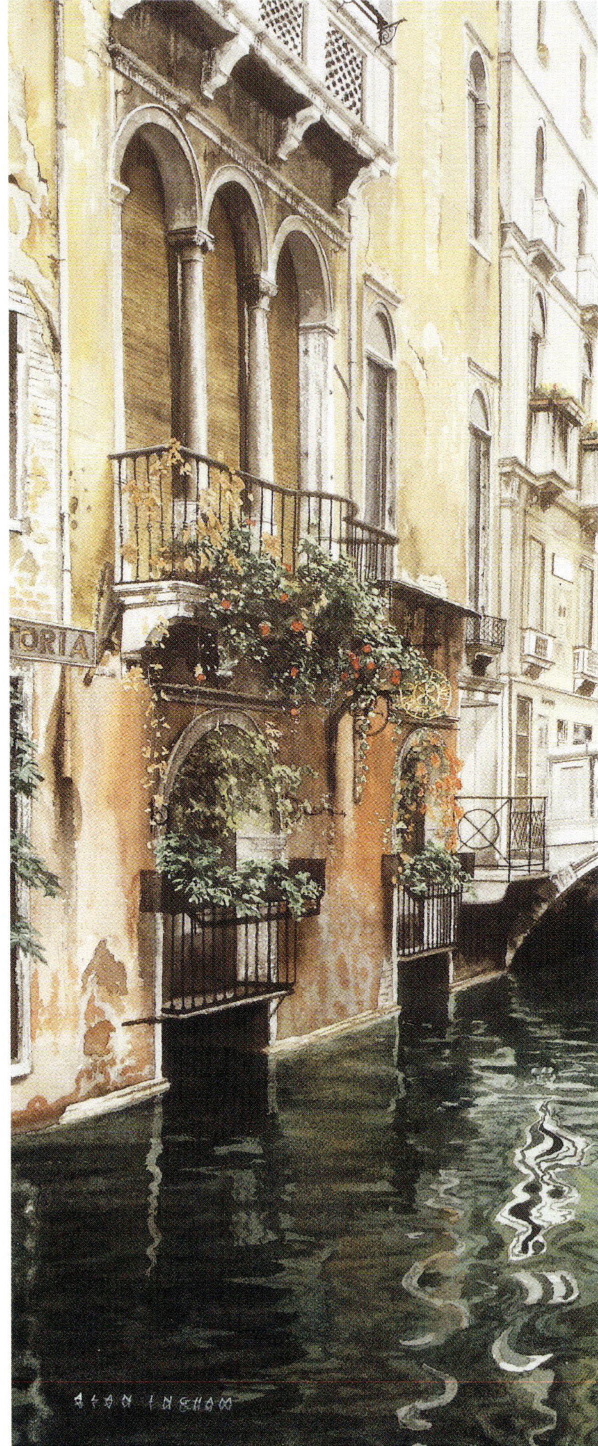

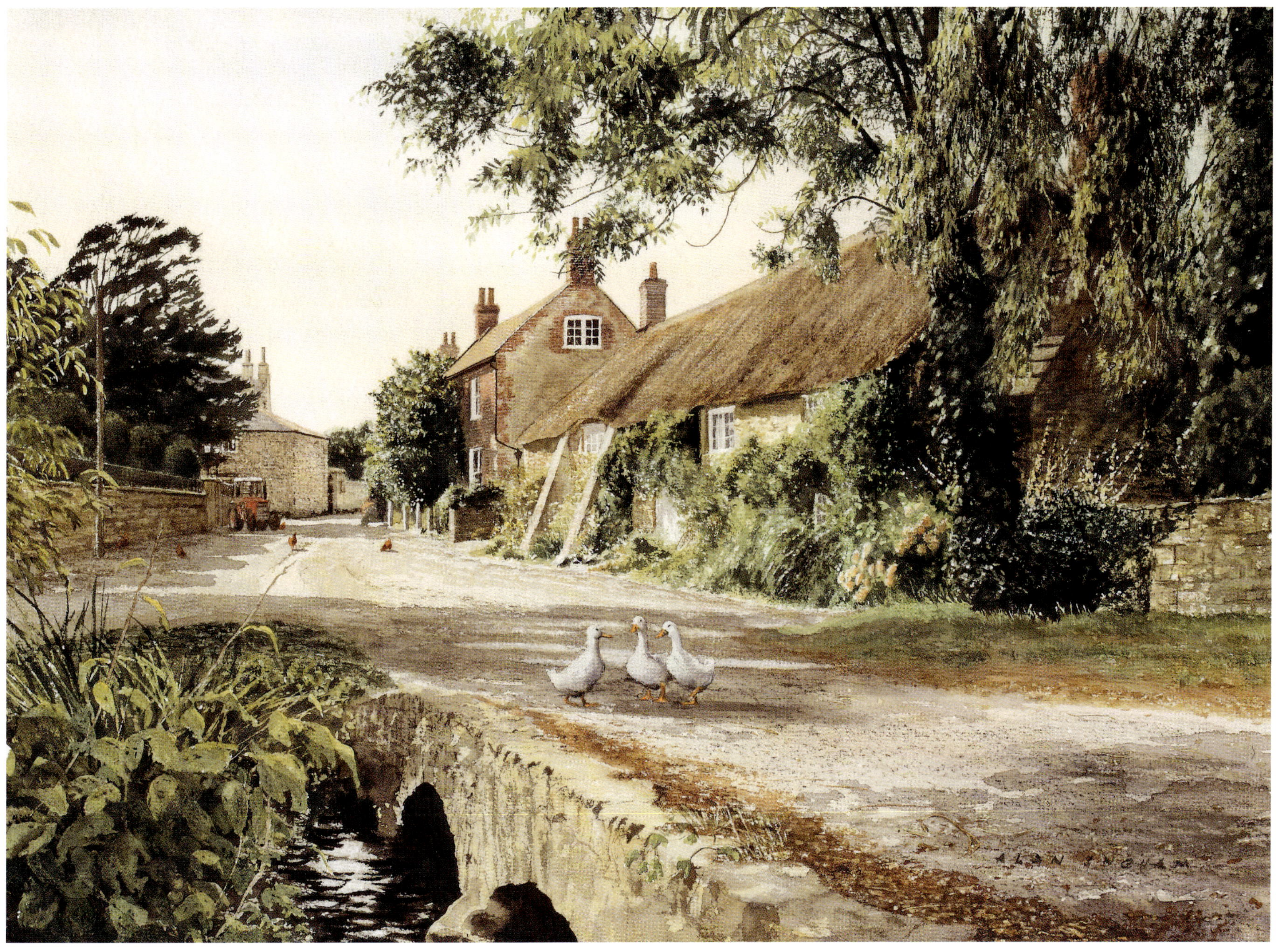

Hob Nobbing, Burton Bradstock, Dorset, 1994.

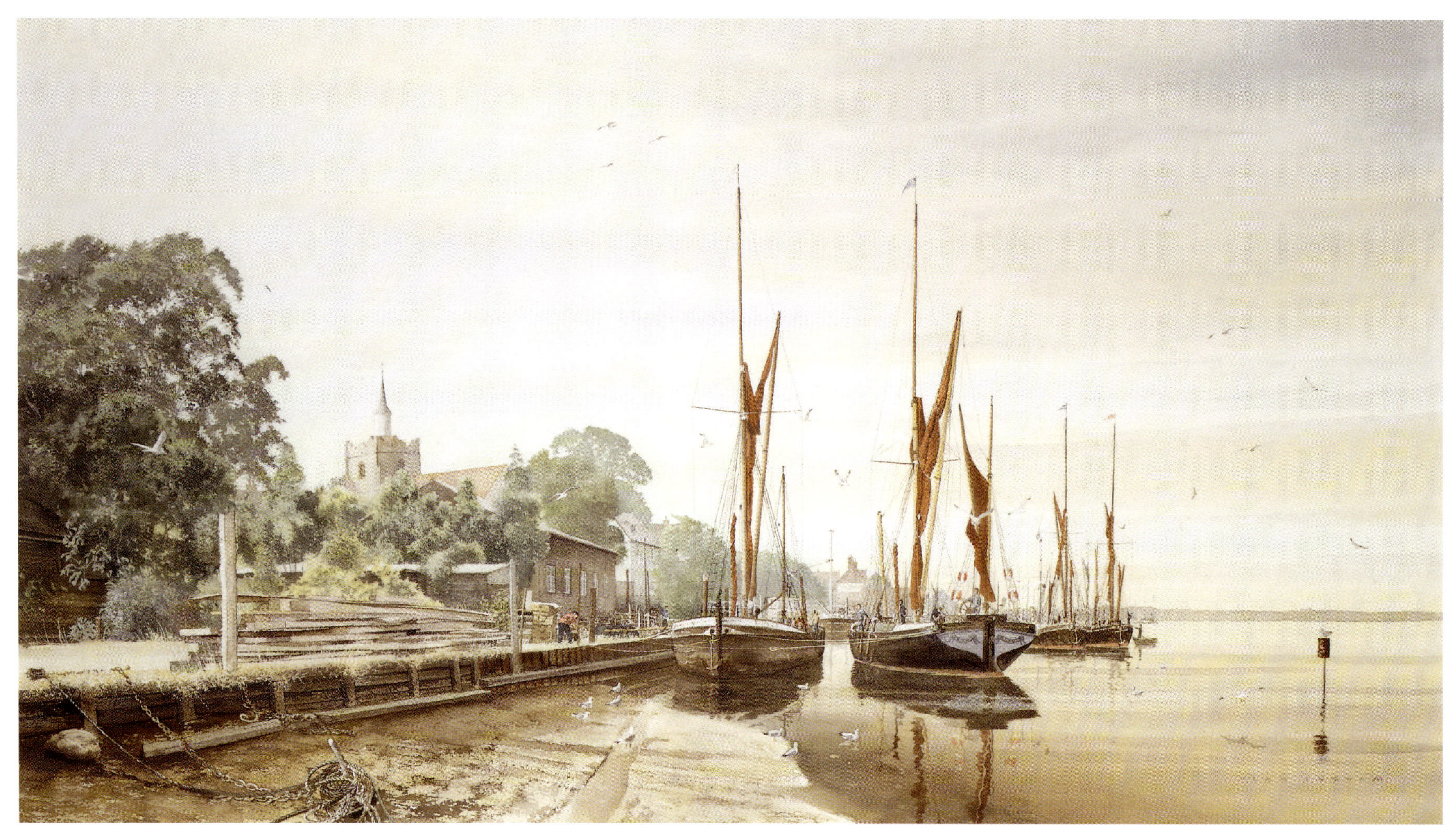

Tying up for the Night, Maldon, Essex, 1994.

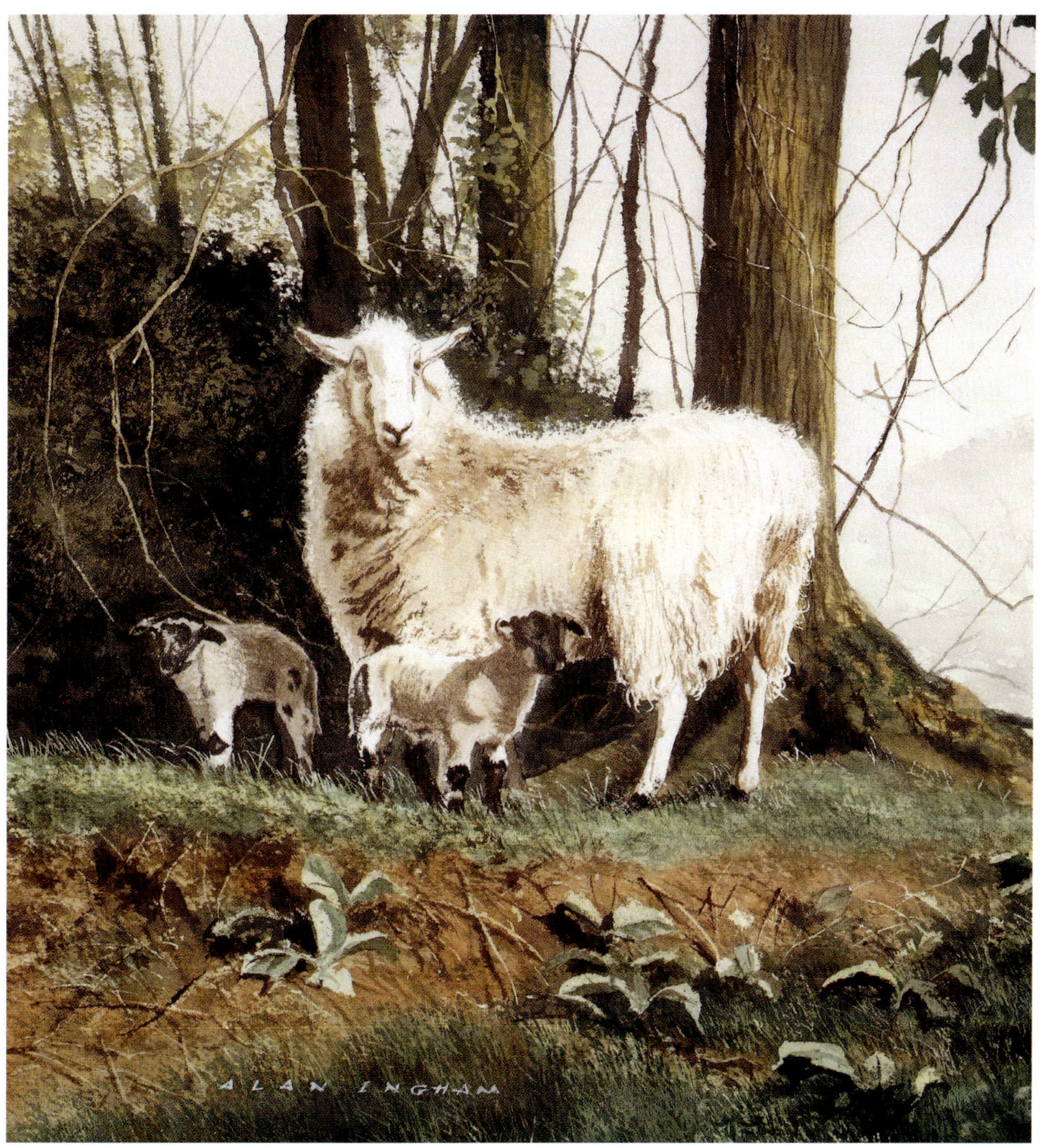

Spring Lambs, Benty Grange, Derbyshire, 1995.

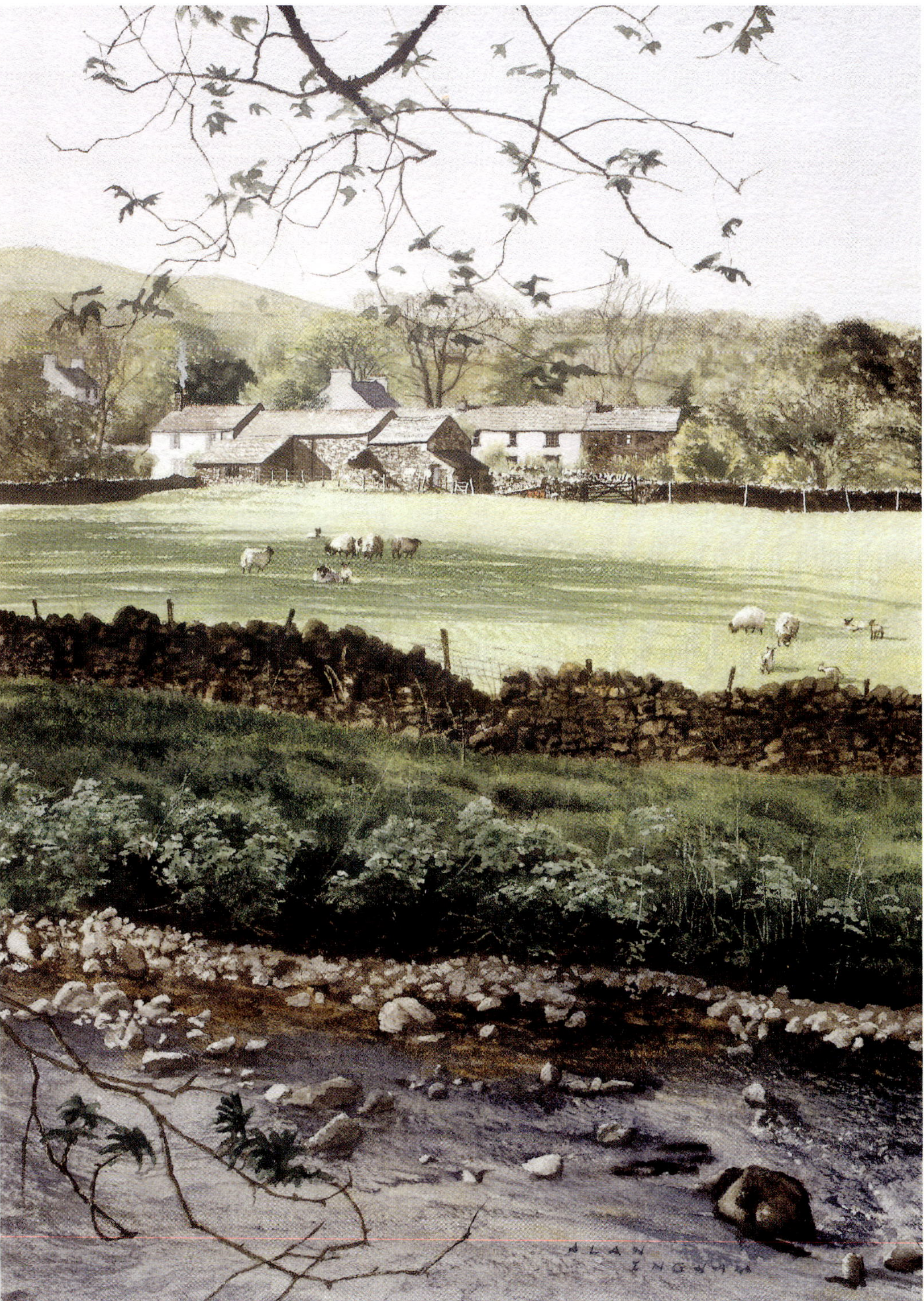

The Grass is Greener, Deepdale Beck, Yorkshire, 1995.

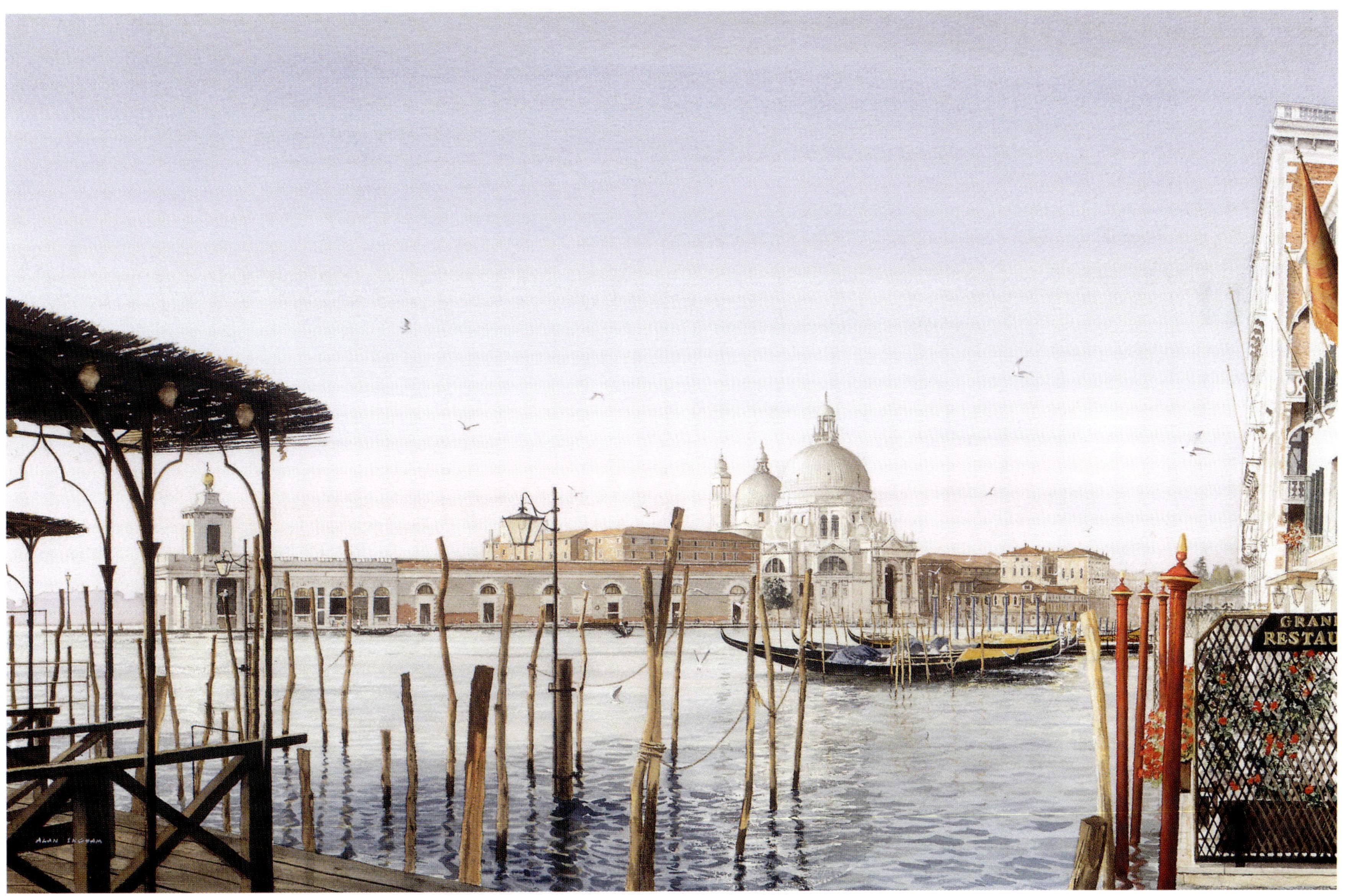

Santa Maria della Salute, Venice, 1996.

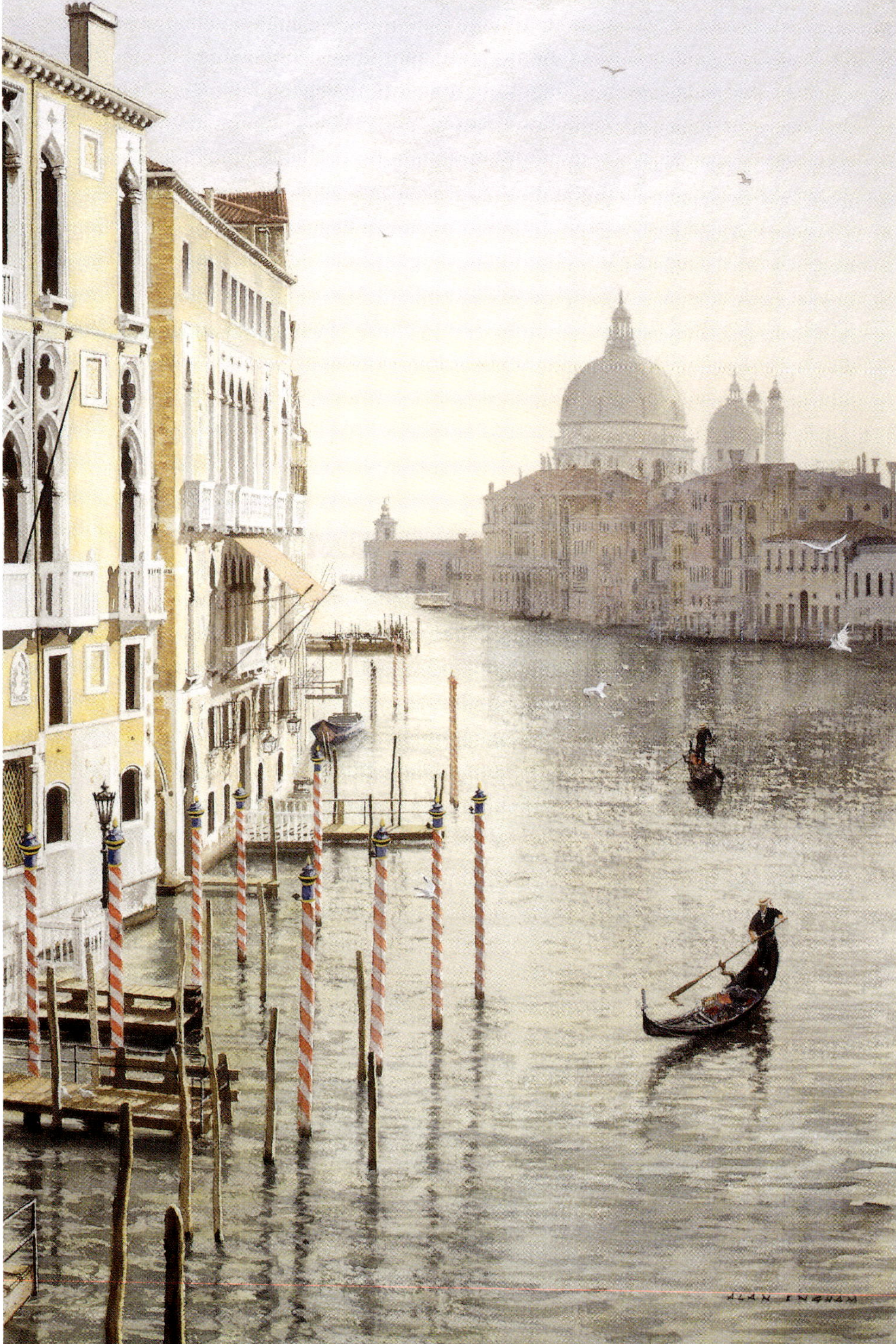

La Serenissima, Venice, 1995.

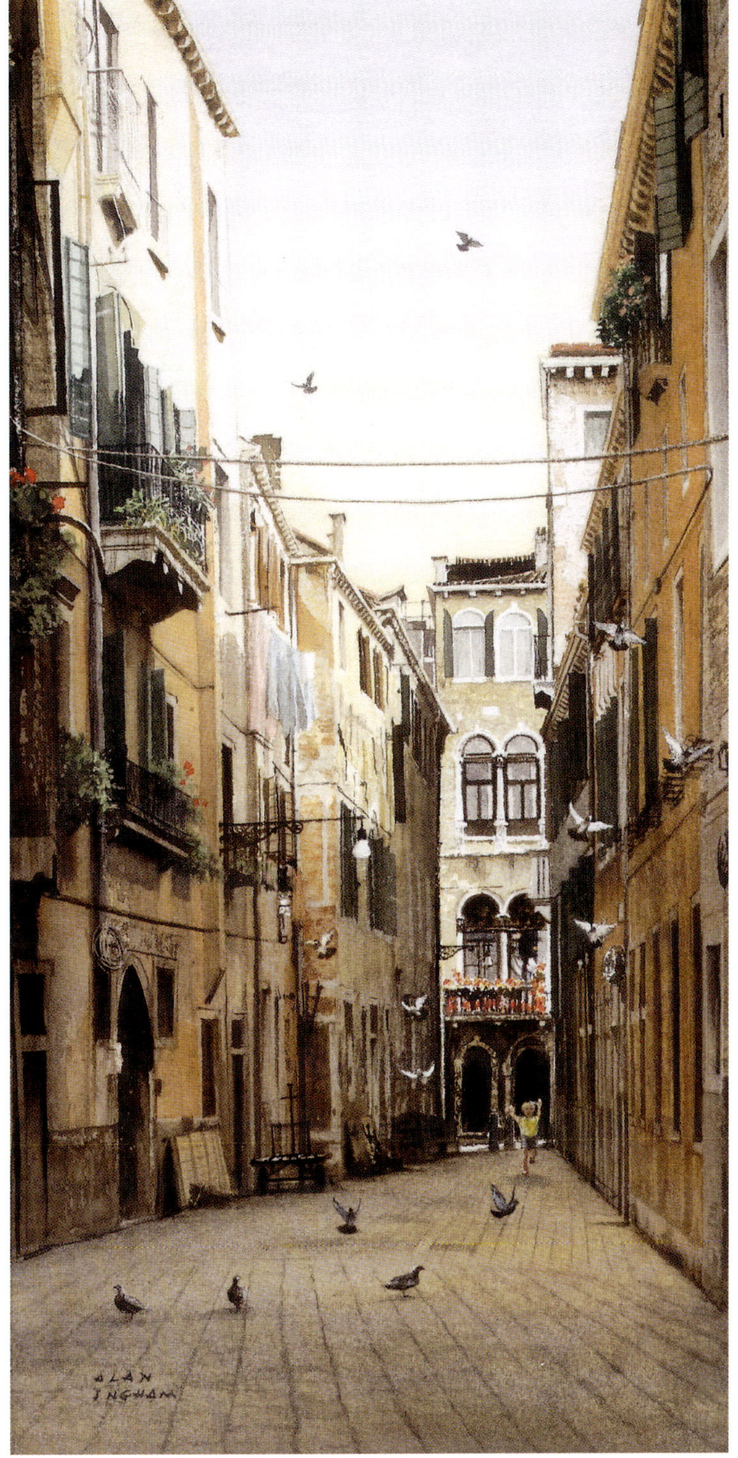

Calle del Assassin, Venice, 1995.

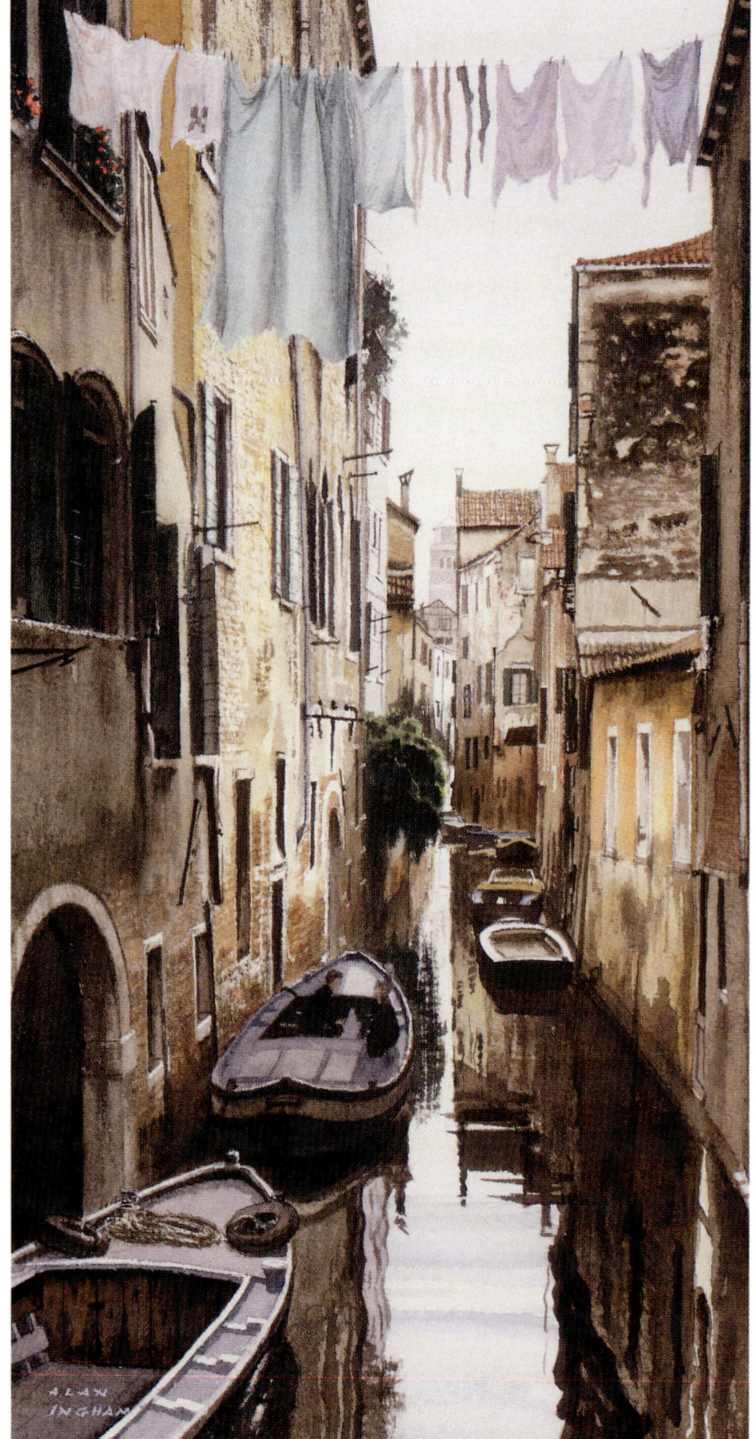

Canal Scorcio, Venice, 1995.

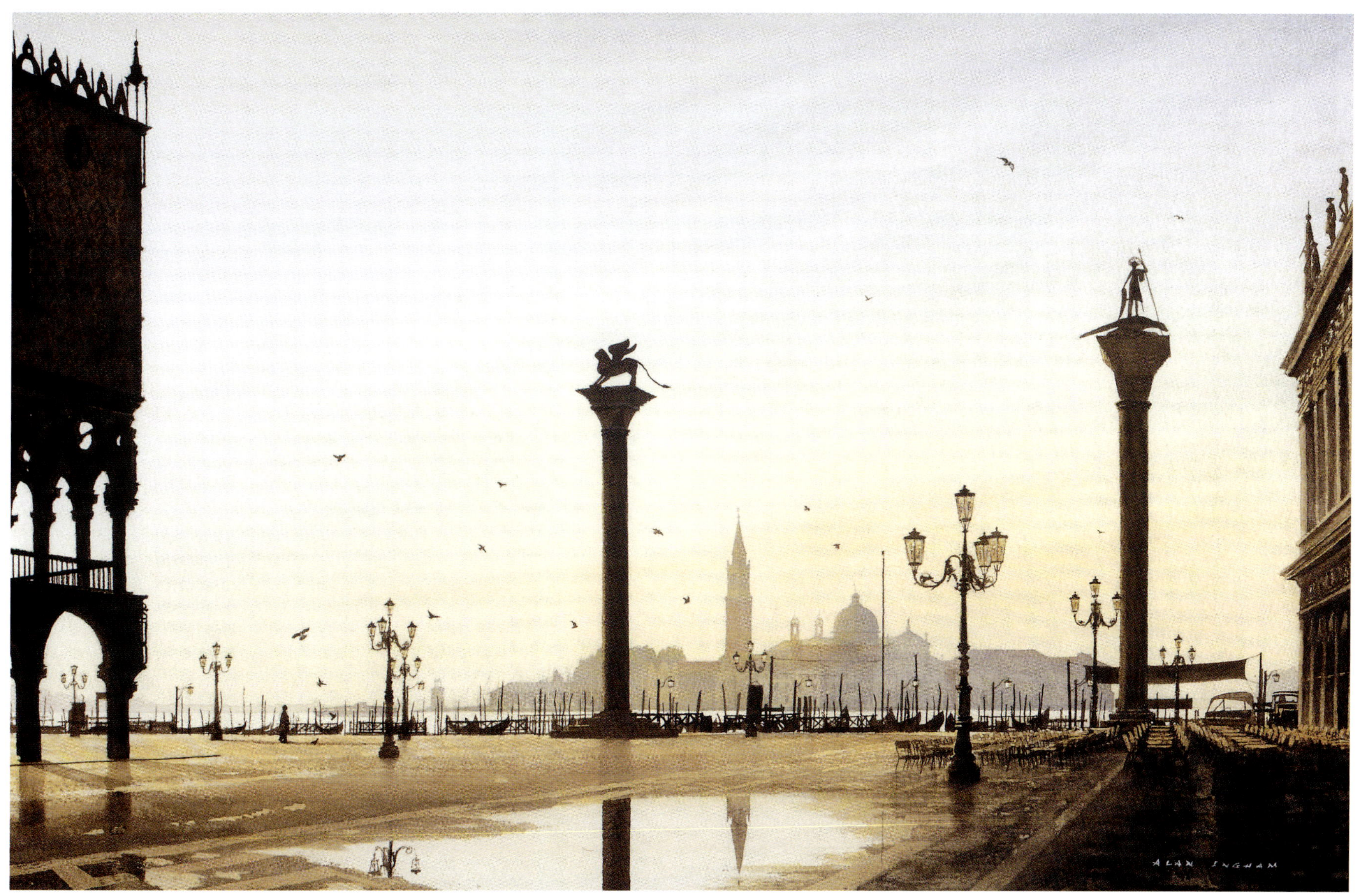

Venetian Sunrise, Venice, 1995

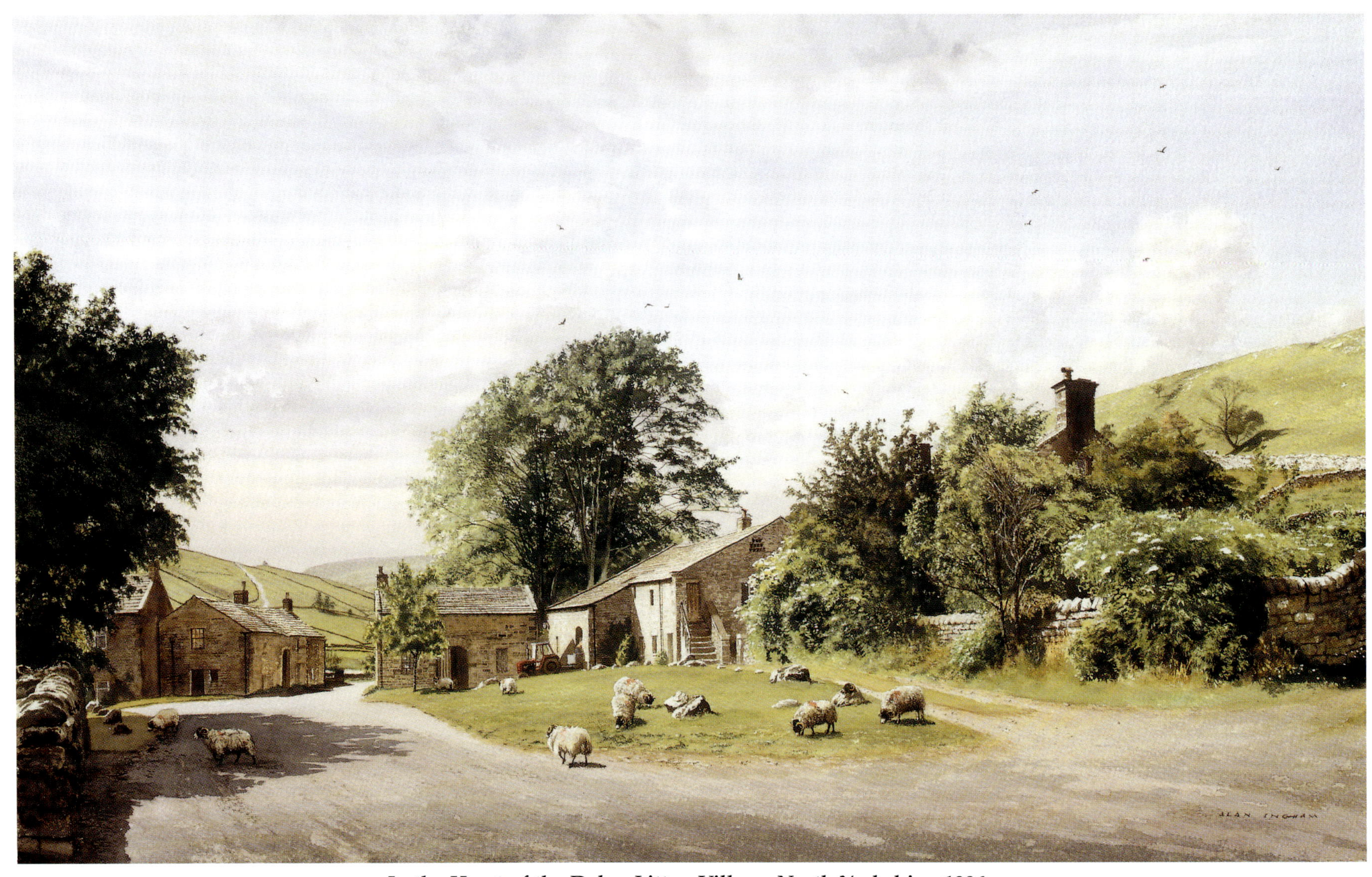

In the Heart of the Dales, Litton Village, North Yorkshire, 1996.

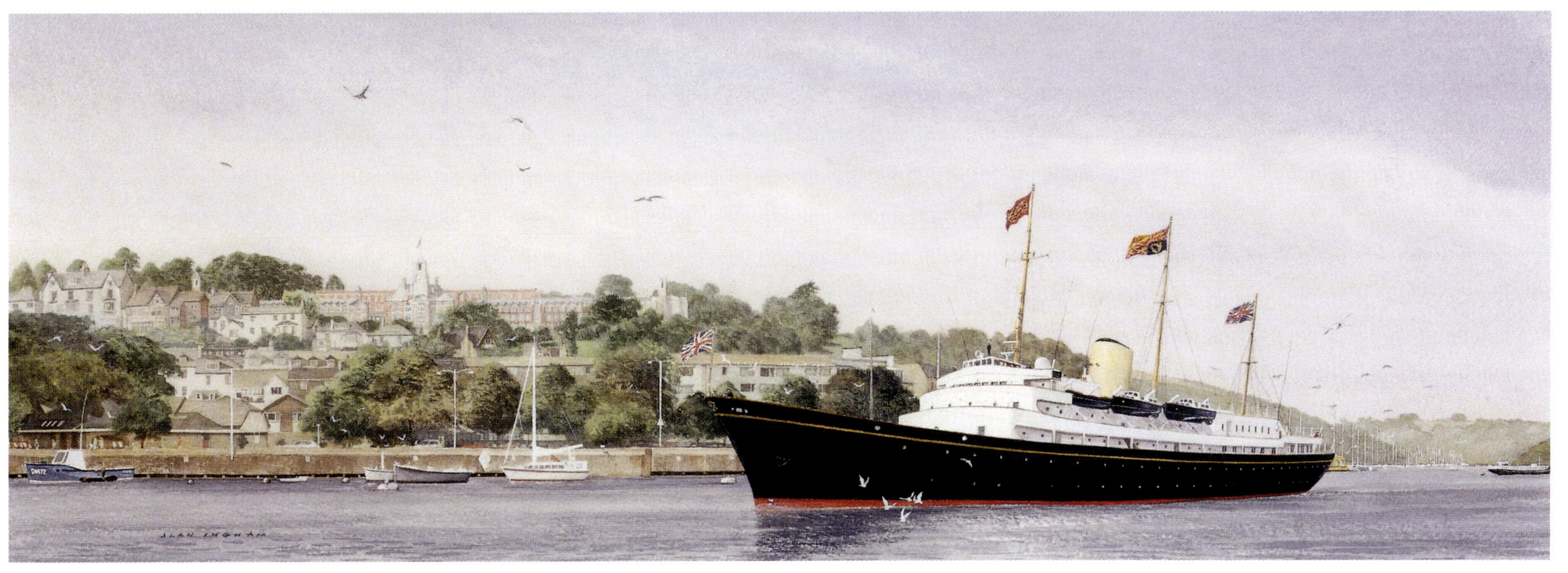

Britannias Two, Royal Naval College, Dartmouth, Devon, 1996.

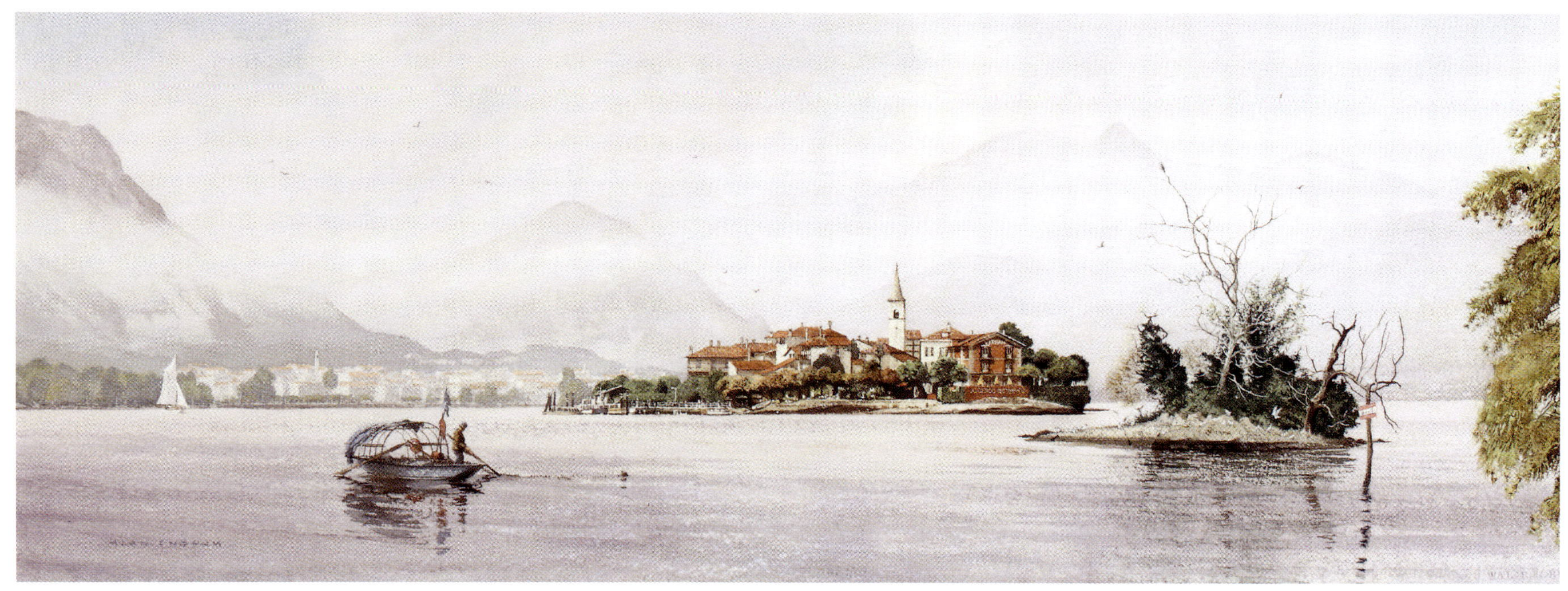

Isola dei Pestcatoria, Lake Maggiore, Italy, 1997.

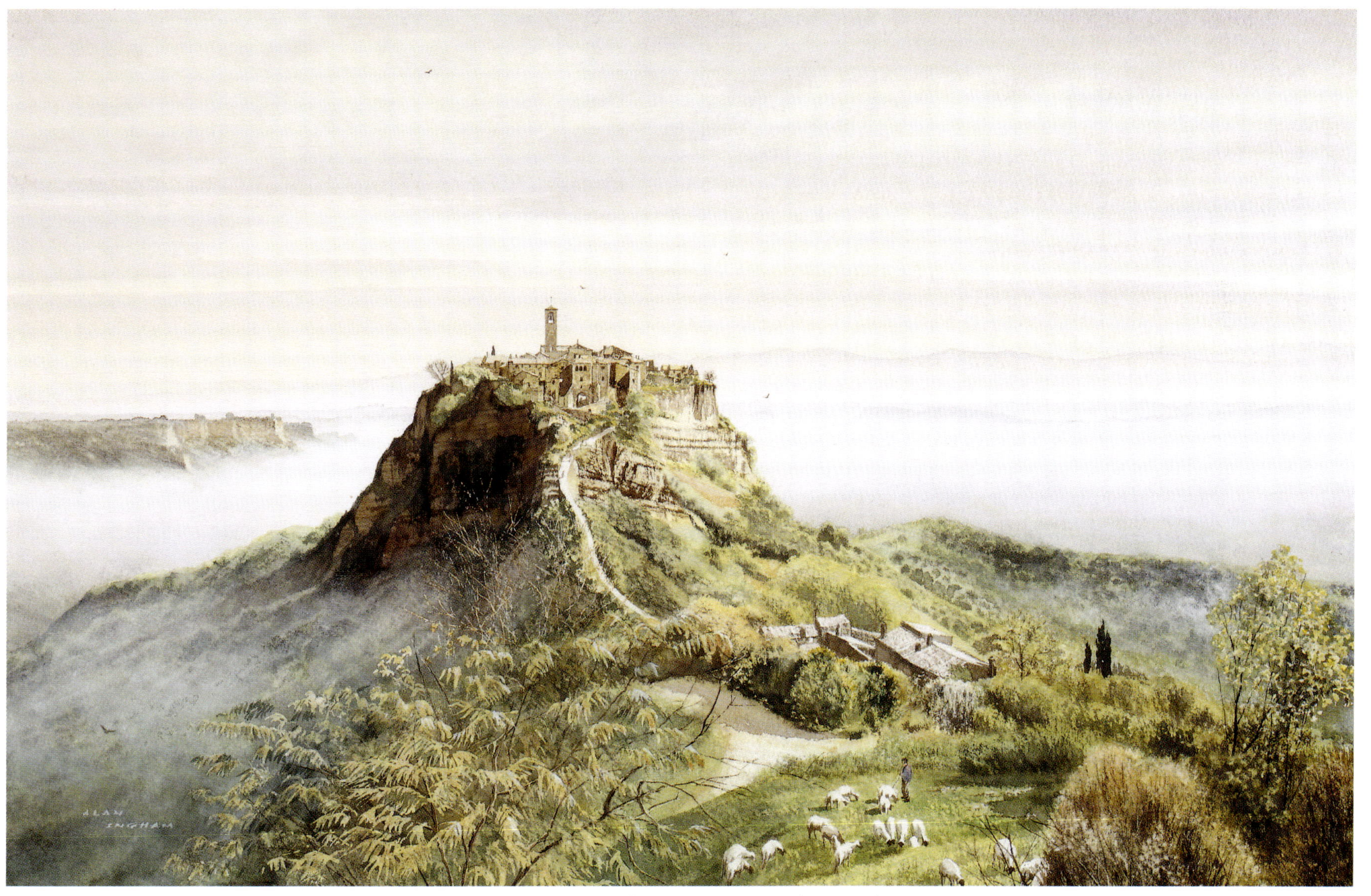

Lost Horizon, Civita di Bagnoregio, Umbria, Italy, 1997.

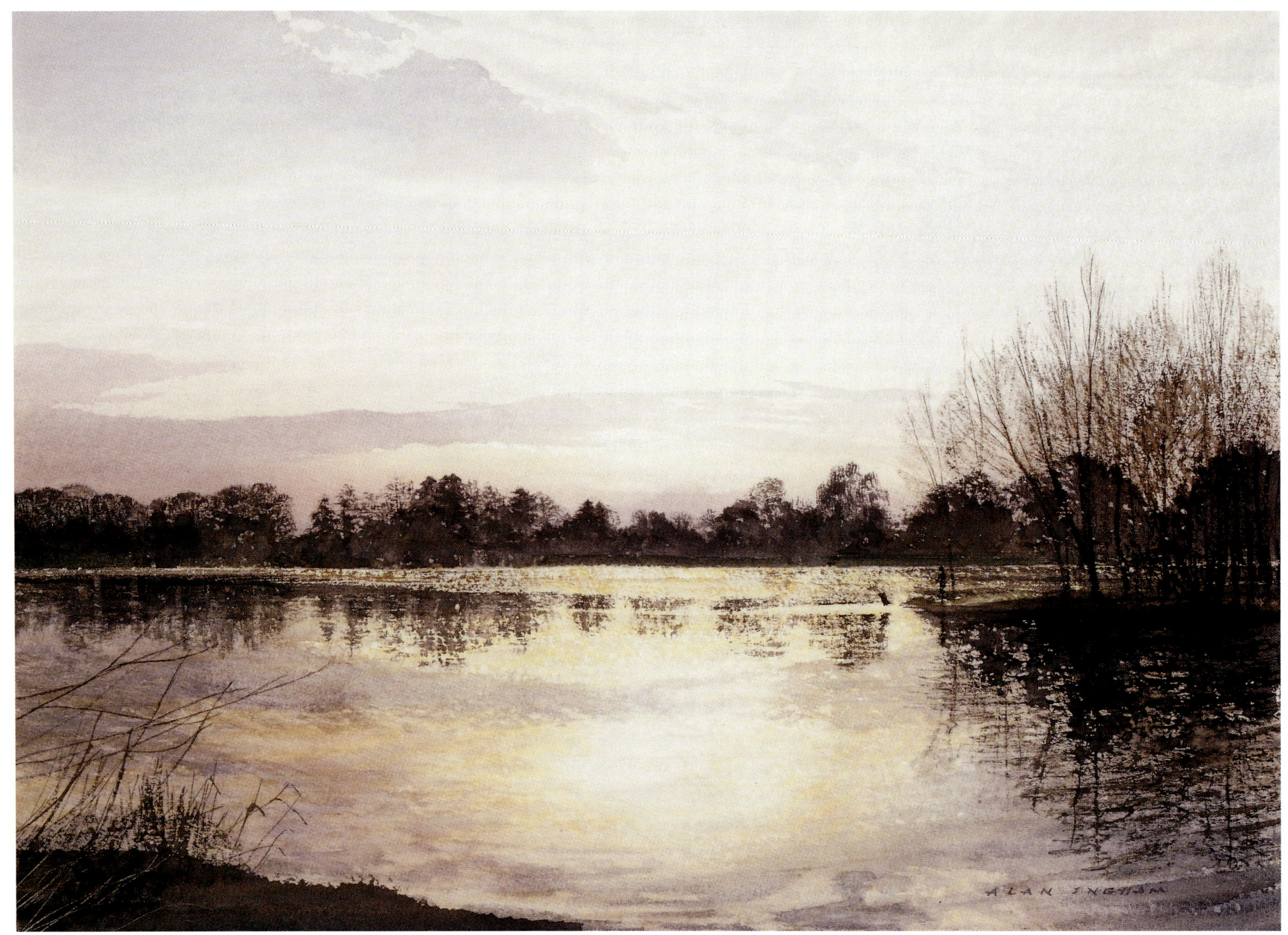

Dreamtime, Broadlands Lake, Romsey, Hampshire, 1998.

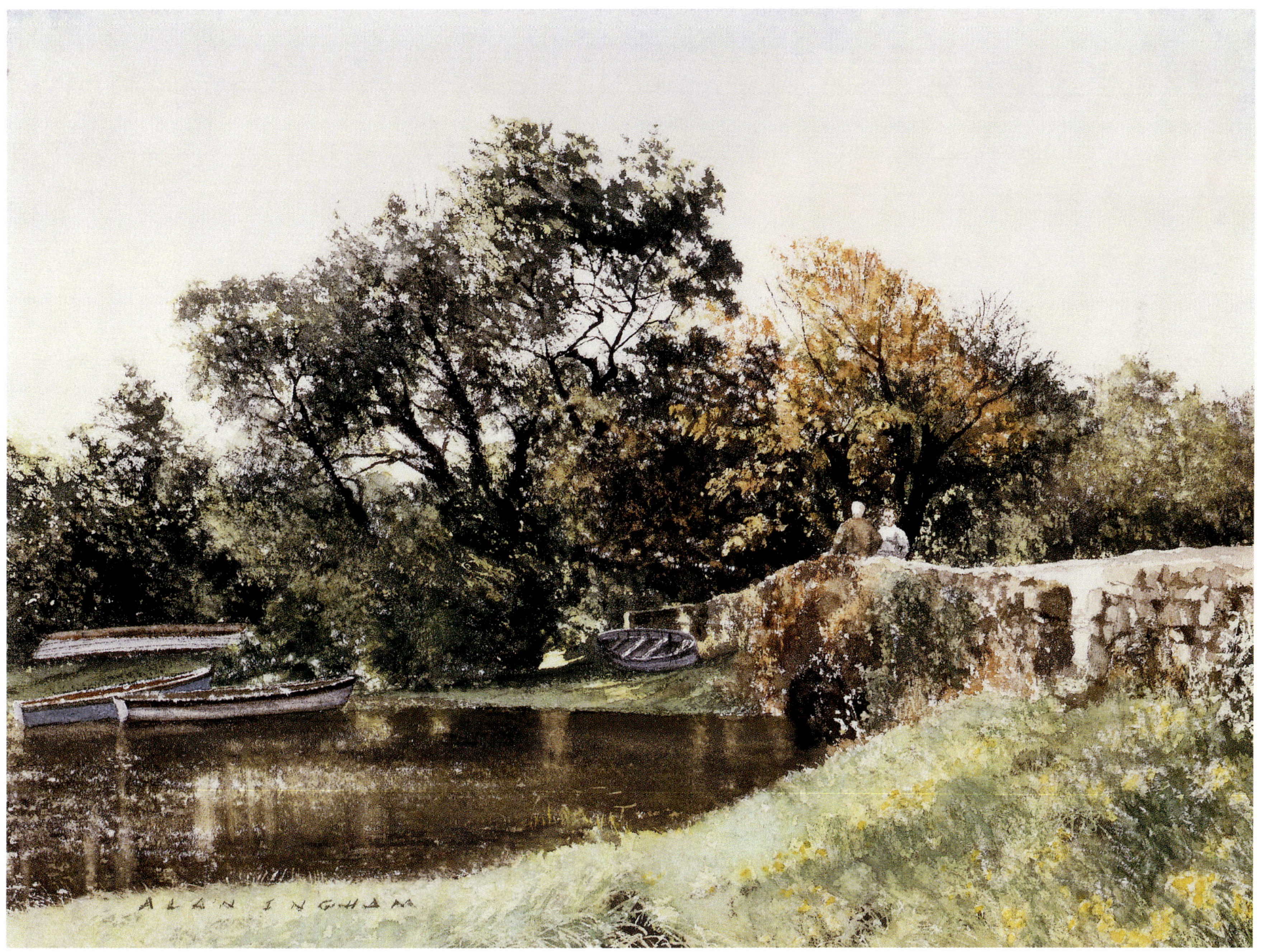

Conversation Piece, Killarney Lakes, Co. Cork, Ireland, 1998.

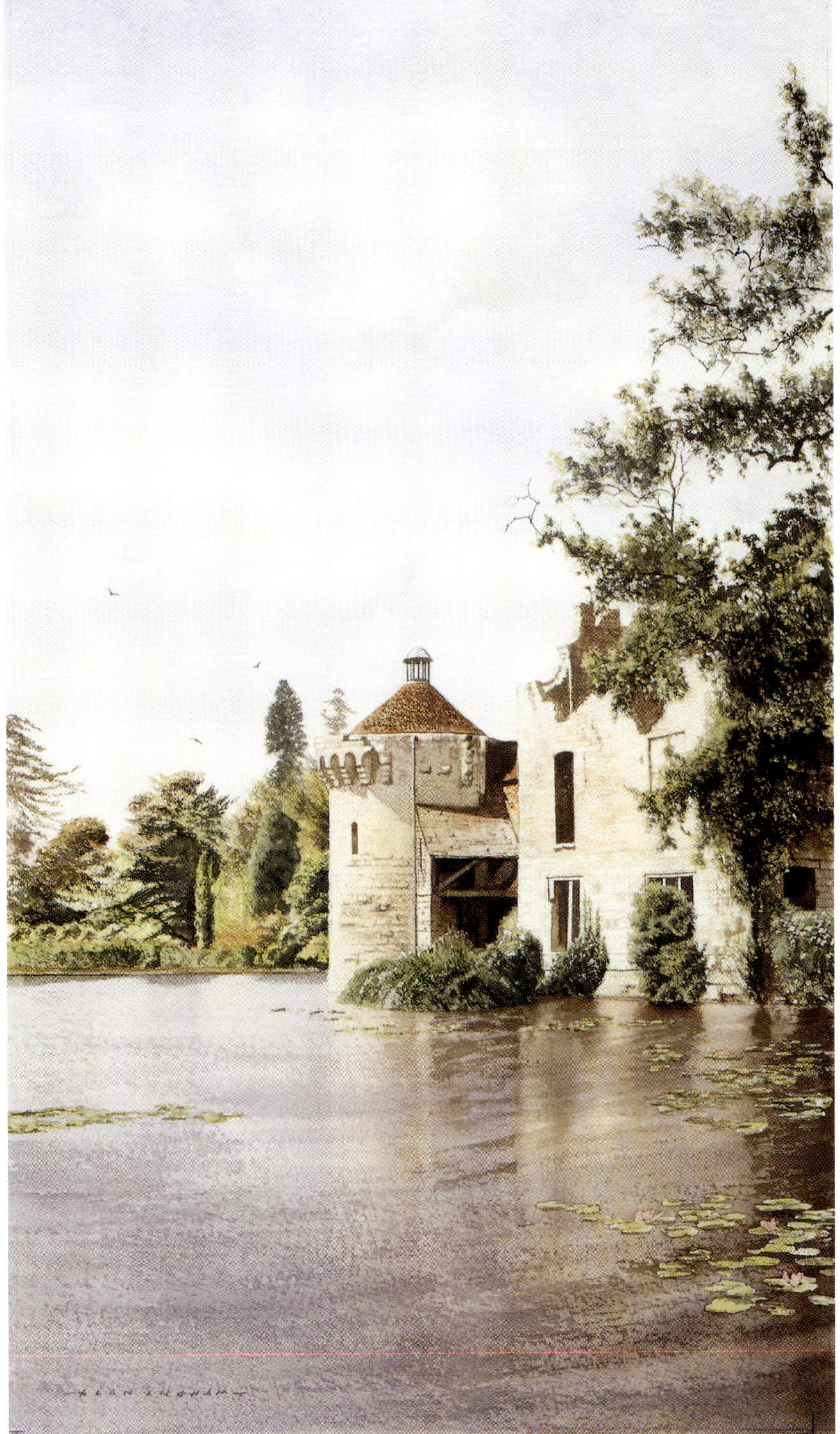

Scotney Castle, Kent, 1998.

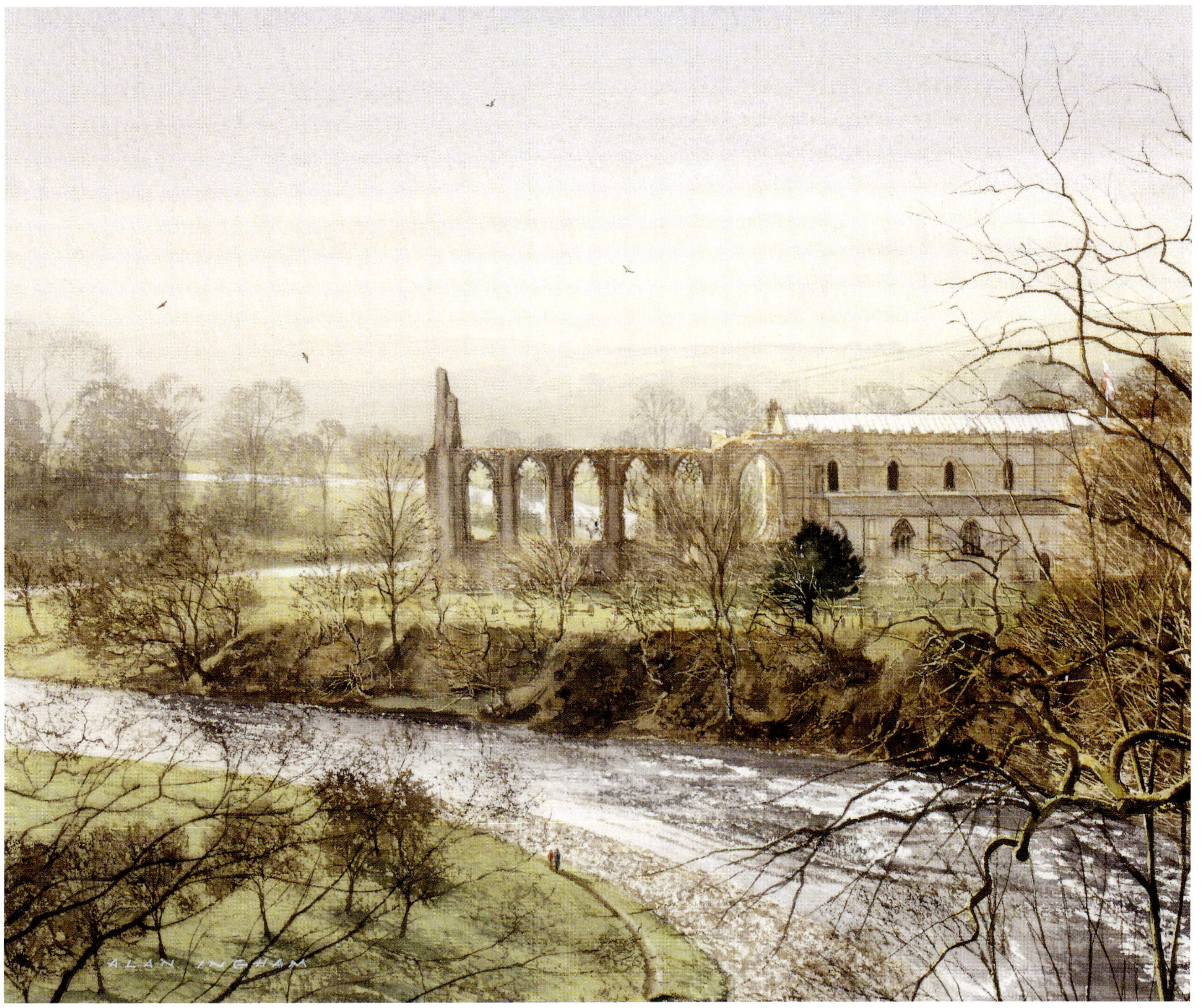

Silent Witness, Bolton Priory and River Wharf, North Yorkshire, 1998.

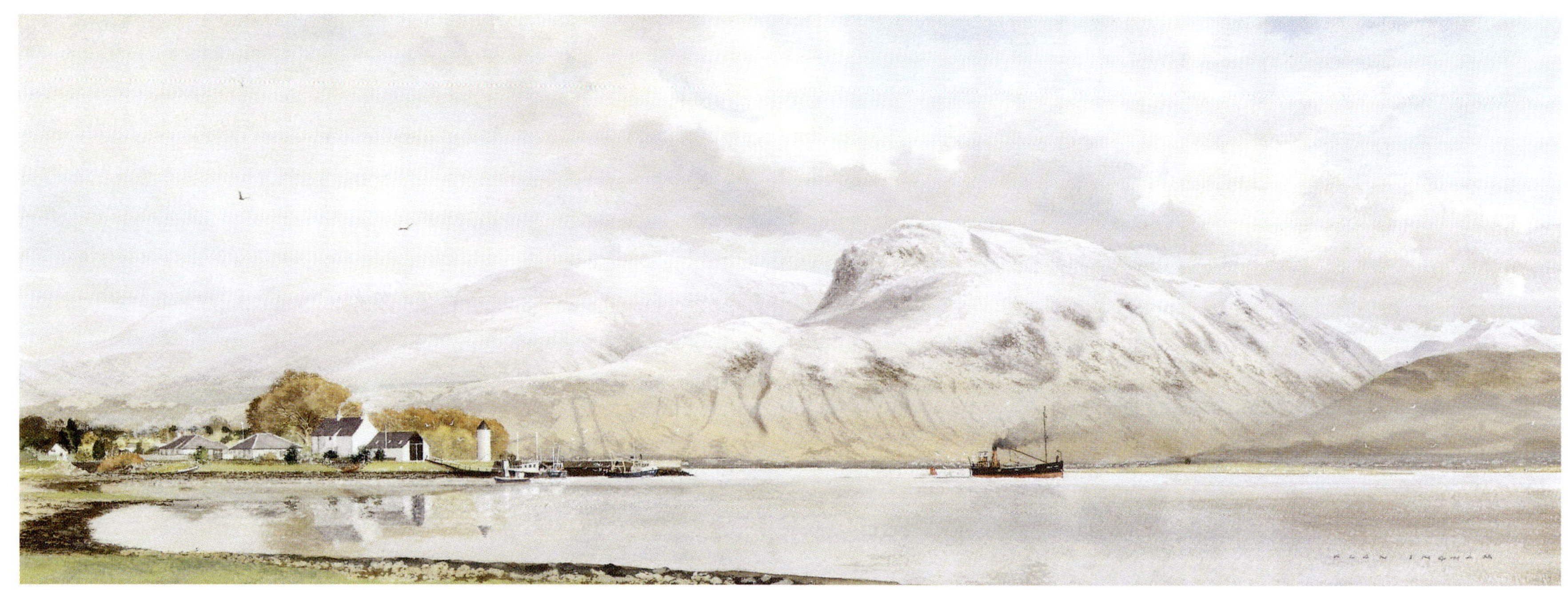

Highland Splendour, Ben Nevis and the Sea Locks at Corpach, Scotland, 1998.

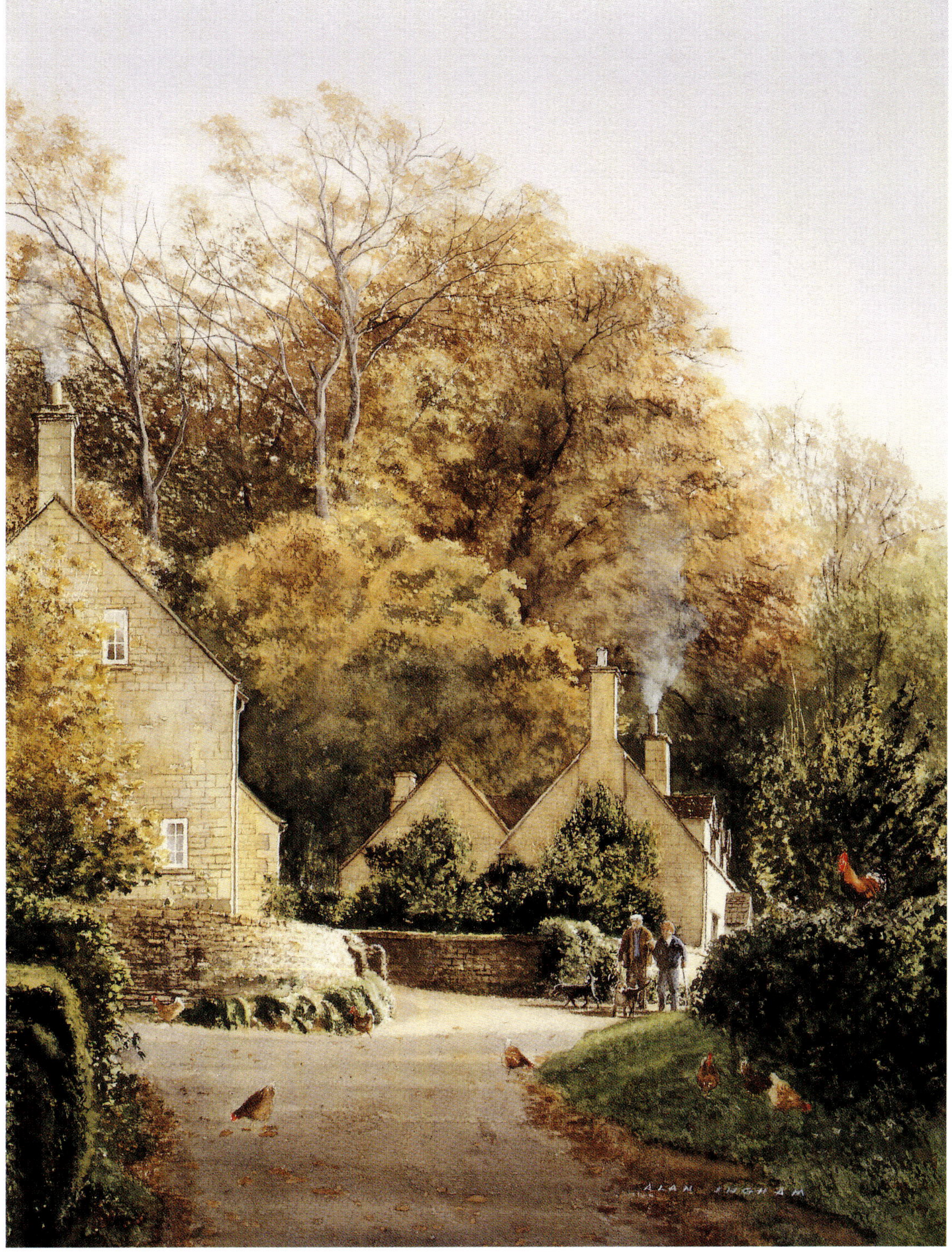

**October Gold,
Stanway,
Gloucestershire, 1998**

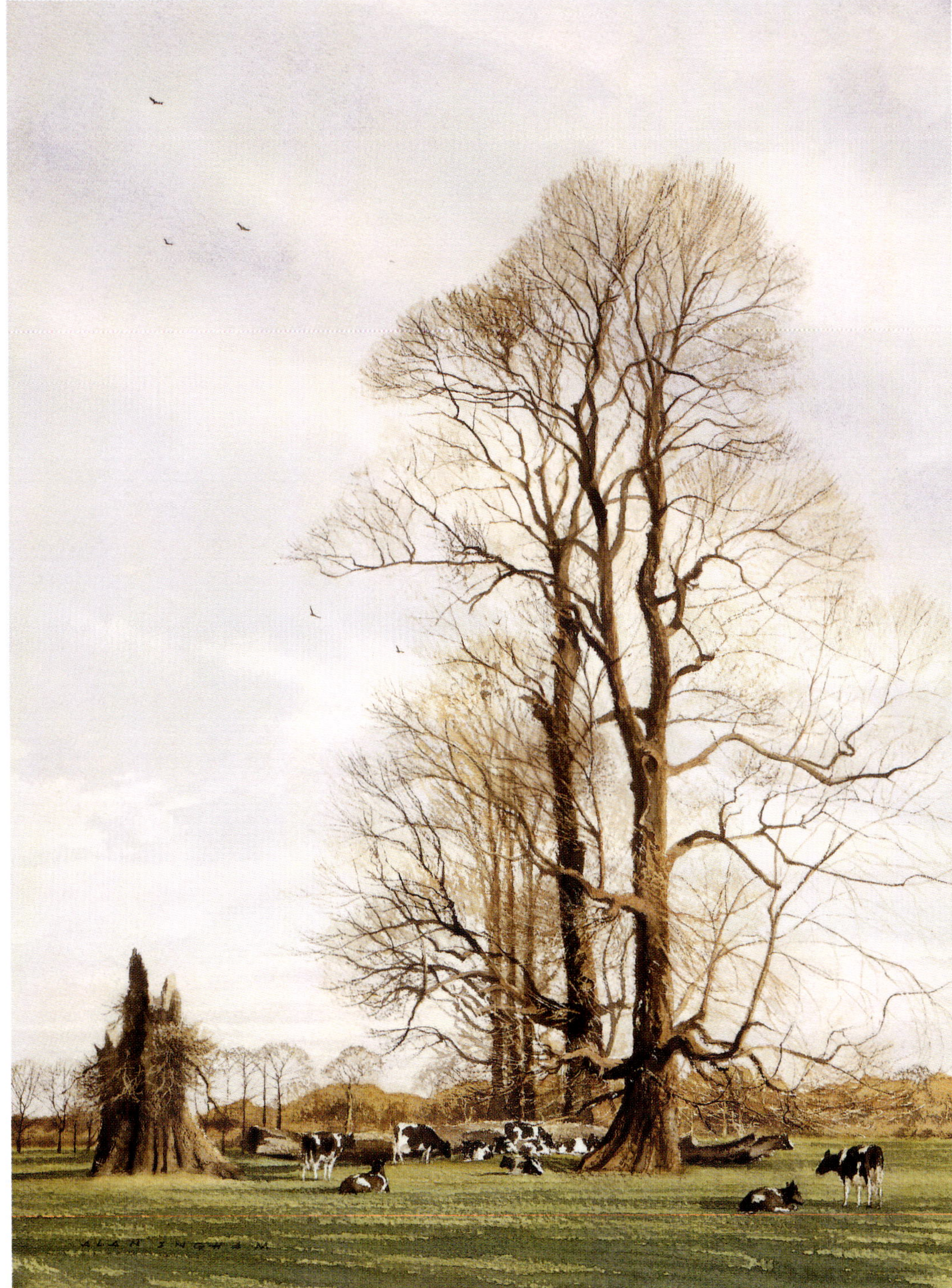

Elegy for the Elm, Brizes Corner, Kelveden Hatch, Essex, 1998.

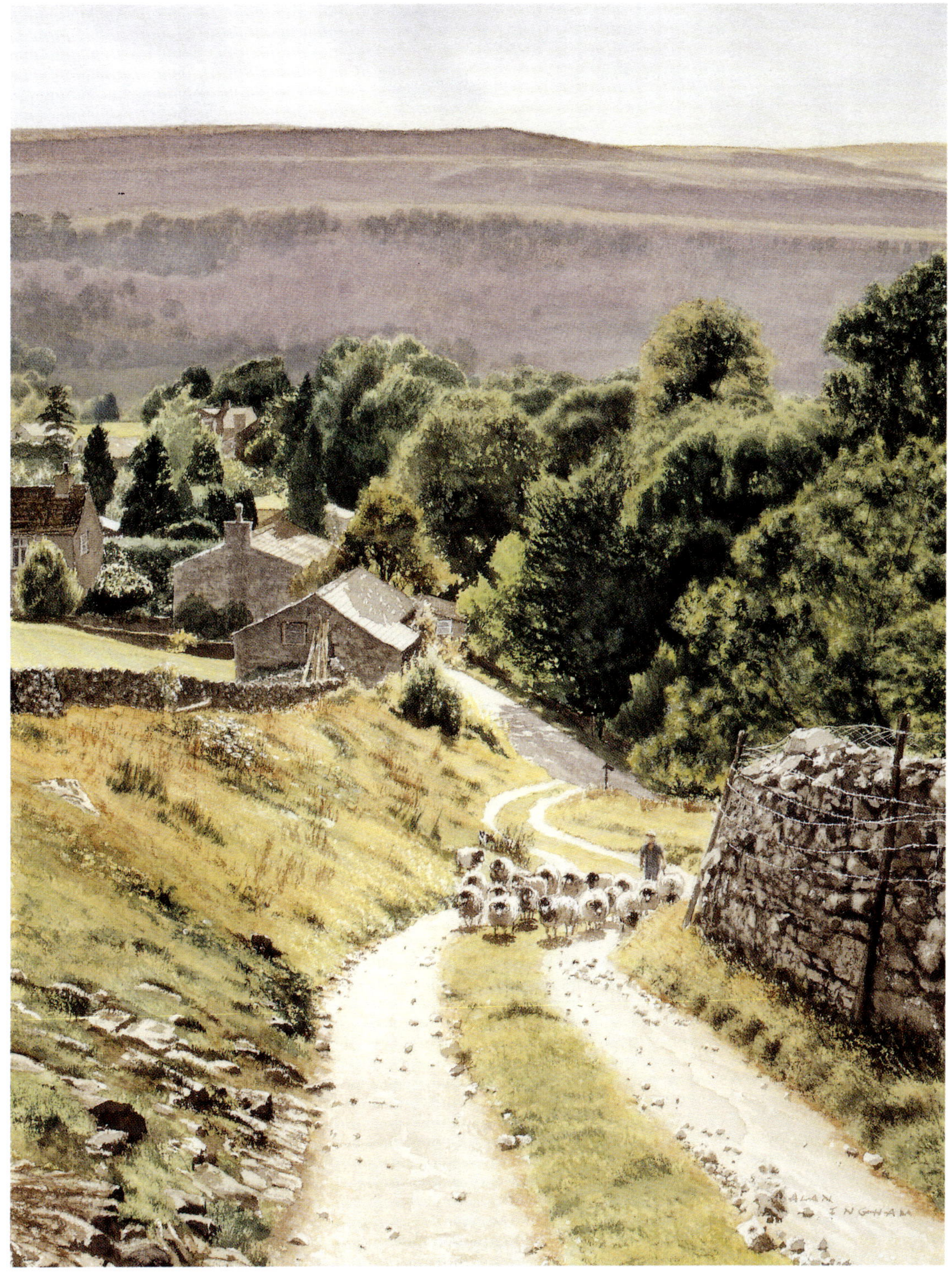

The Drovers Road, Kettlewell in Wharfedale, North Yorkshire, 1998.

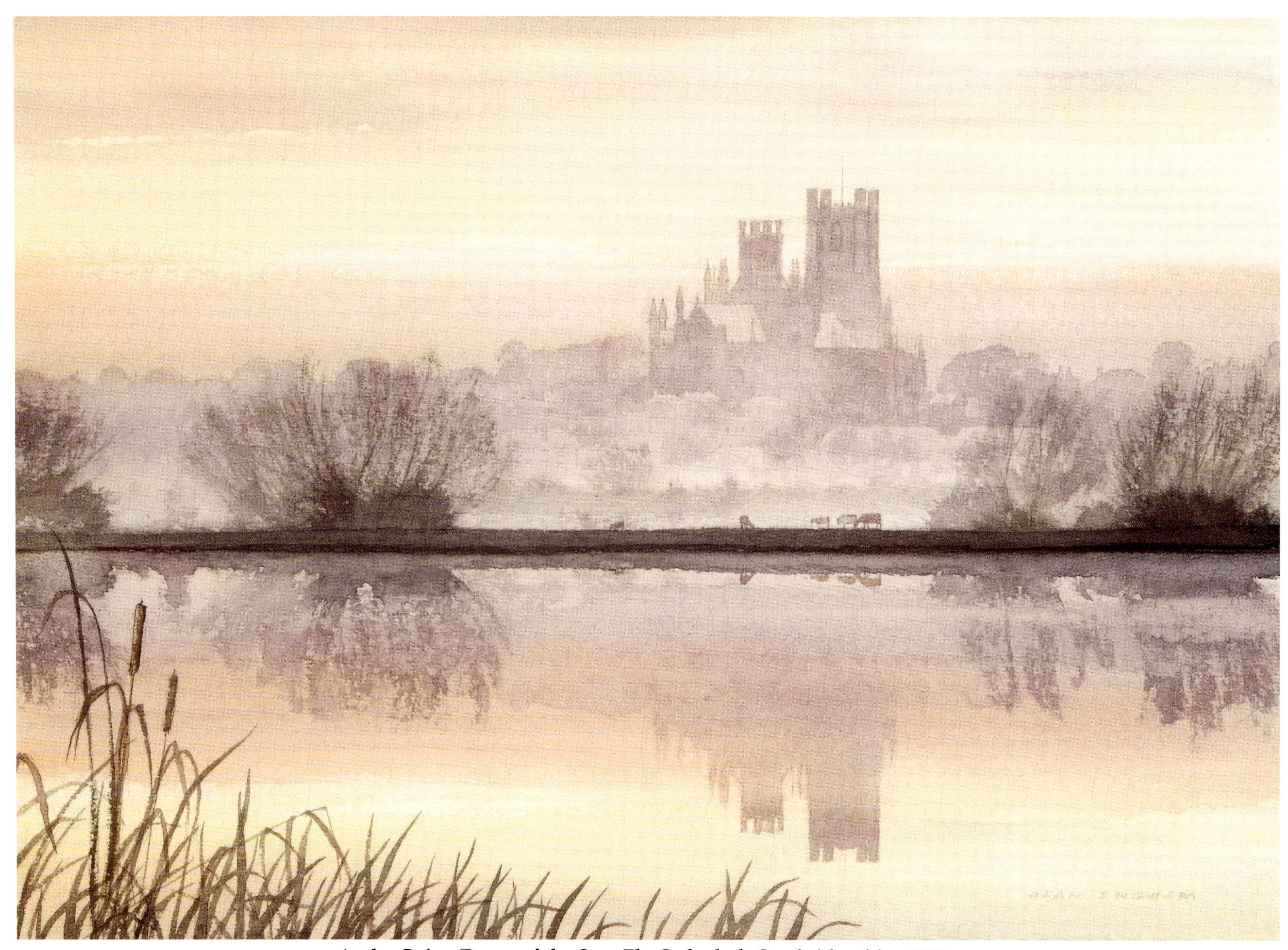

At the Going Down of the Sun, Ely Cathedral, Cambridgeshire, 1998.

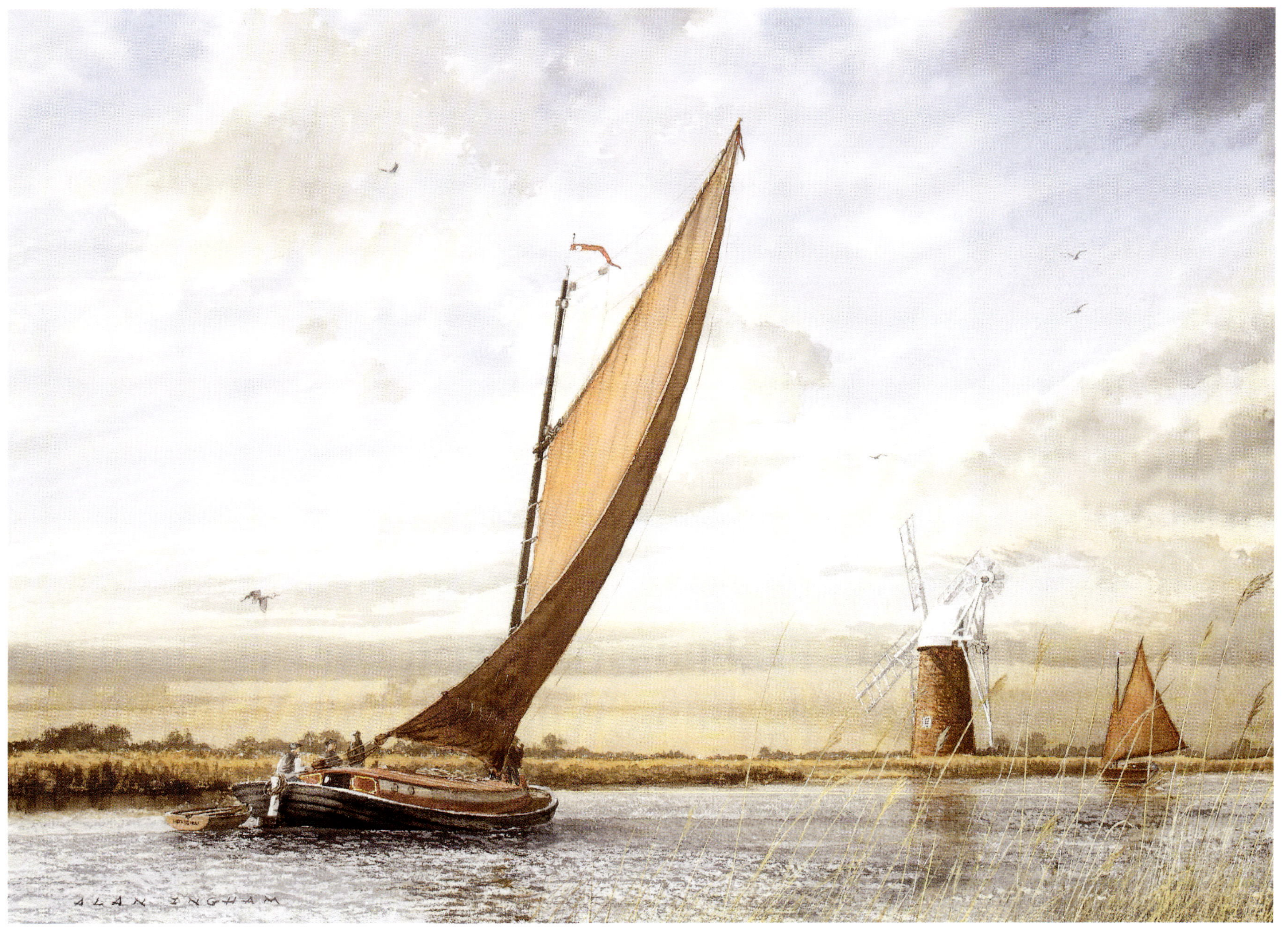

Running Free, Norfolk Broads, 1998.

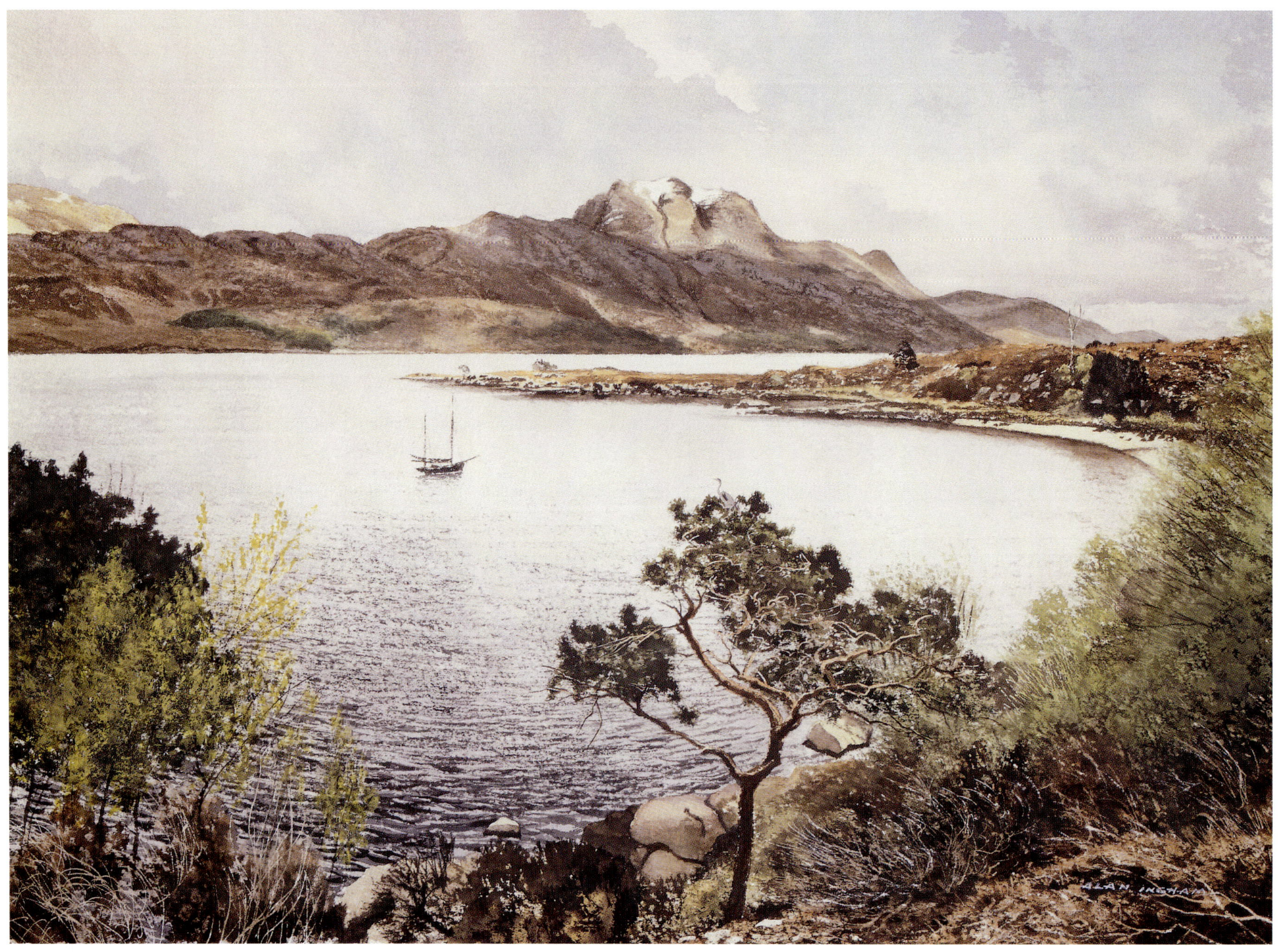

Serenity, Loch Maree and Ben Siloch, Wester Ross, Scotland, 1998.

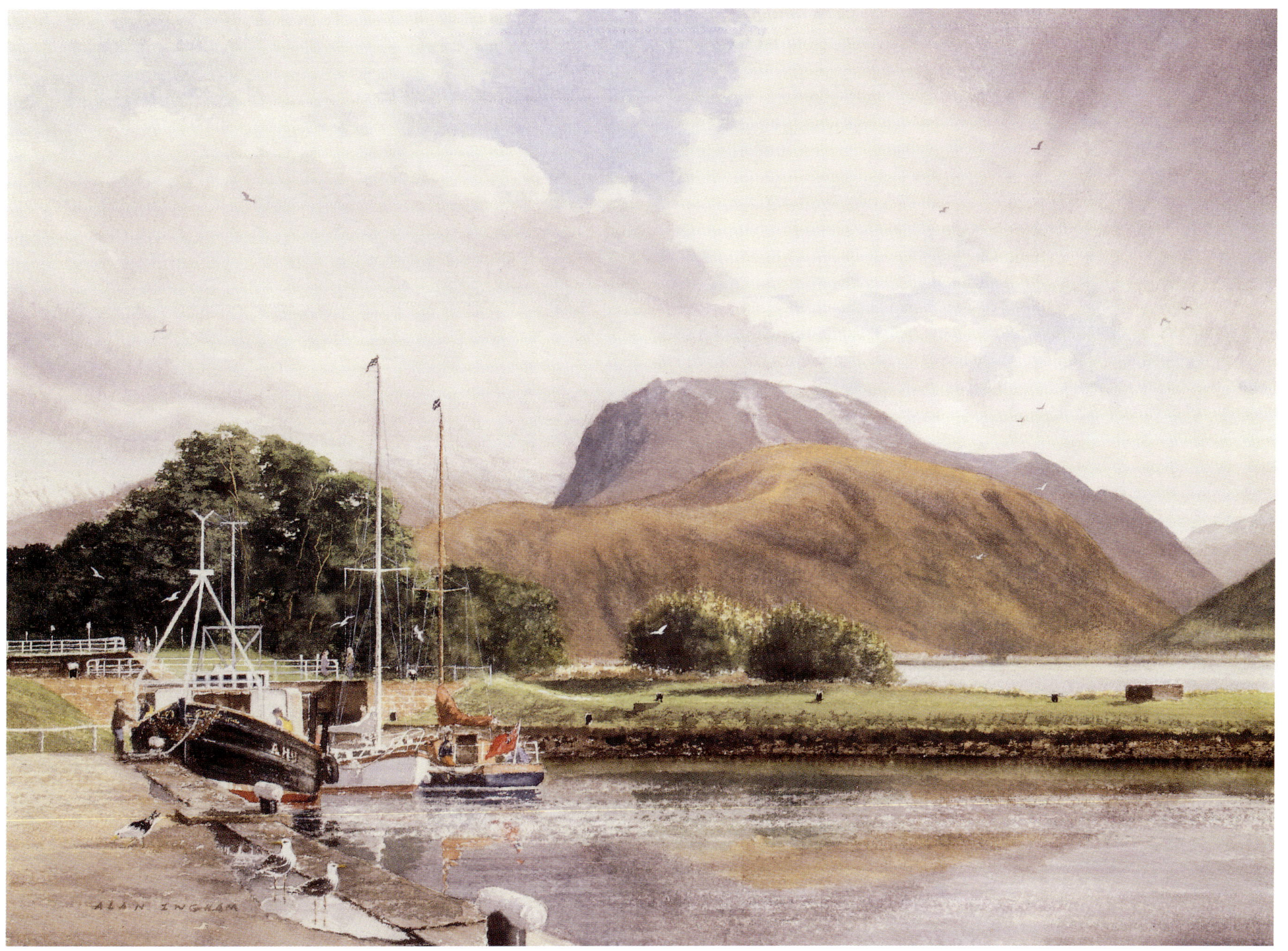

High and Mighty, Ben Nevis from Corpach Basin, Highlands, Scotland, 1998.

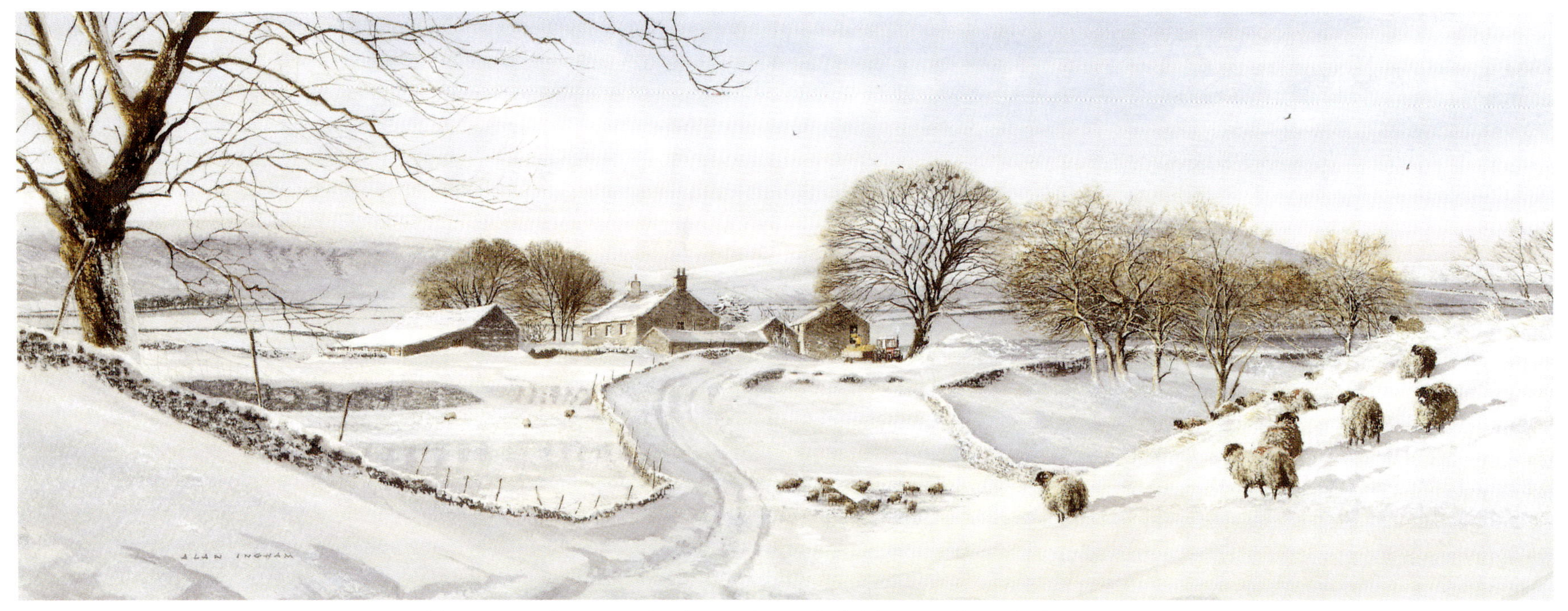

Winter Daydreams, Northcote Farm, Selside, North Yorkshire, 1998.

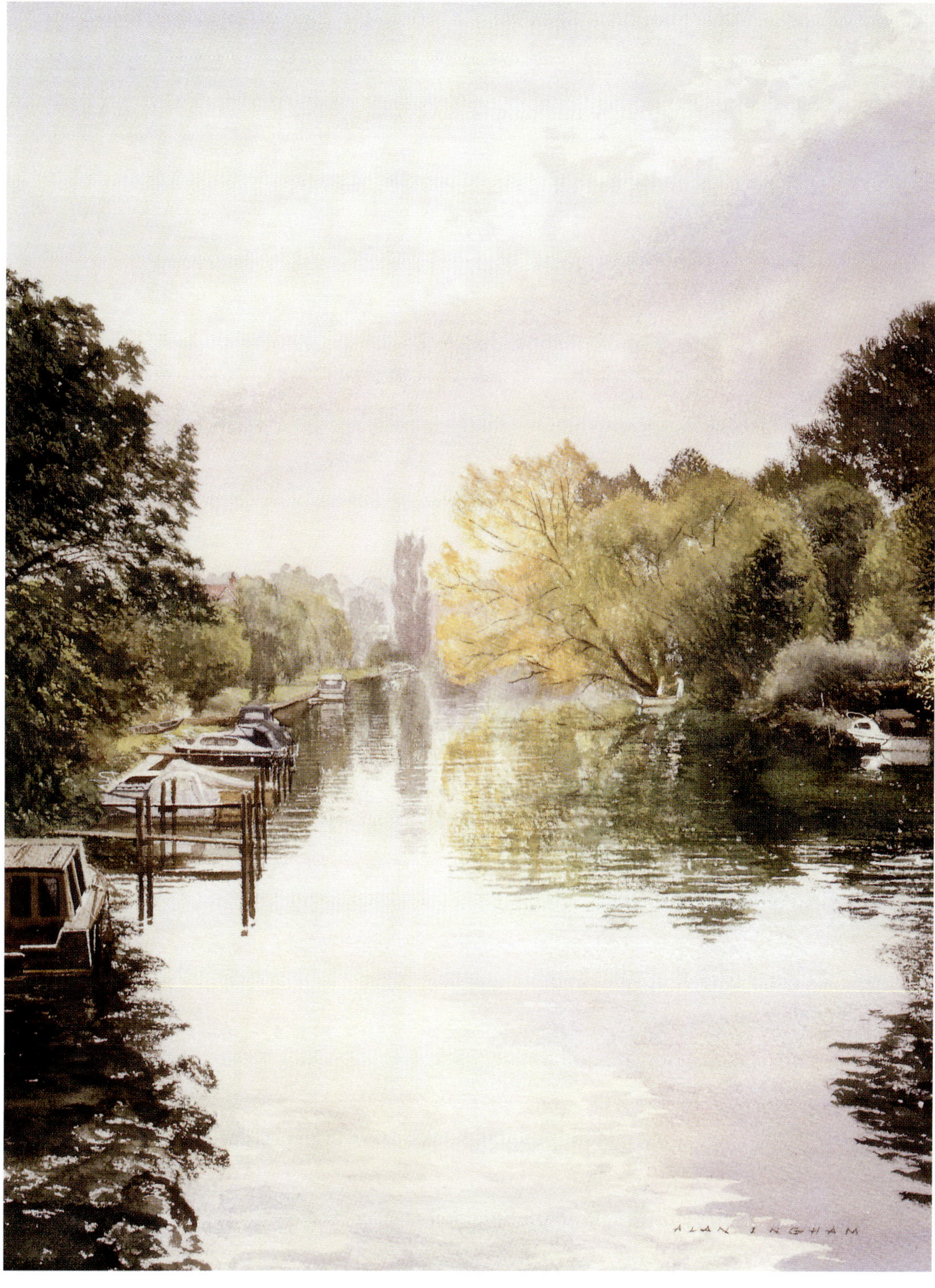

The Tryst, Thames Backwater from Whitchurch Toll Bridge, Oxfordshire, 1998.

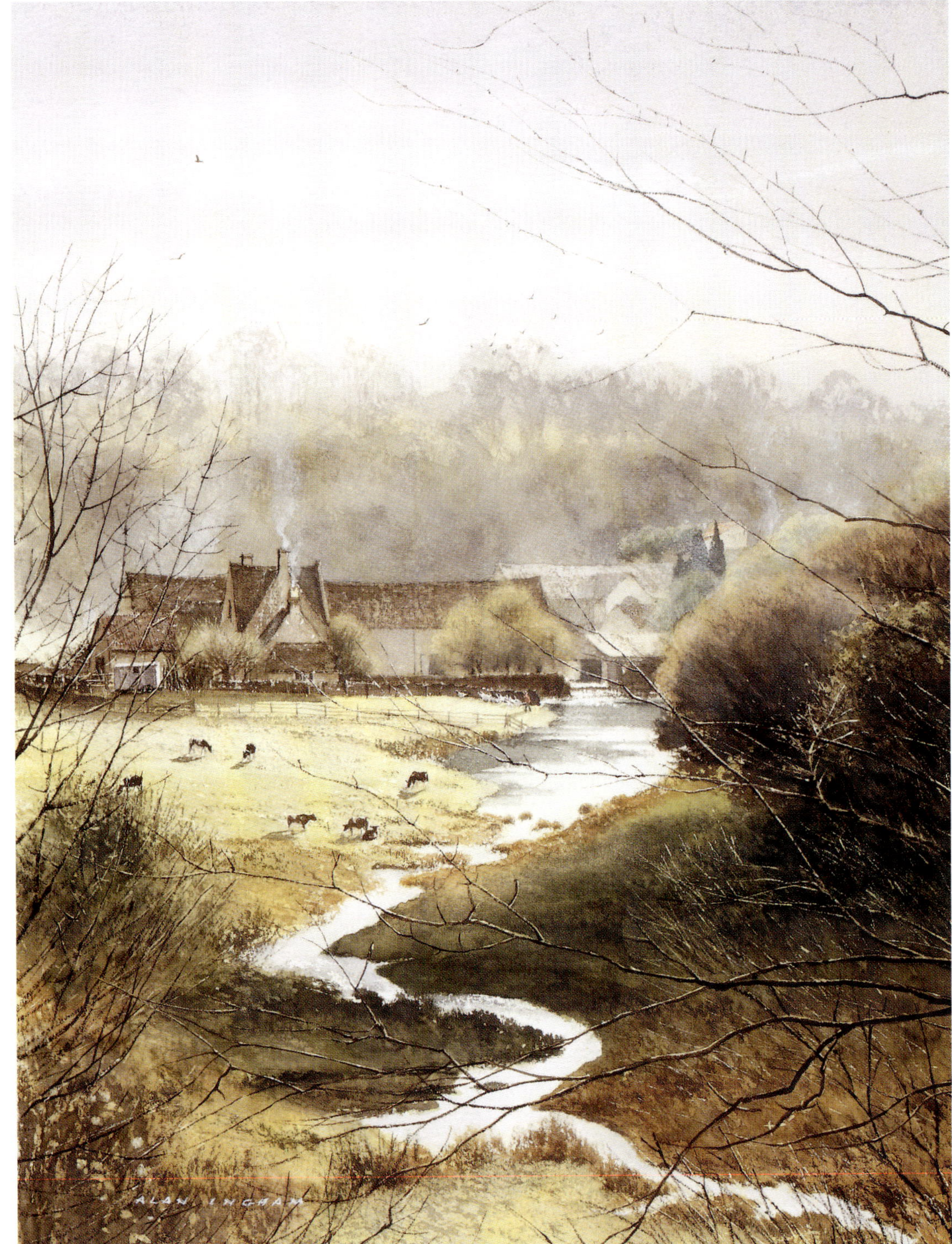

Rosie's Country, Middle Duntisbourne, Gloucestershire, 1998.

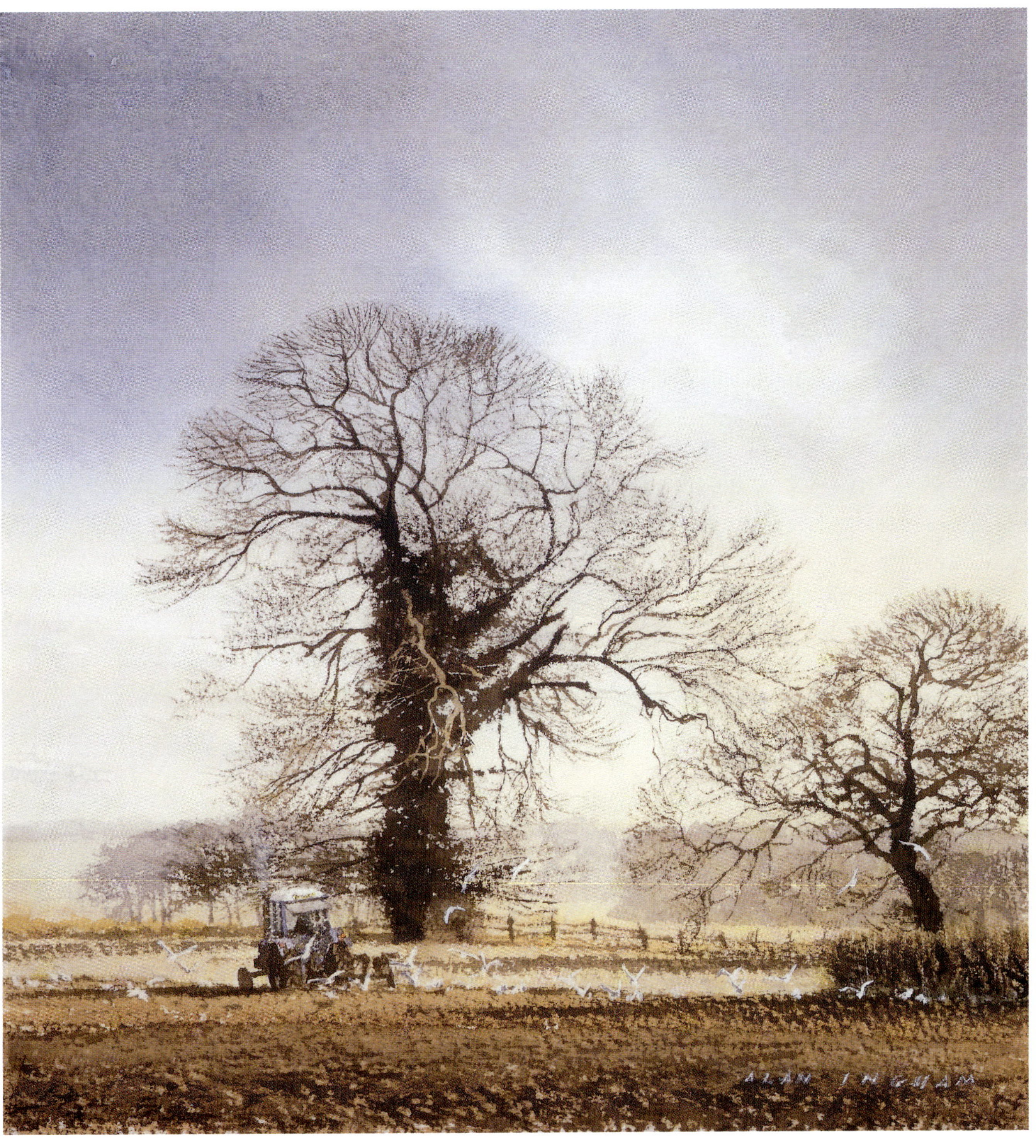

Speed the Plough, near Watlington, Oxfordshire, 1999.

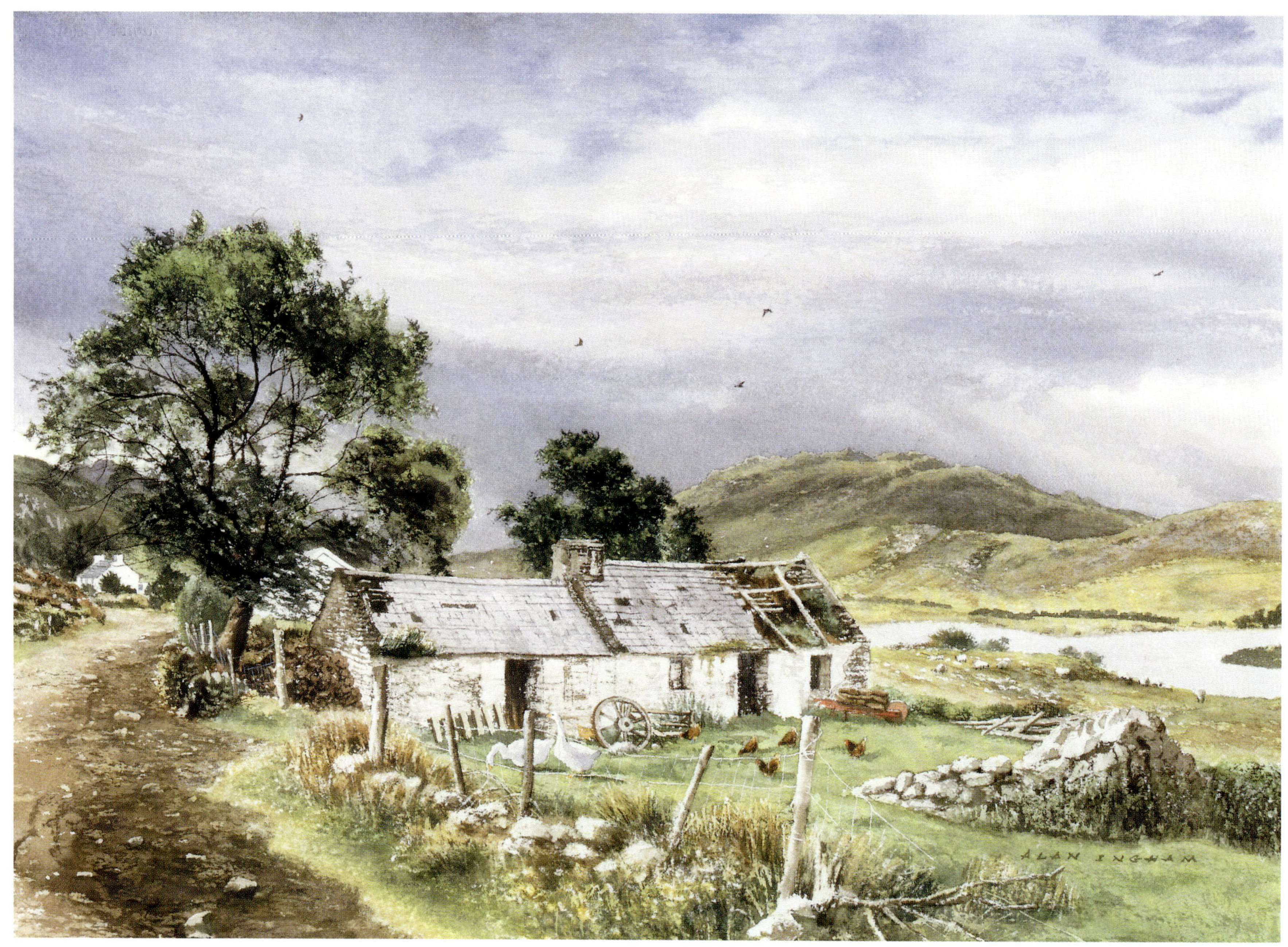

A Relic of Old Ireland, near Kilgarvan, Co. Cork, Ireland, 1998.

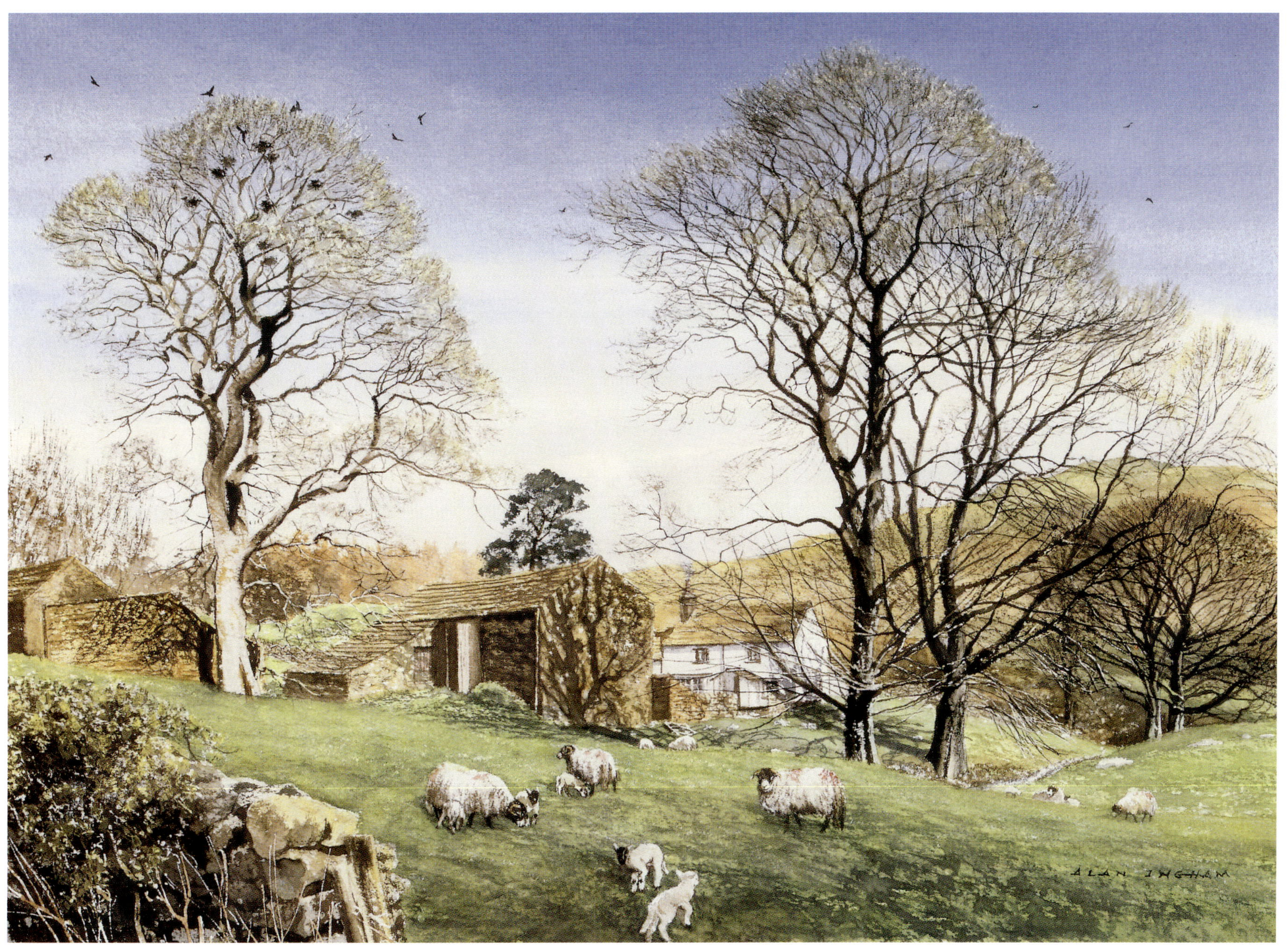

The Nursery Slopes, Longlands Fell, Cumbria, 1999.

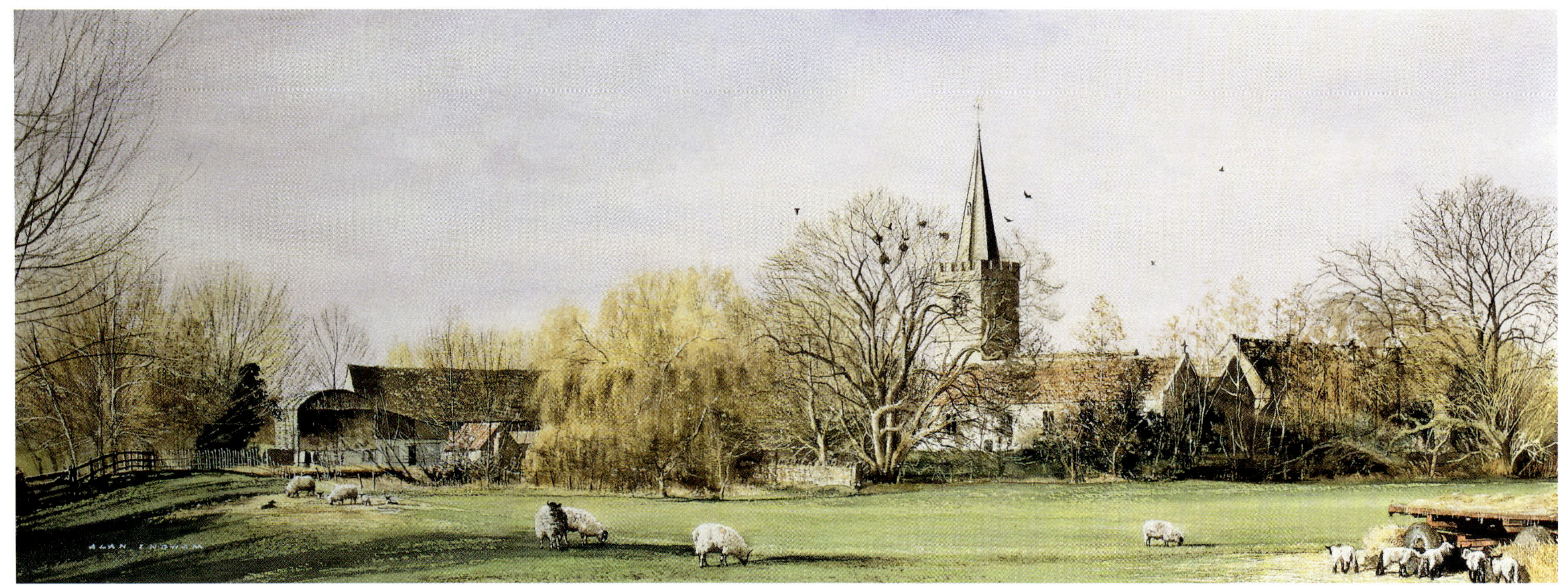

Without a Care in the World, Ashleworth Court, Gloucestershire, 1999.

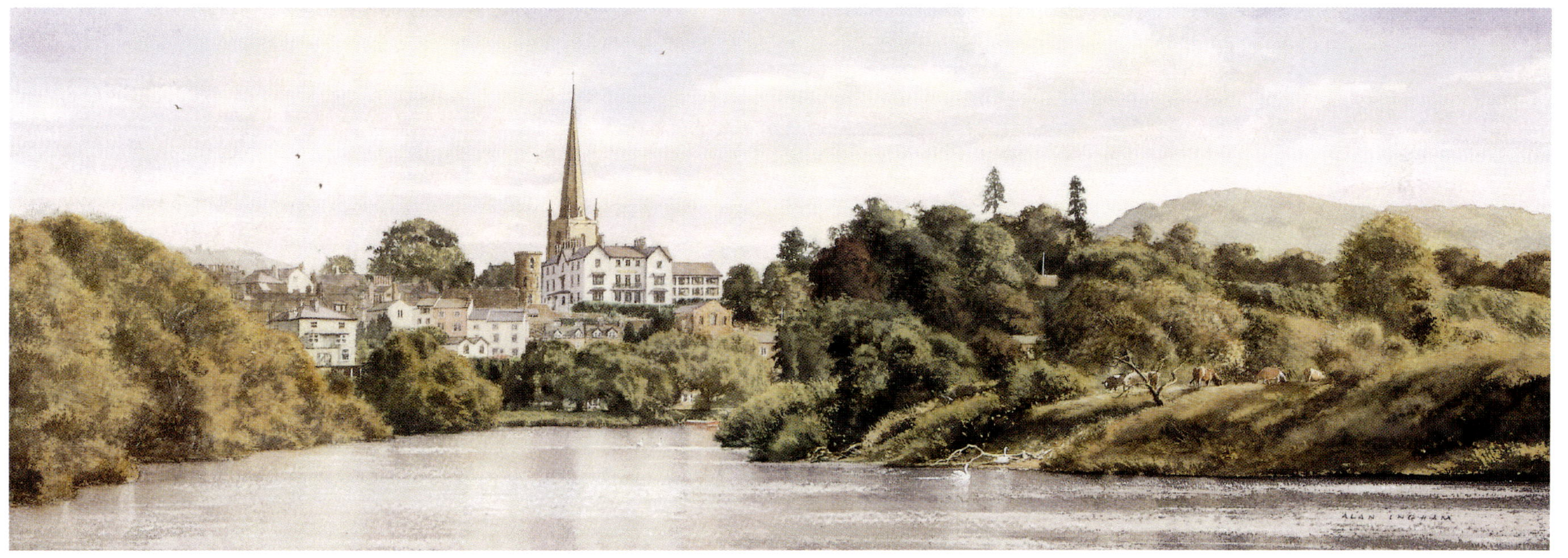

Out of Time, Ross-on-Wye, Herefordshire, 1999.

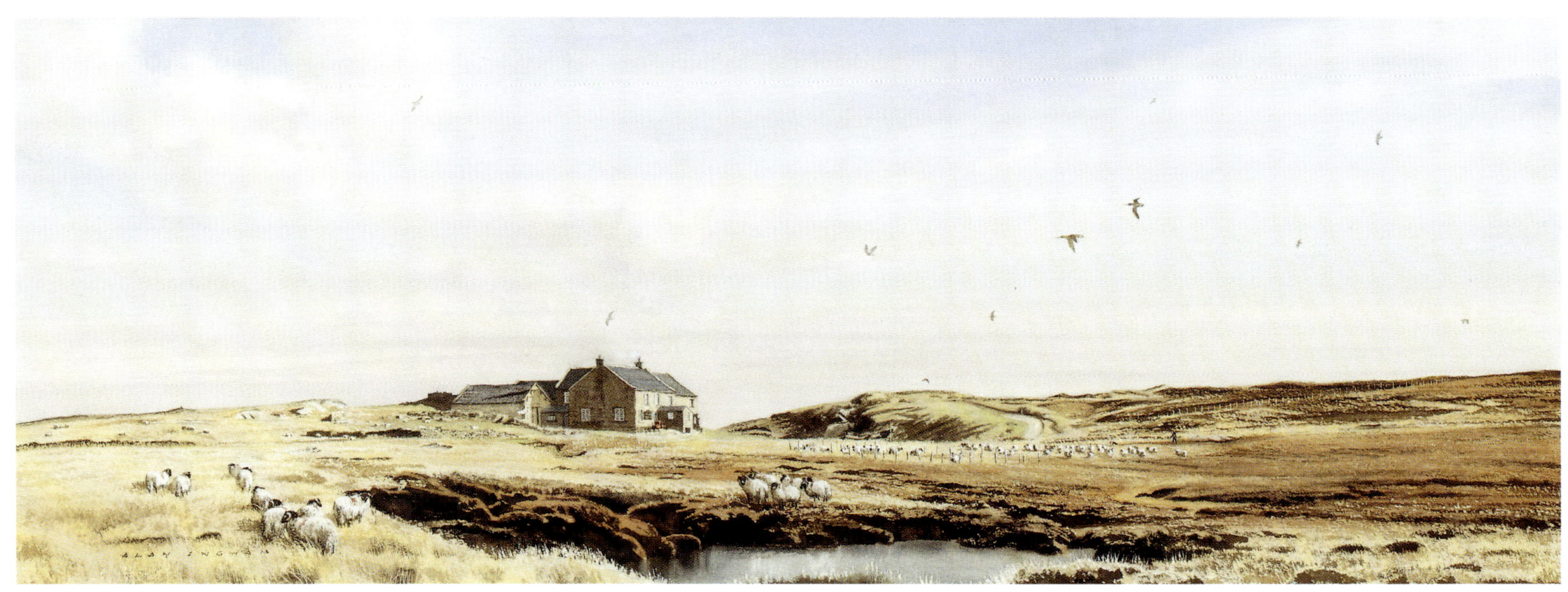

Cry of the Curlew, Tan Hill and Stonesdale Moor, North Yorkshire, 1999.

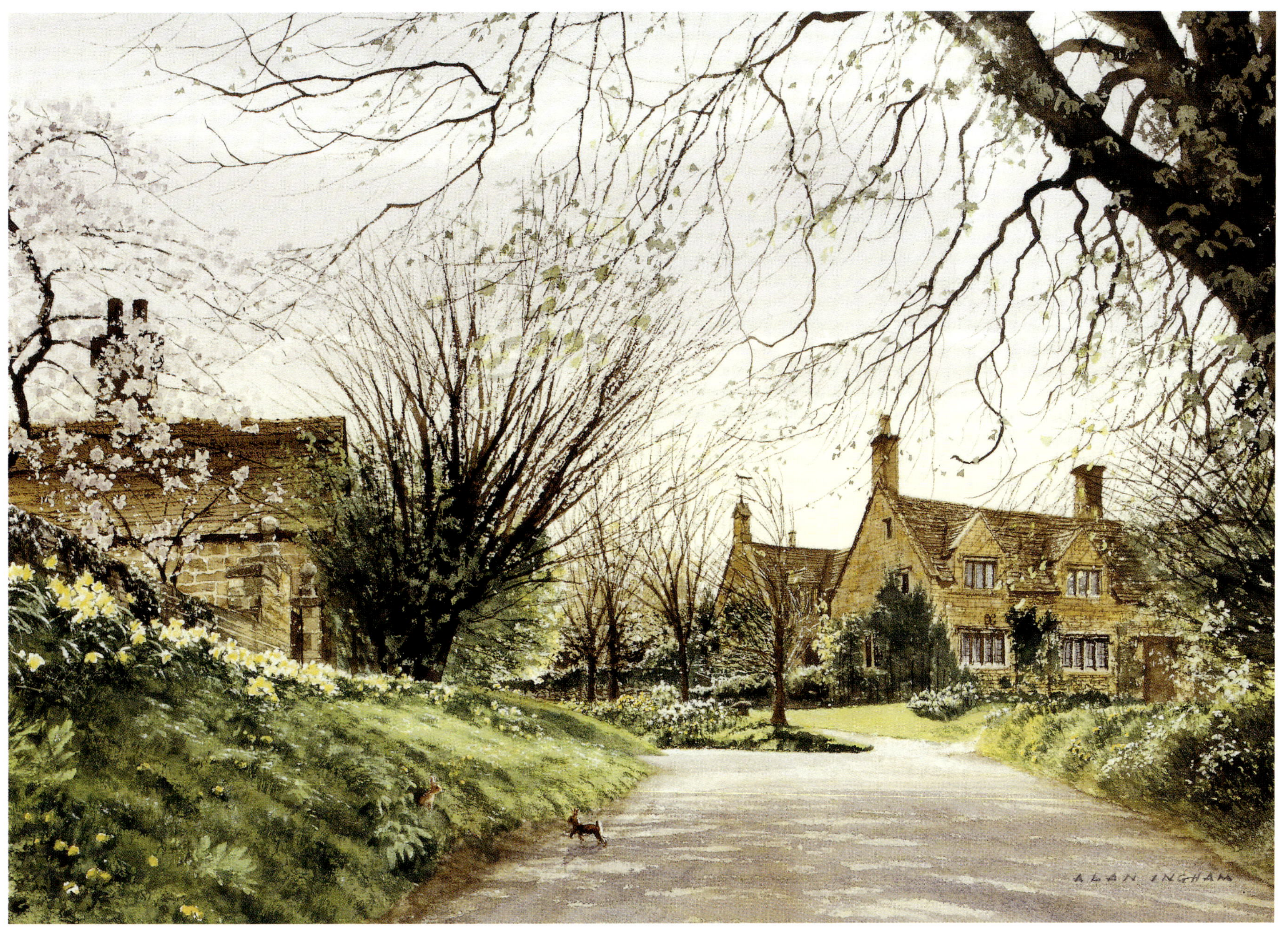

Oh! to be in England, Saintbury, Gloucestershire, 1999.

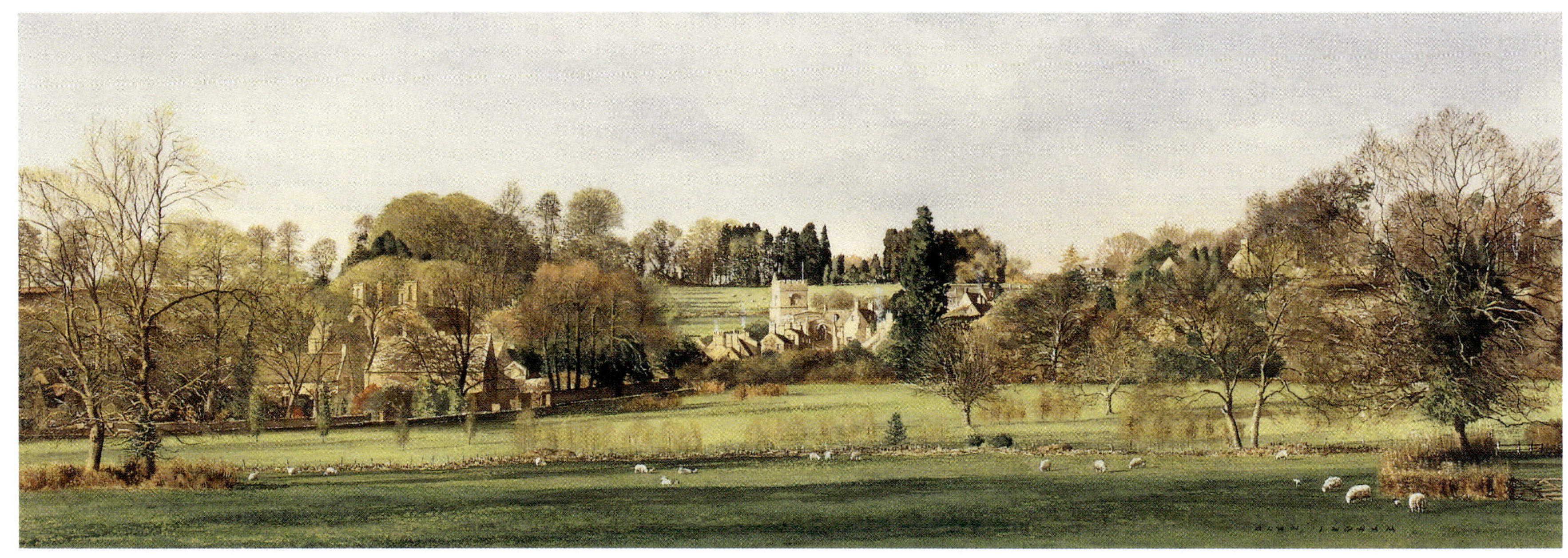

Village England, Bourton-on-the-Hill, Gloucestershire, 1999.

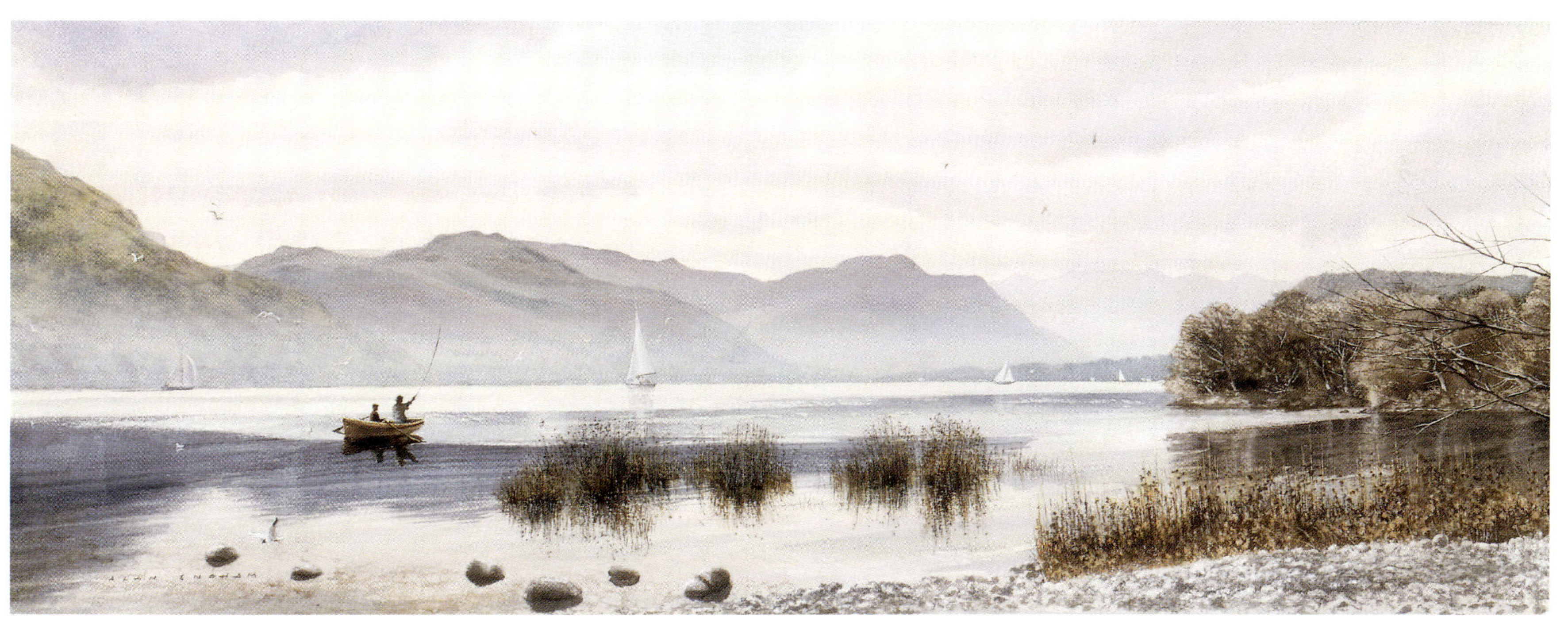

Castaways, Ullswater, Cumbria, 1999.

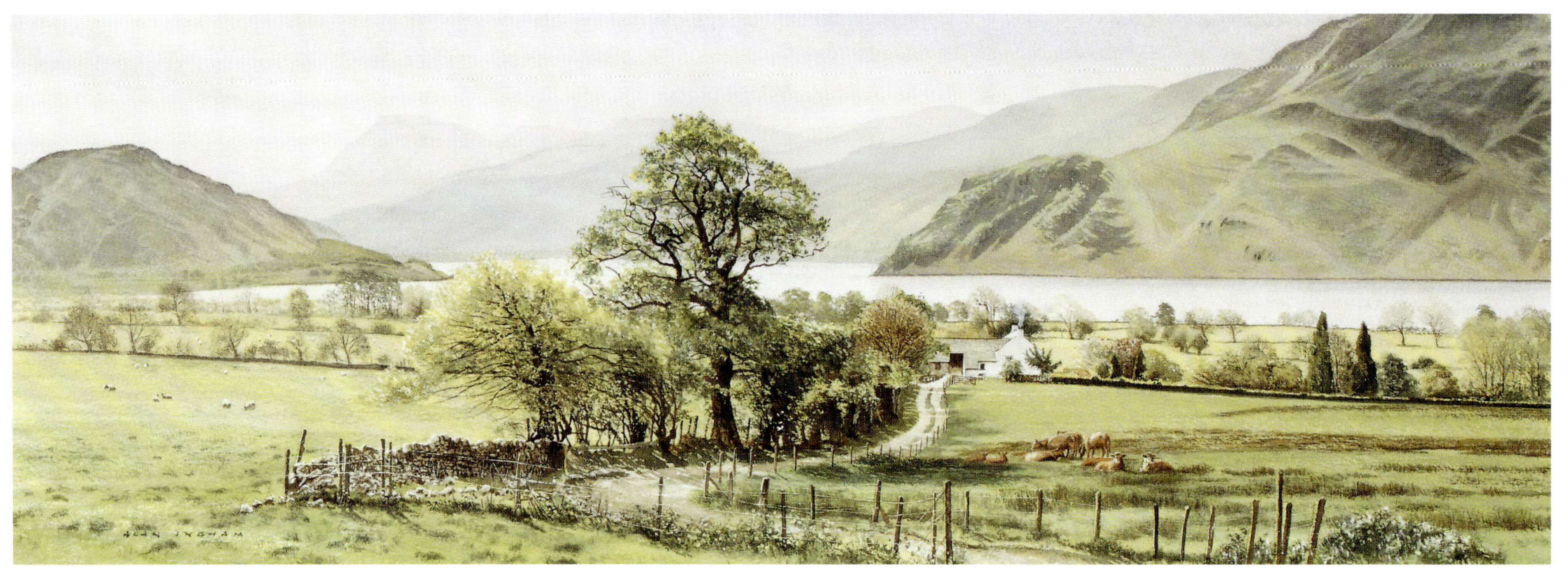

At Peace, Beck Foot Farm, Ennerdale, Cumbria, 1999.

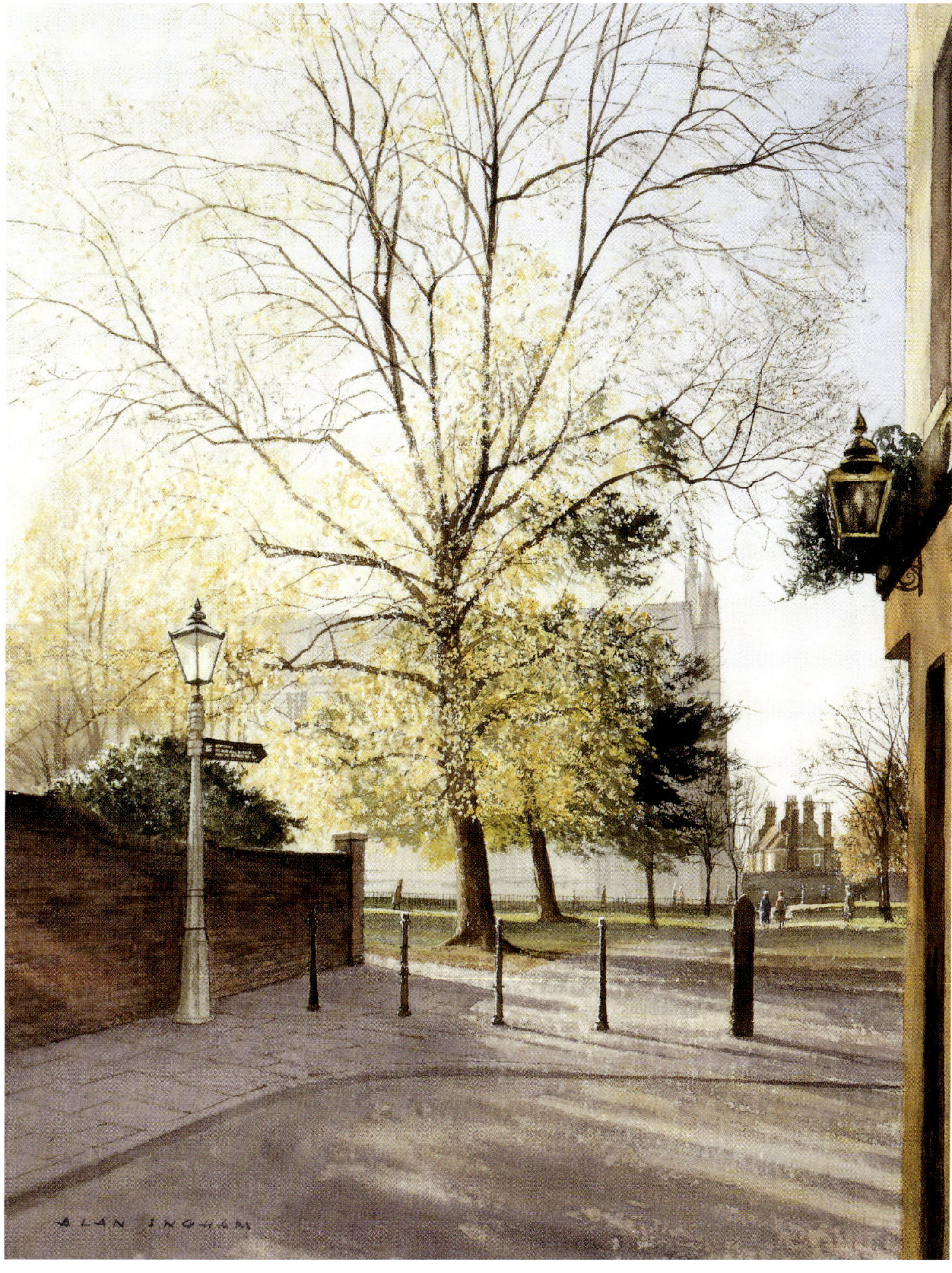

Cathedral Close, Winchester, Hampshire, 2000.

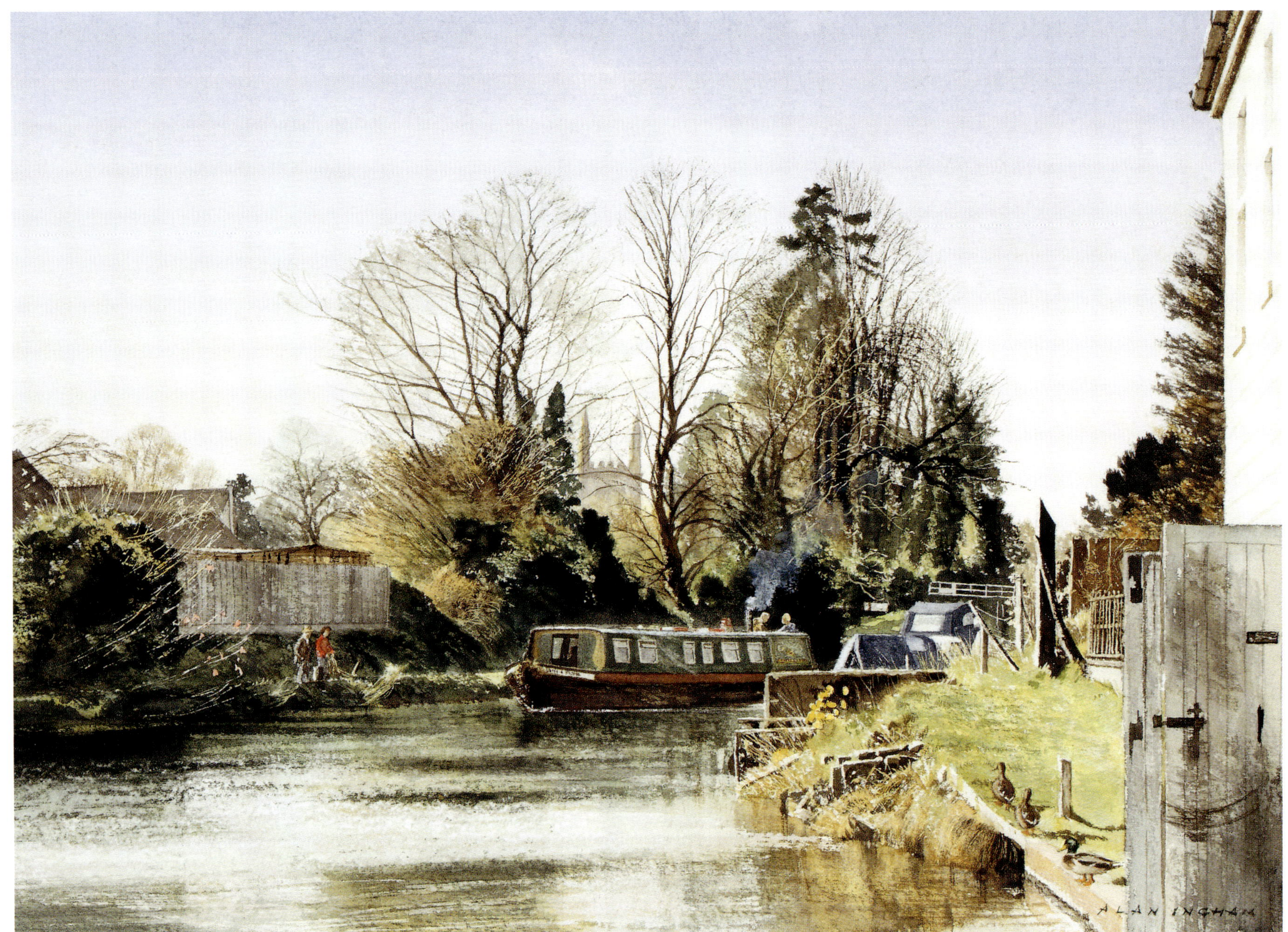

This is the Life! Kennet and Avon Canal, Bathampton, Avon, 2000.

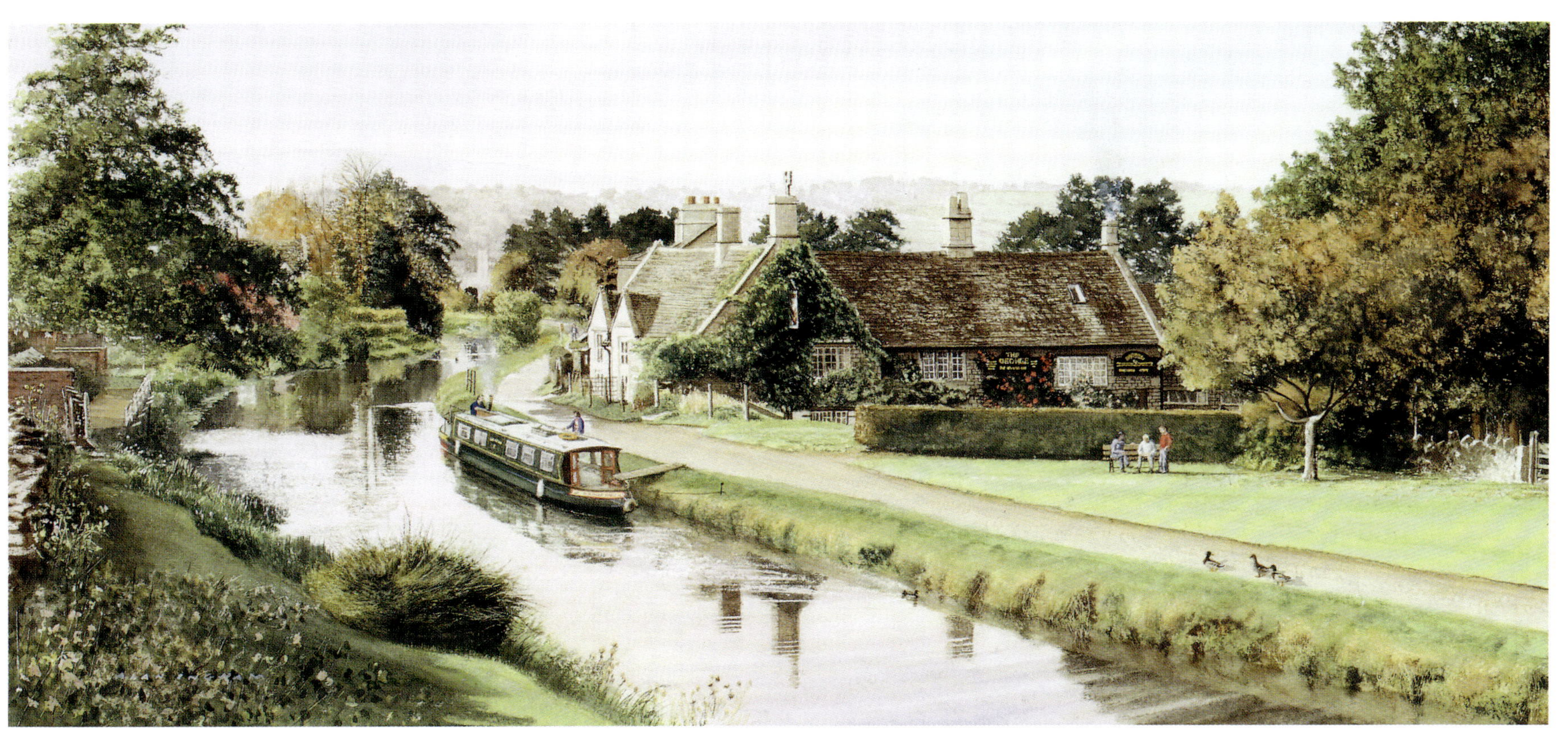

Time for Reflection, The George Inn, Kennet and Avon Canal, Bathampton, Avon, 2000.

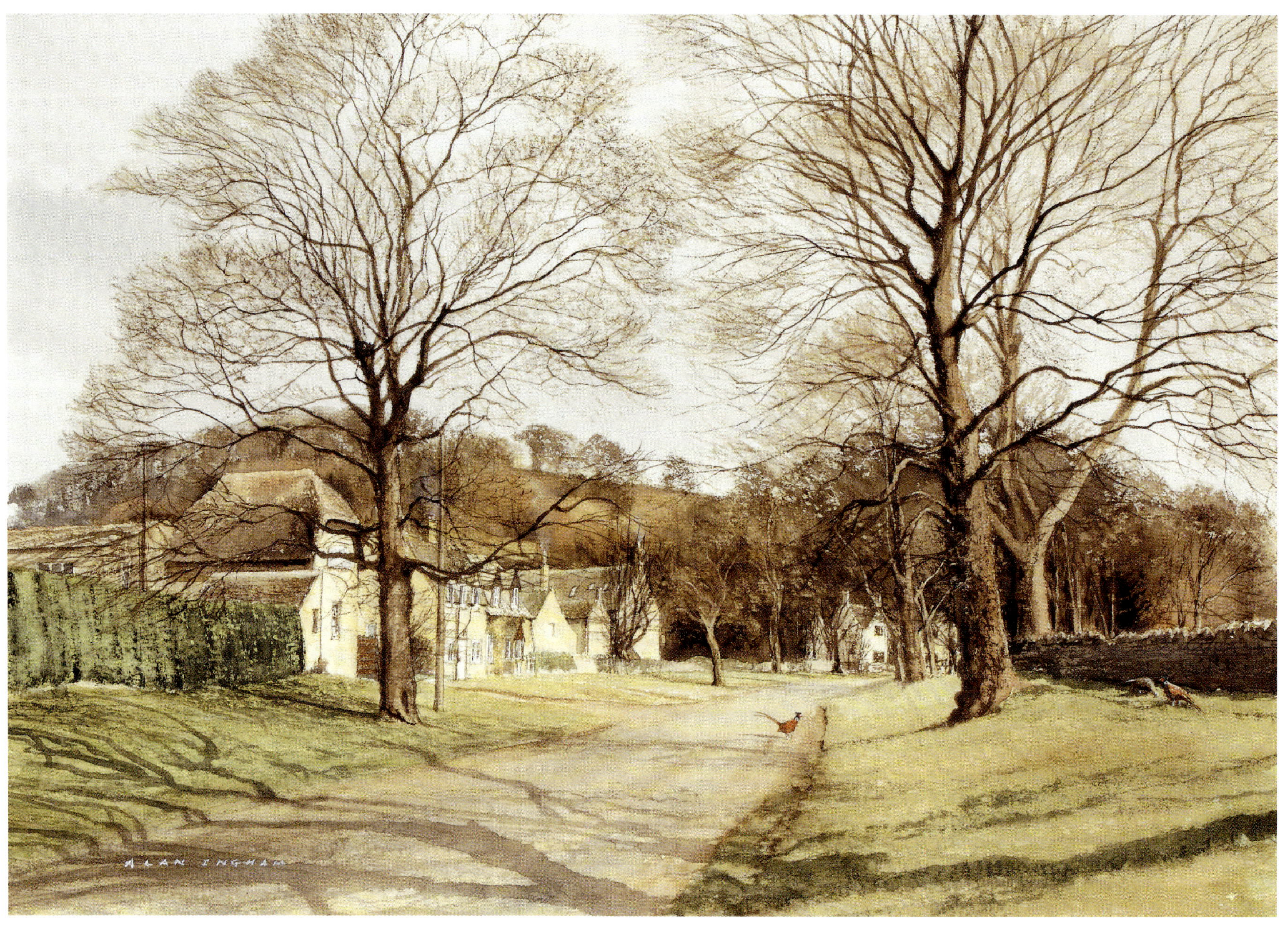

Waiting for Spring, Buckland, Gloucestershire, 2000.

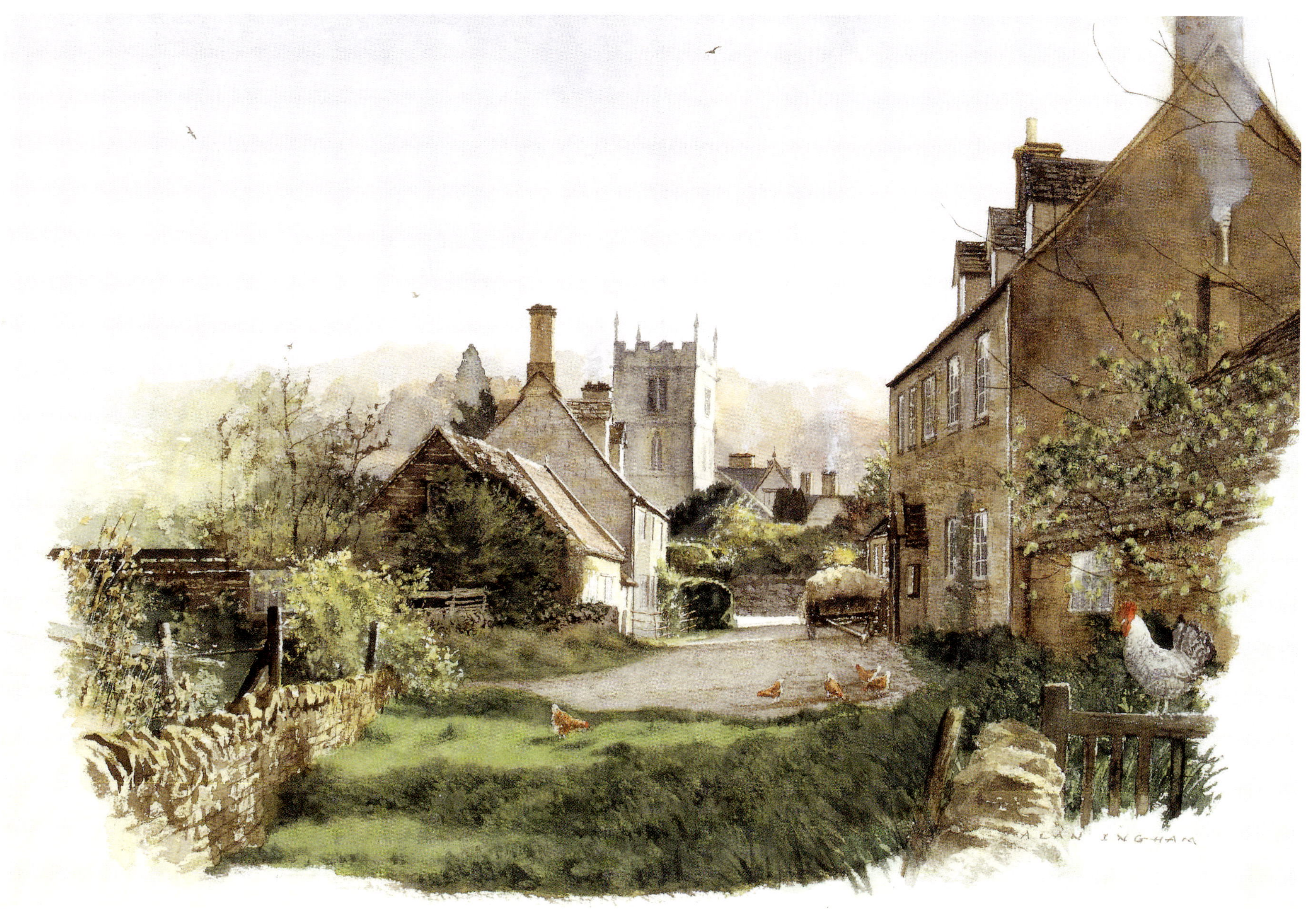

Cock O'The Walk, Stanway, Gloucestershire, 2000.

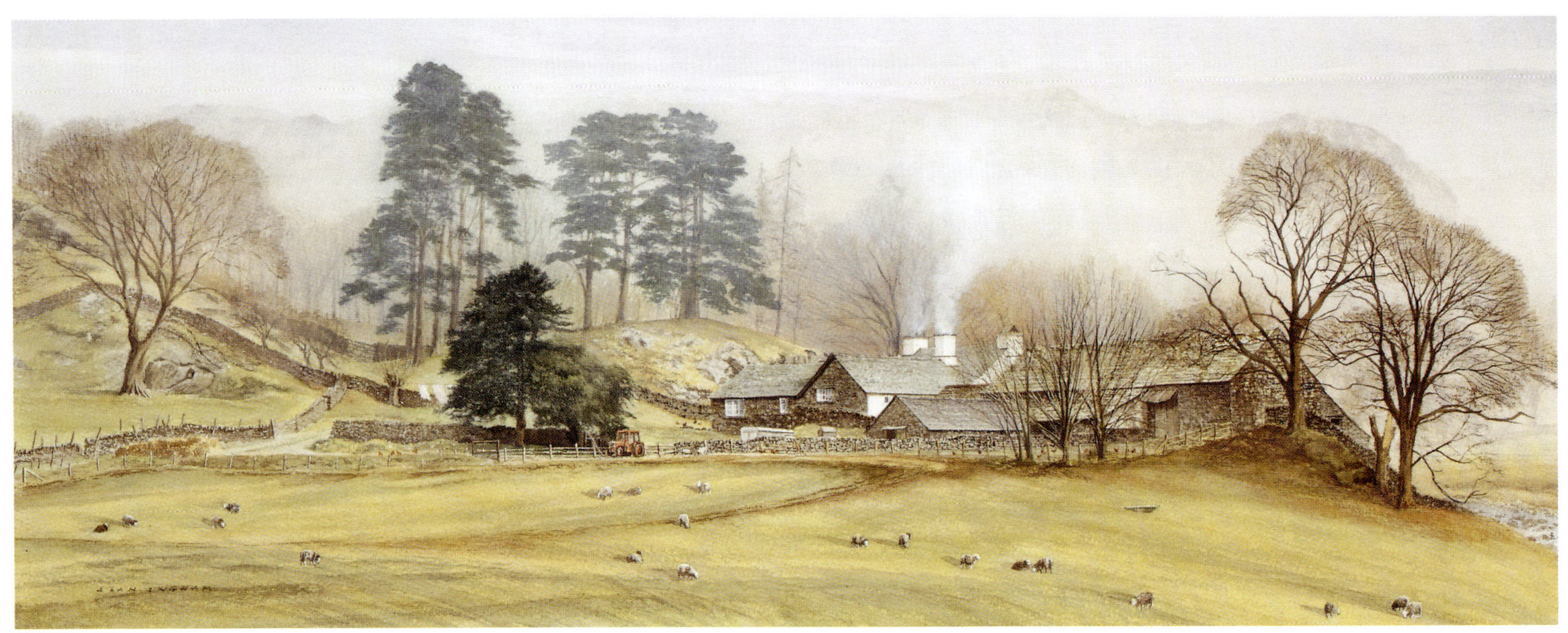

October Mist, Yew Tree House Farm, Yewdale, Cumbria, 2001.

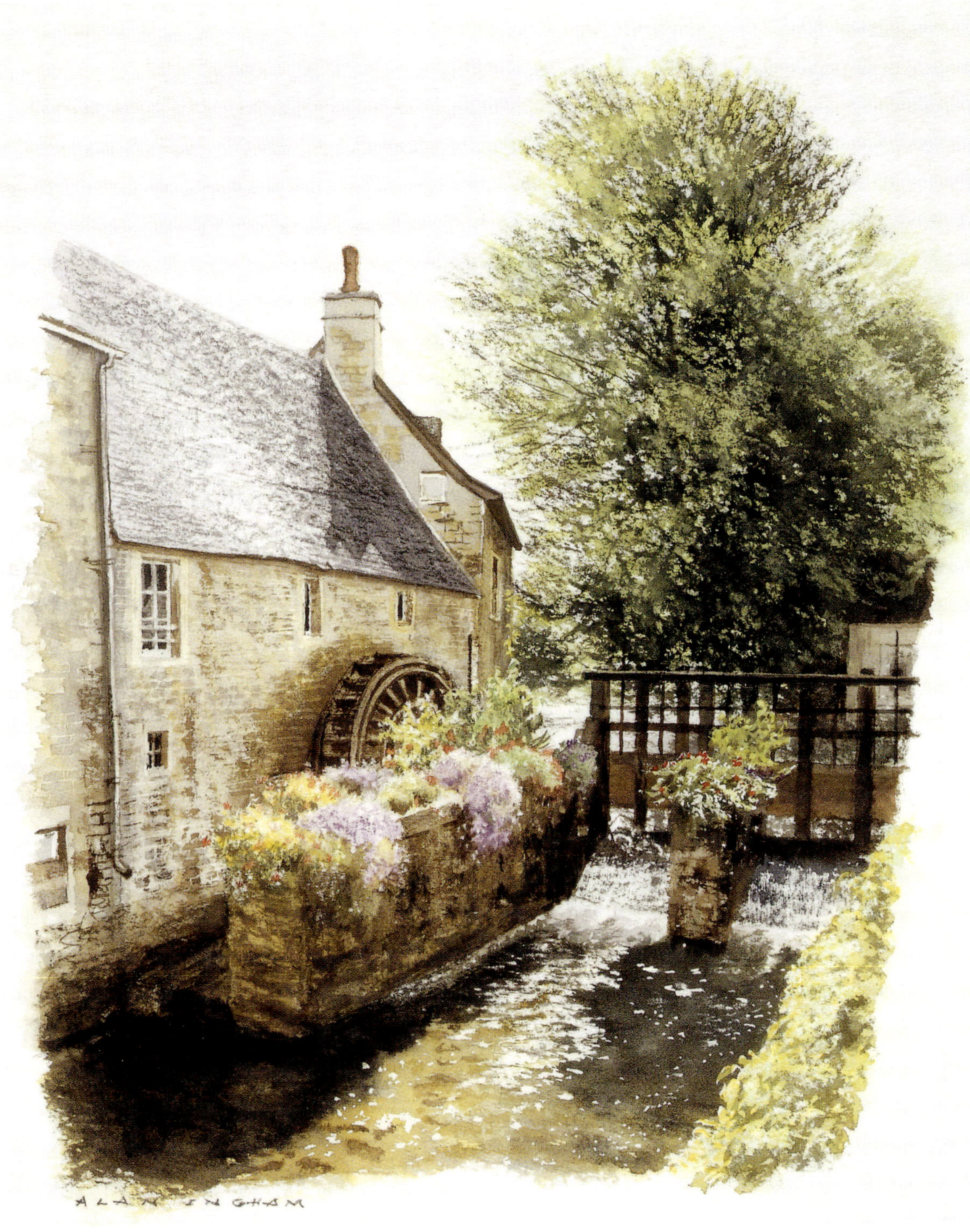

The Old Mill Stream, Bayeux, Normandy, France, 2000.

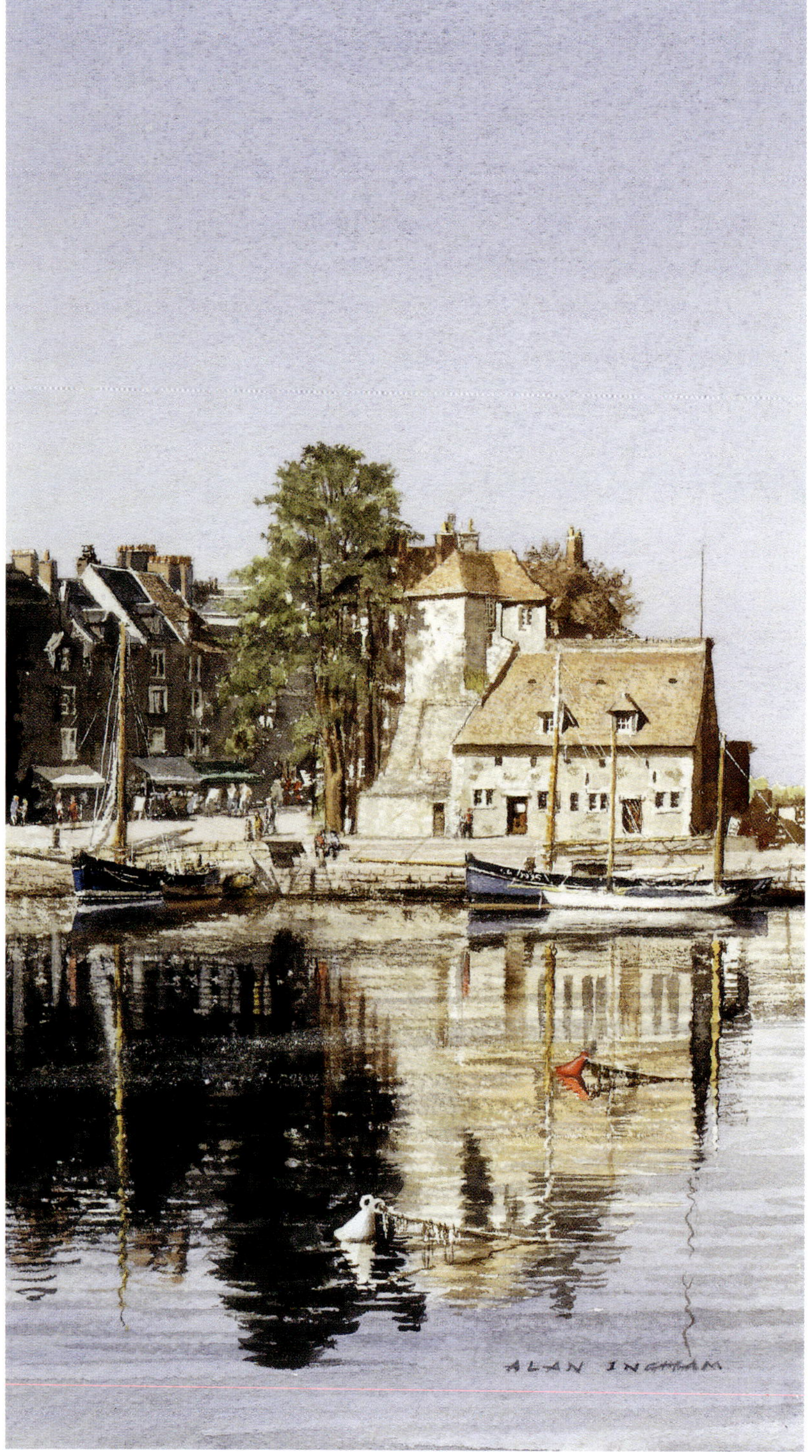

Honfleur Old Harbour, Normandy, France, 2000.

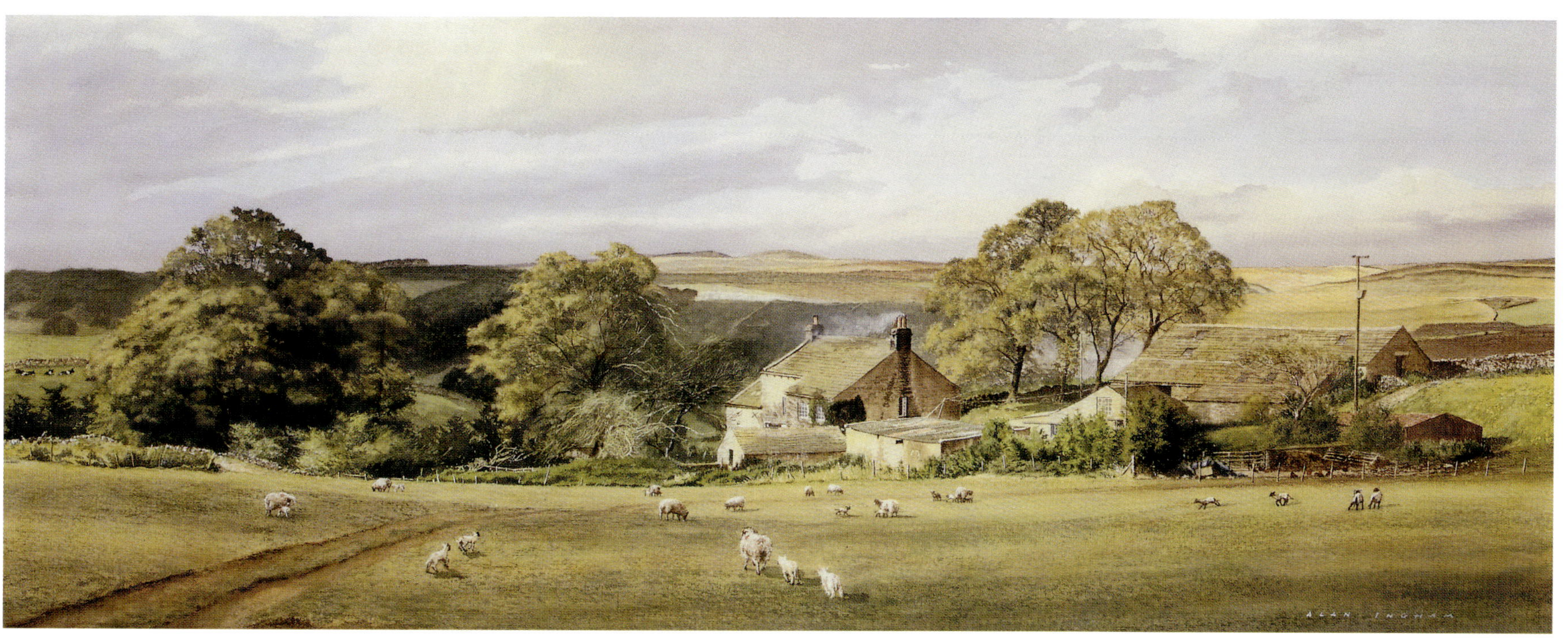

Here Comes the Sun, Langerton House Farm, near Burnsall, North Yorkshire, 2000.

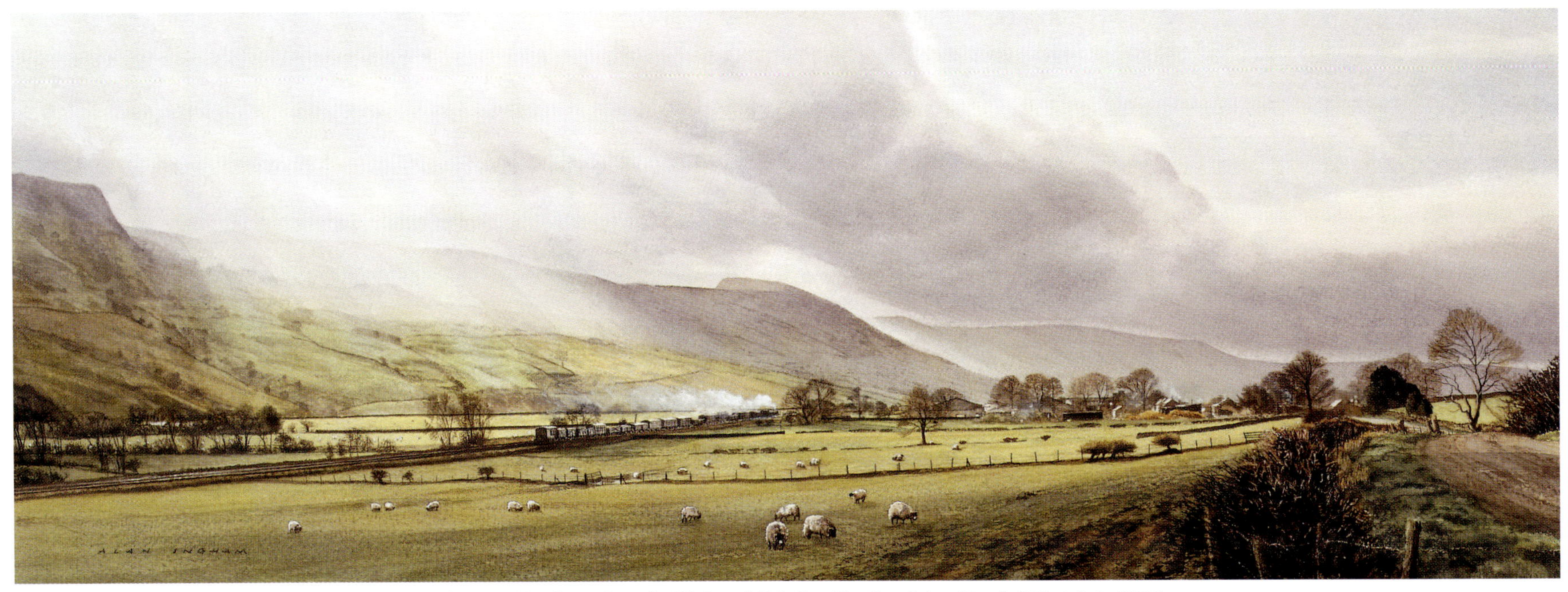

Sunburst, Nether Booth, Vale of Edale, Derbyshire Peak District, 2001.

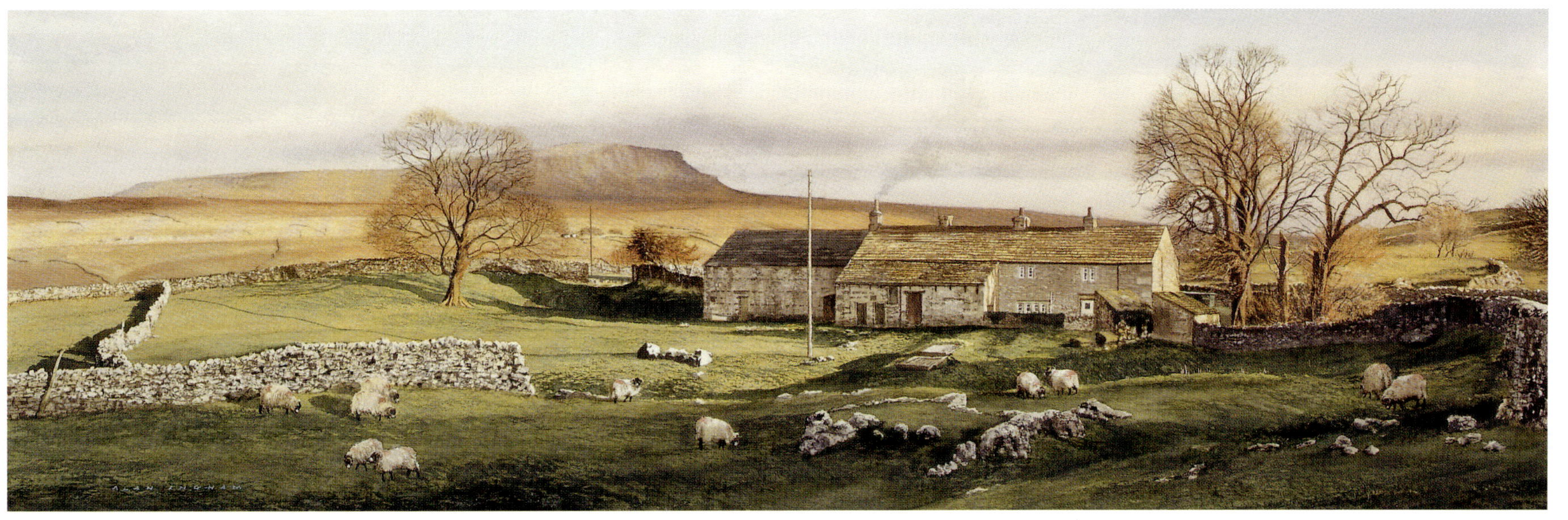

Evening Shadows, Pen-y-Ghent Hill from Selside, Ribblesdale, NorthYorkshire.

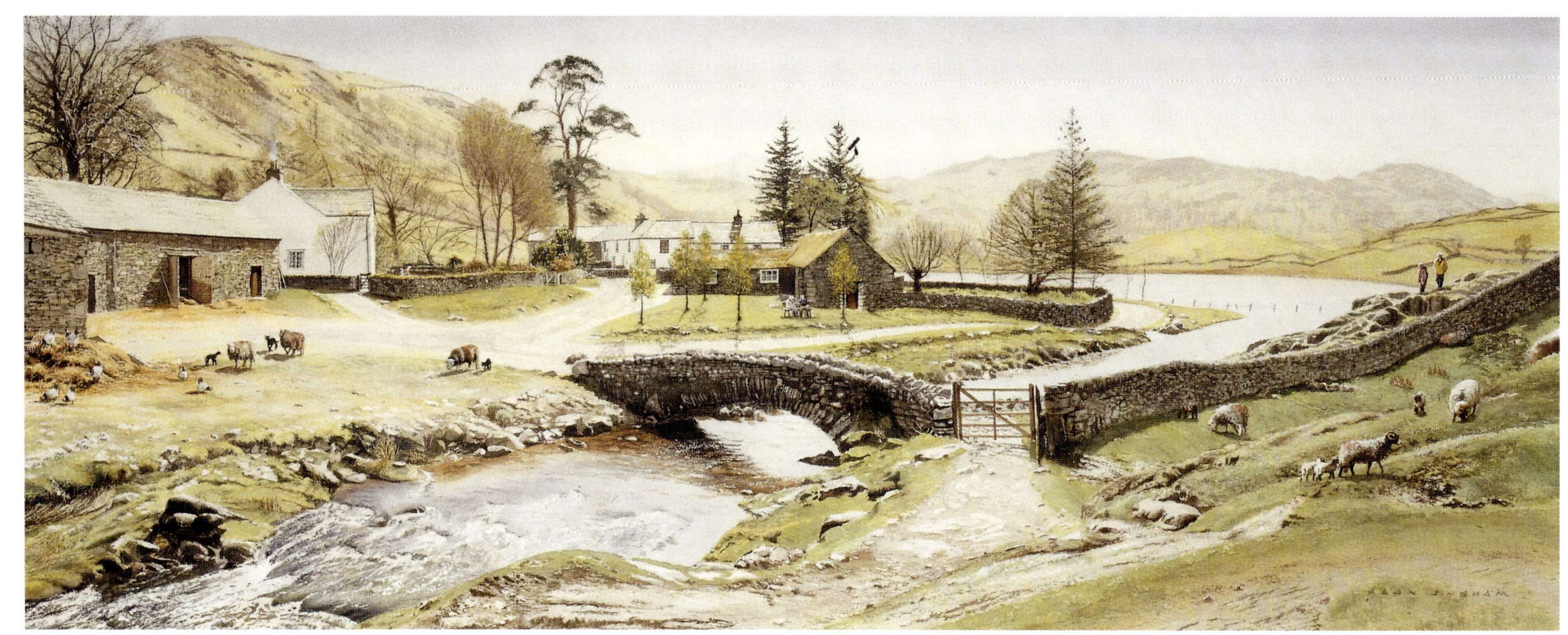

Perfect Harmony, Watendlath, Cumbria, 2001.

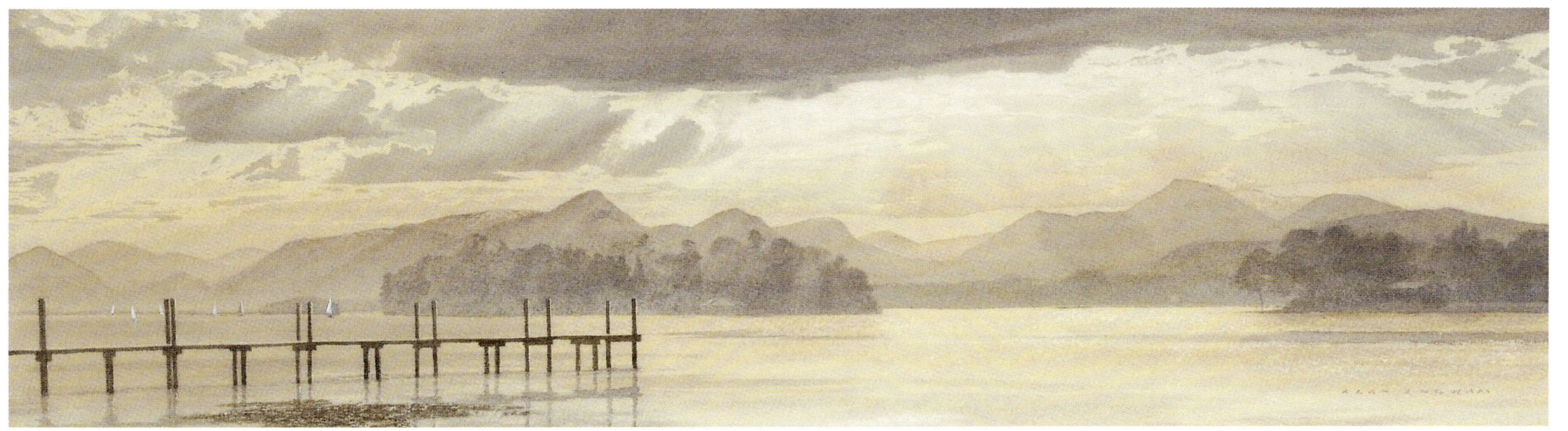

All is Calm, Derwentwater, Cumbria, 2001.

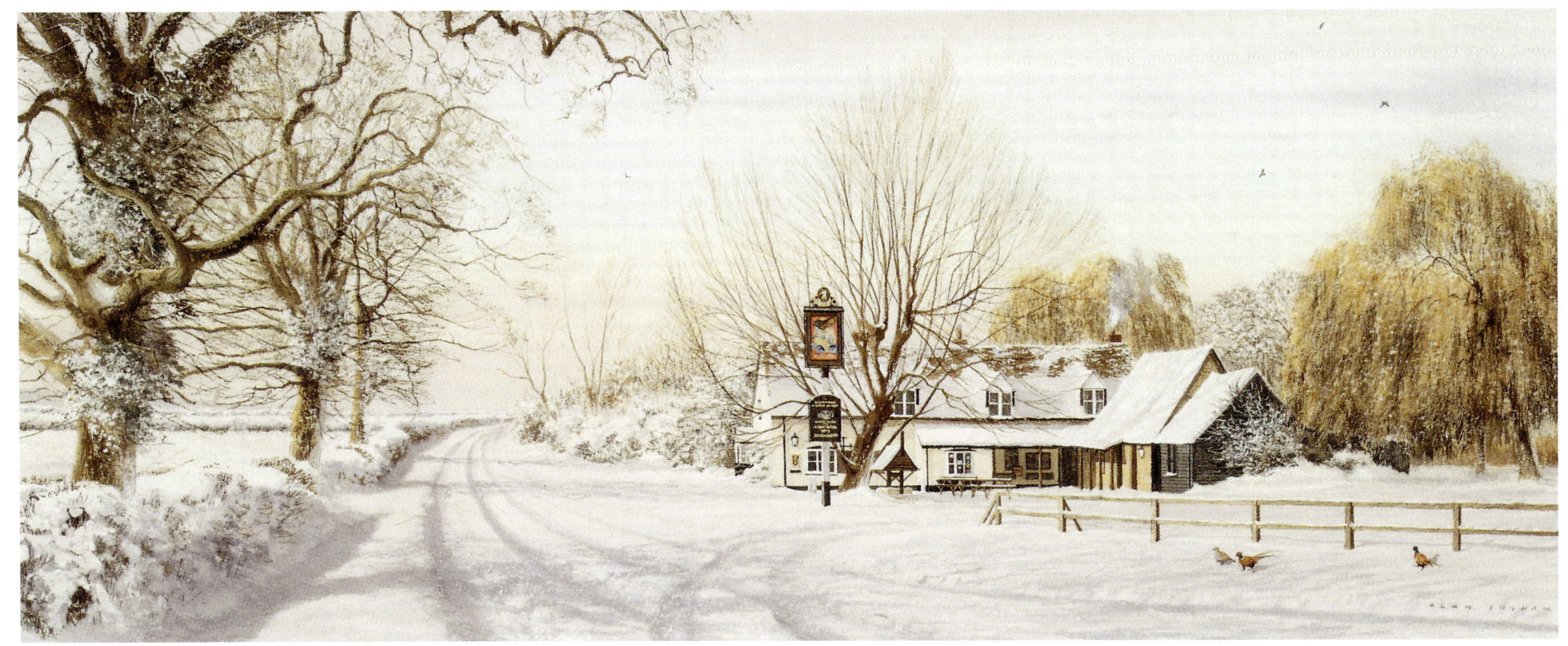

The Quiet Time, Hobnails Inn, Little Washbourne, Gloucestershire, 2001.

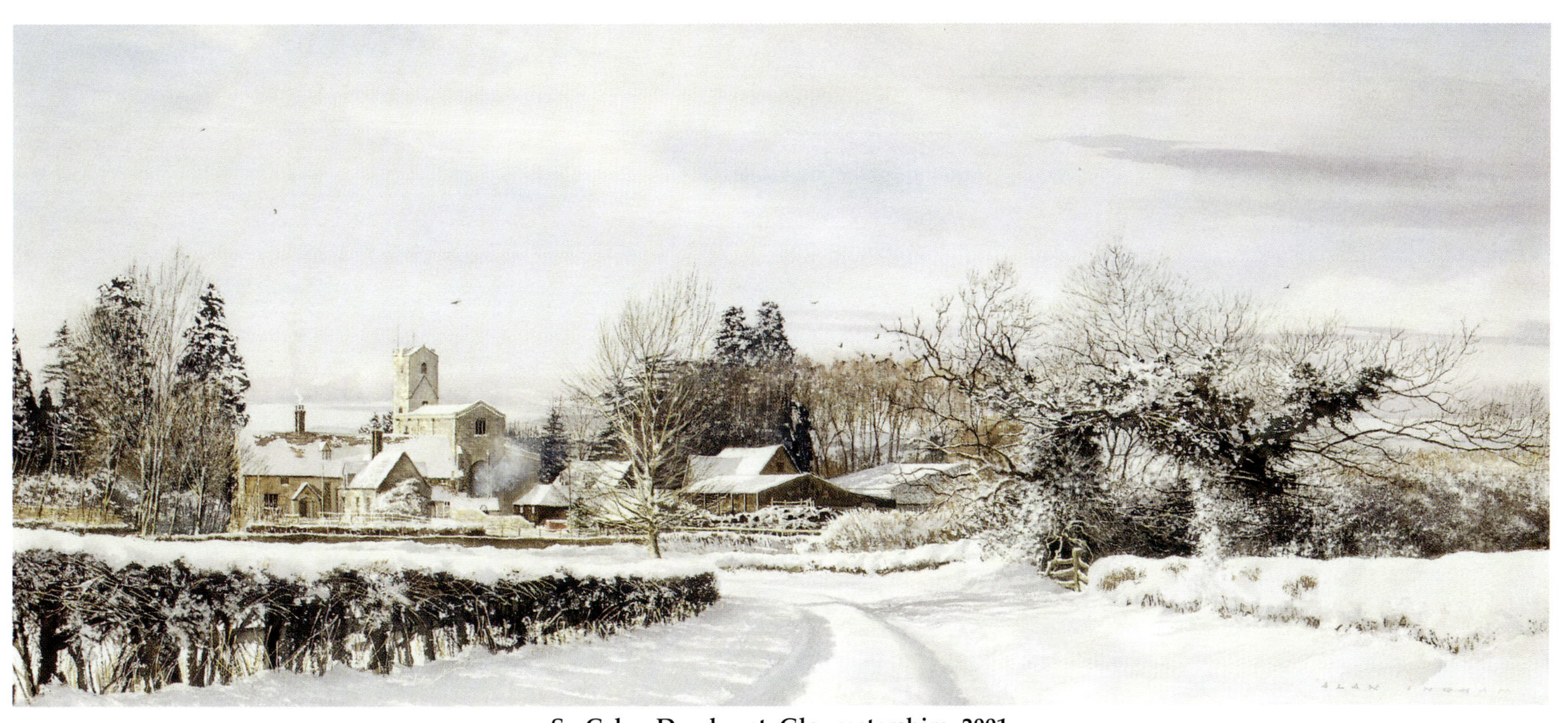

So Calm, Deerhurst, Gloucestershire, 2001.

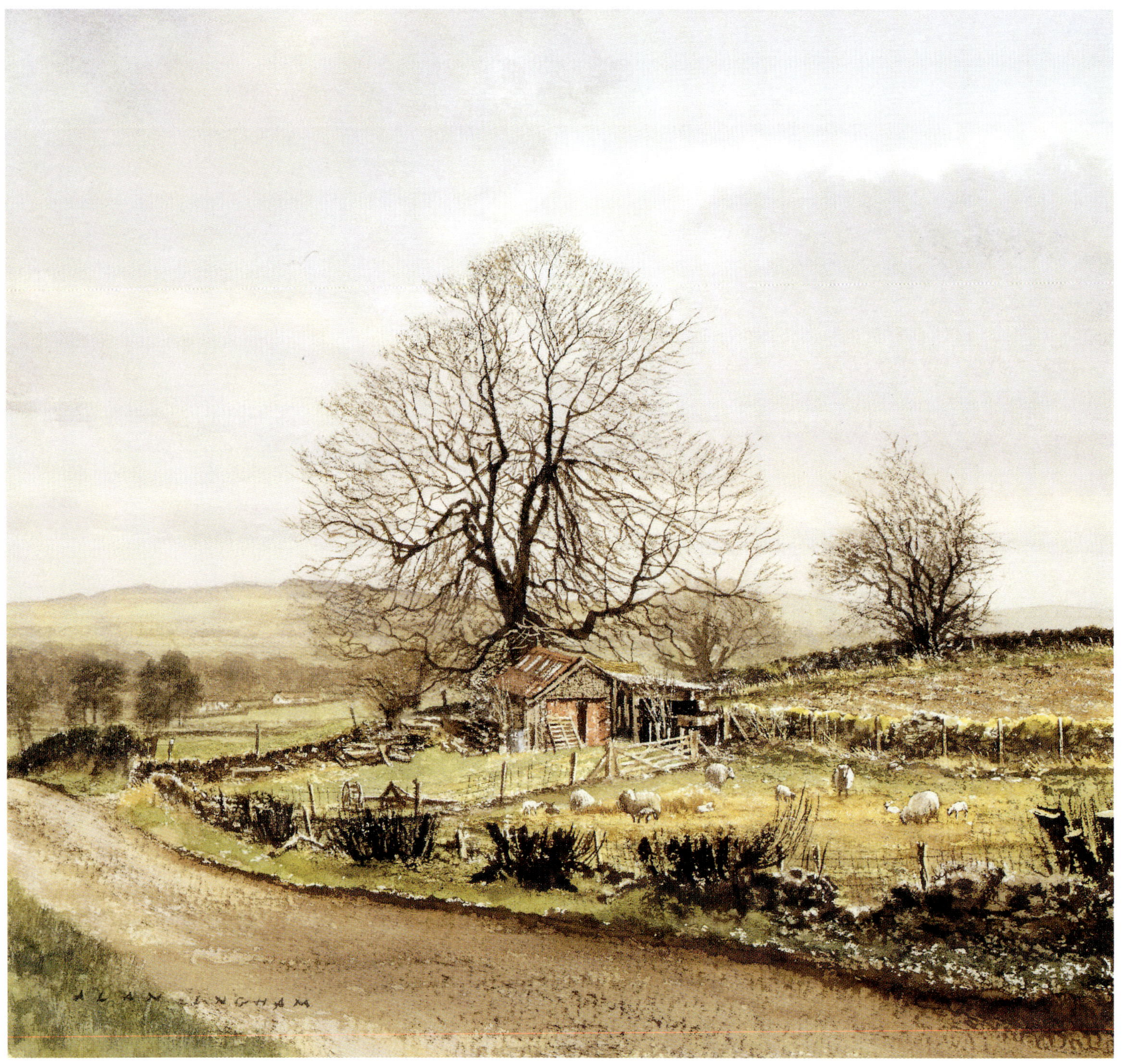

The Sheepfold, near Chewton Mendip, Somerset, 2001.

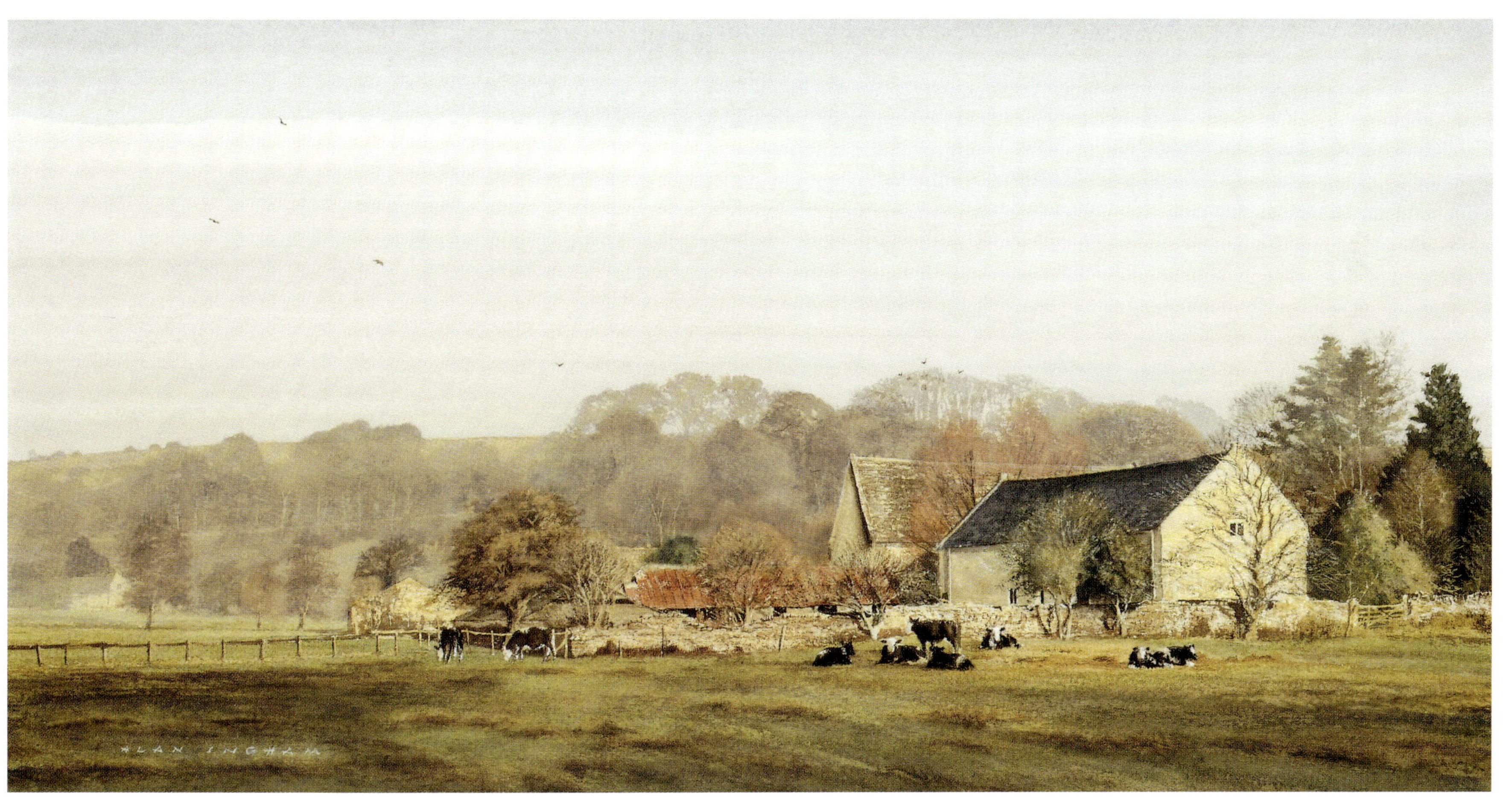

Chewing the Cud, Whittington, Gloucestershire, 2001.

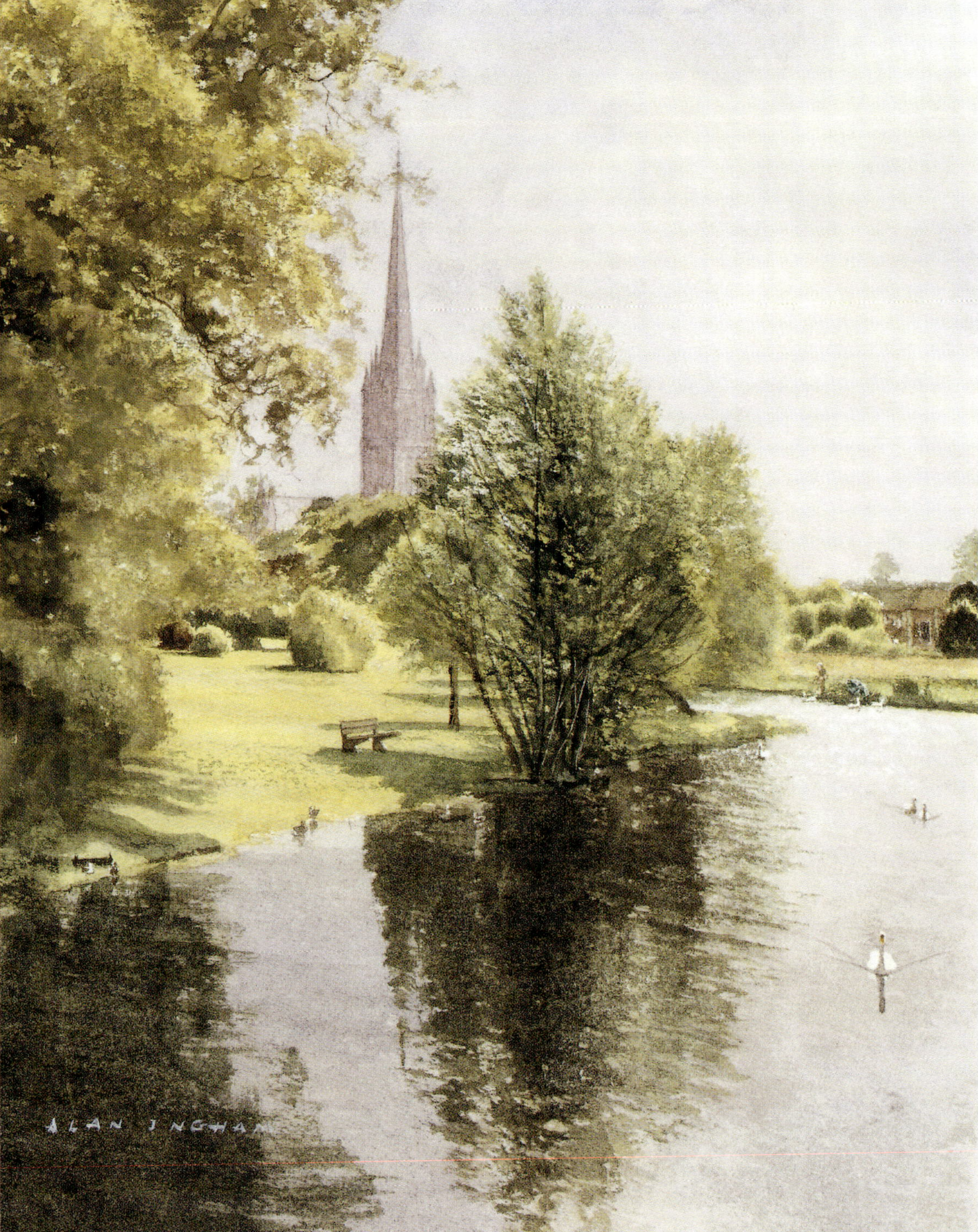

**The Vacant Seat,
Salisbury Cathedral,
Wiltshire, 2001.**

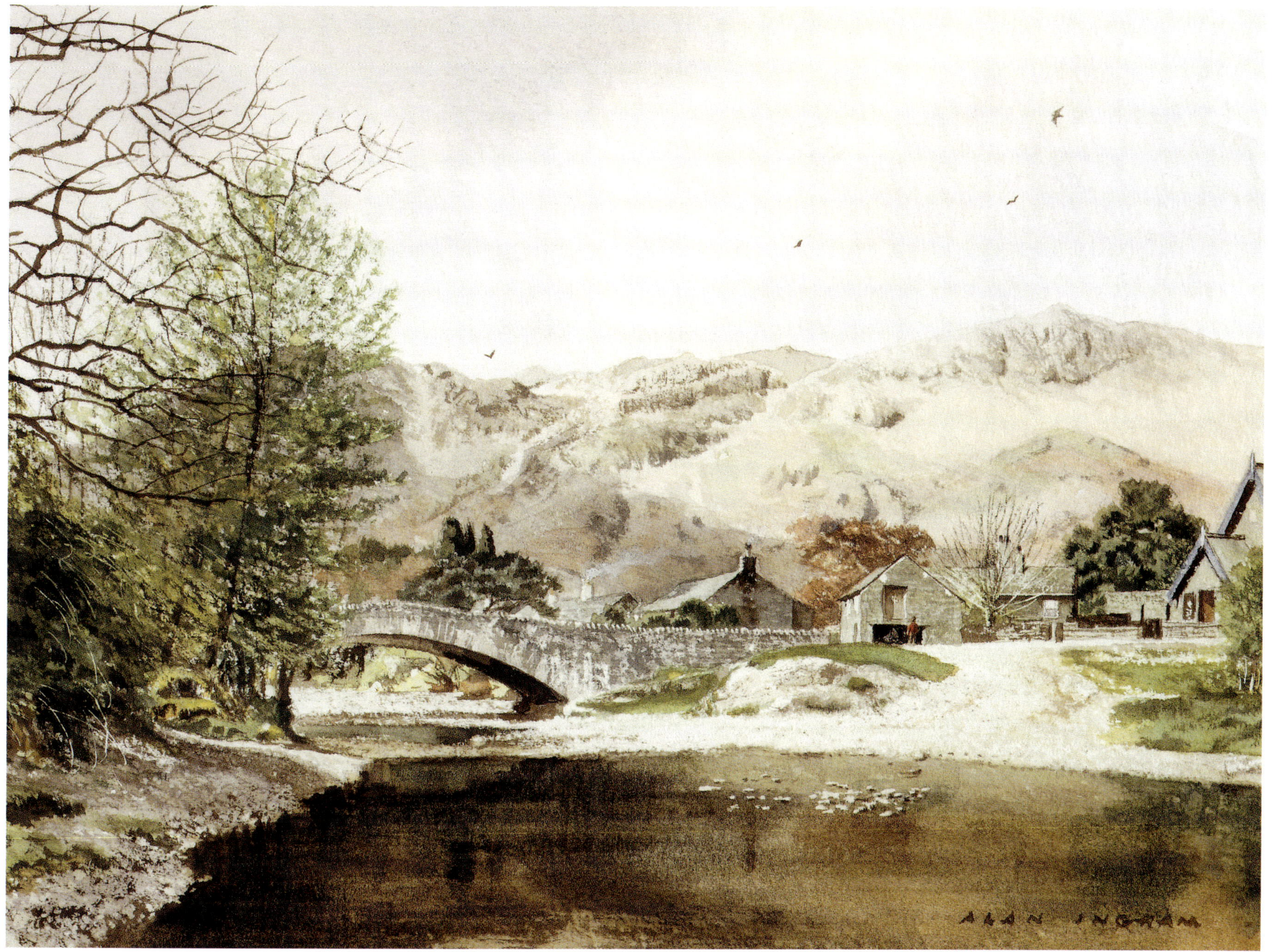

Lakeland in Springtime, Grange-in-Borrowdale, Cumbria, 2000.

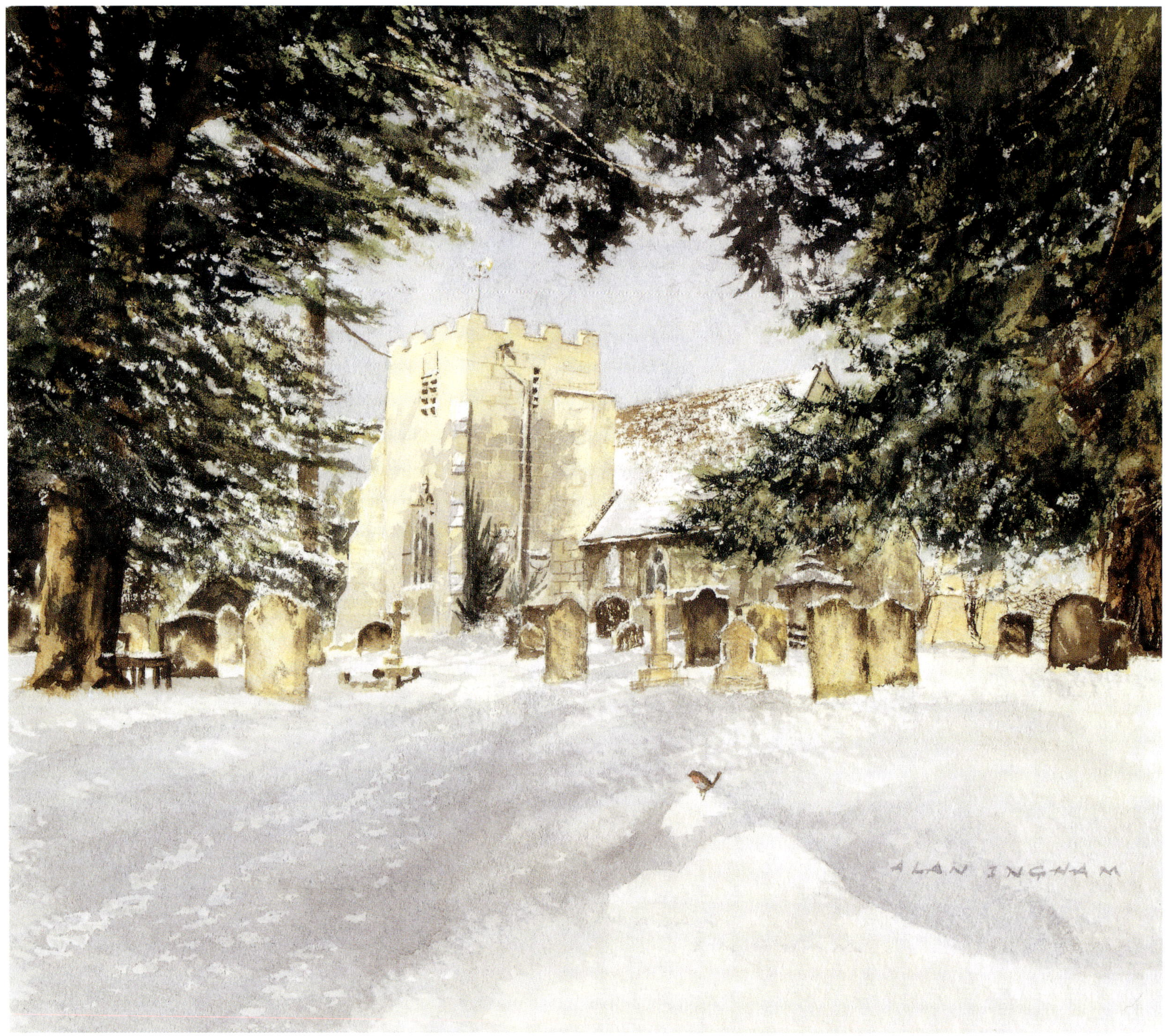

A Country Churchyard, Staverton, Gloucestershire, 2000.

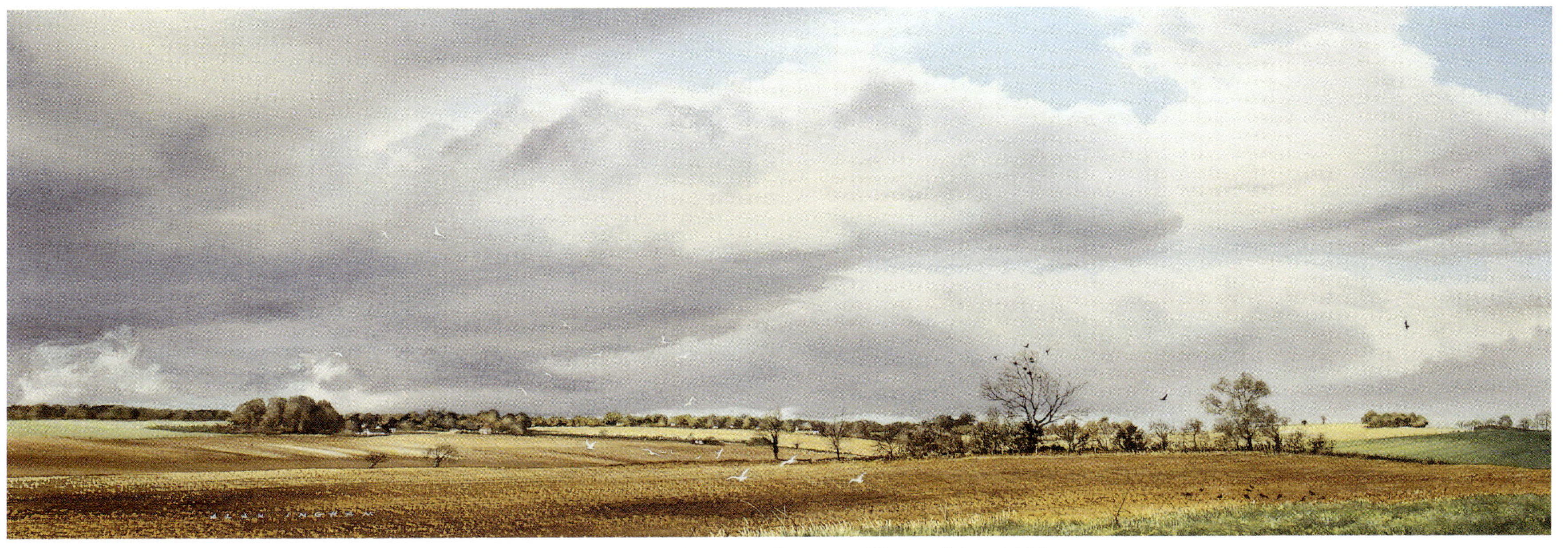

Landscape Bright, near Romsey, Hampshire, 2001.

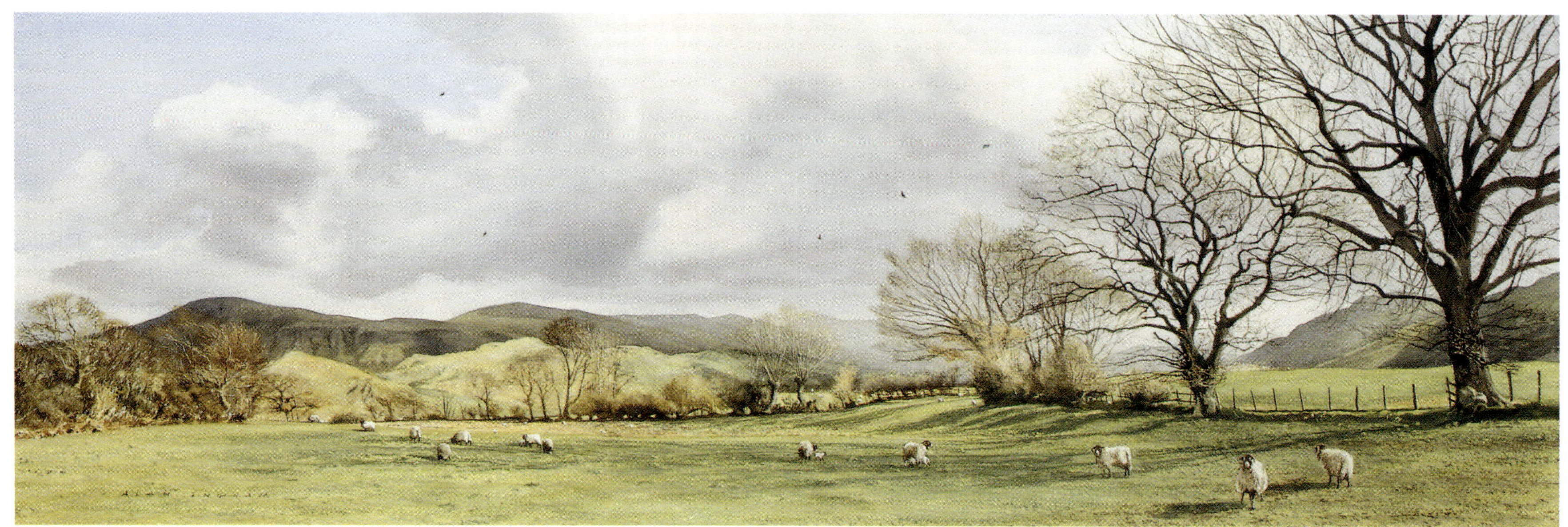

The High Pasture, near Castlerigg, Cumbria, 2001.

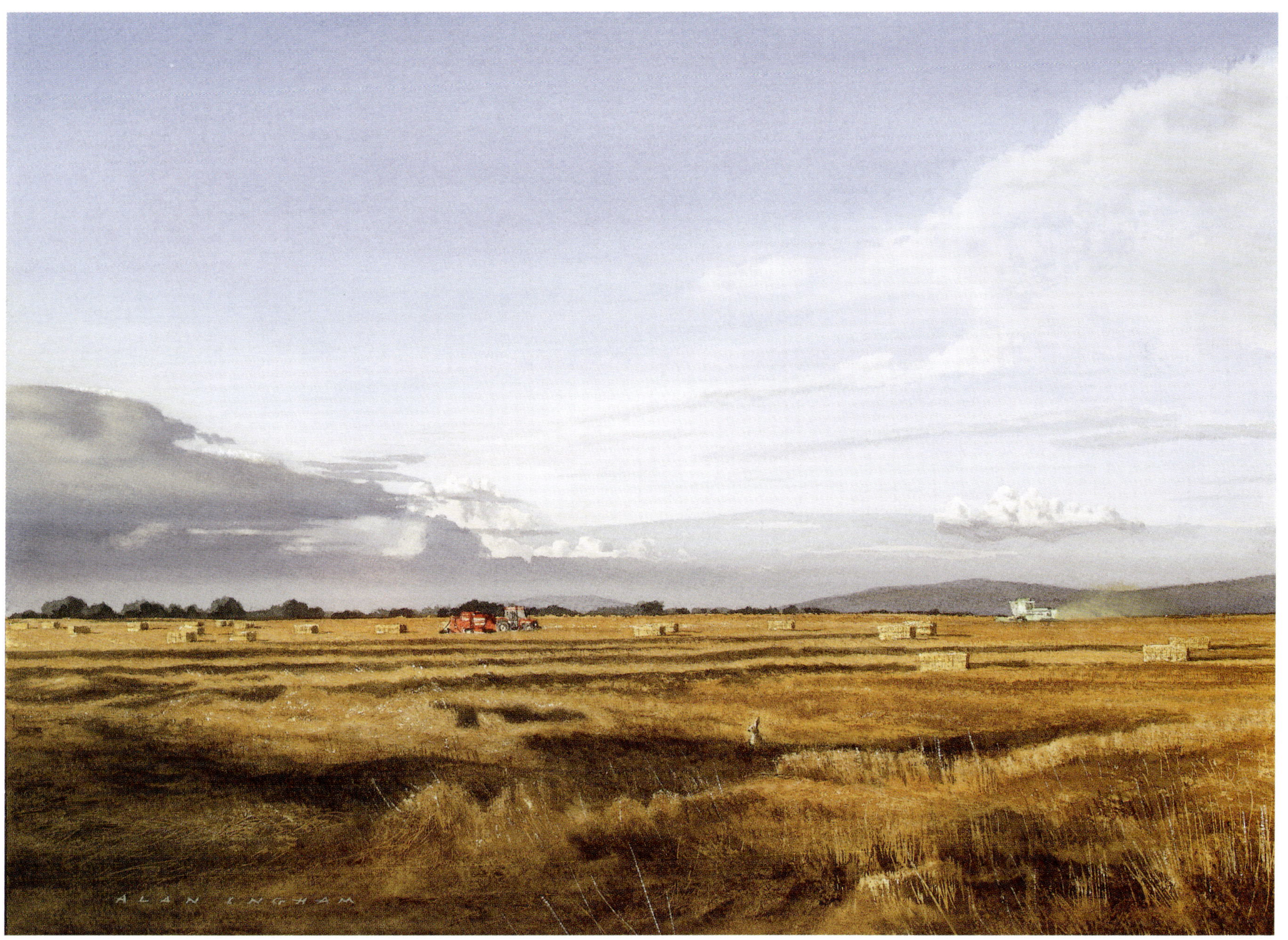

Harvest Almost Home, Staverton, Gloucestershire, 2001.

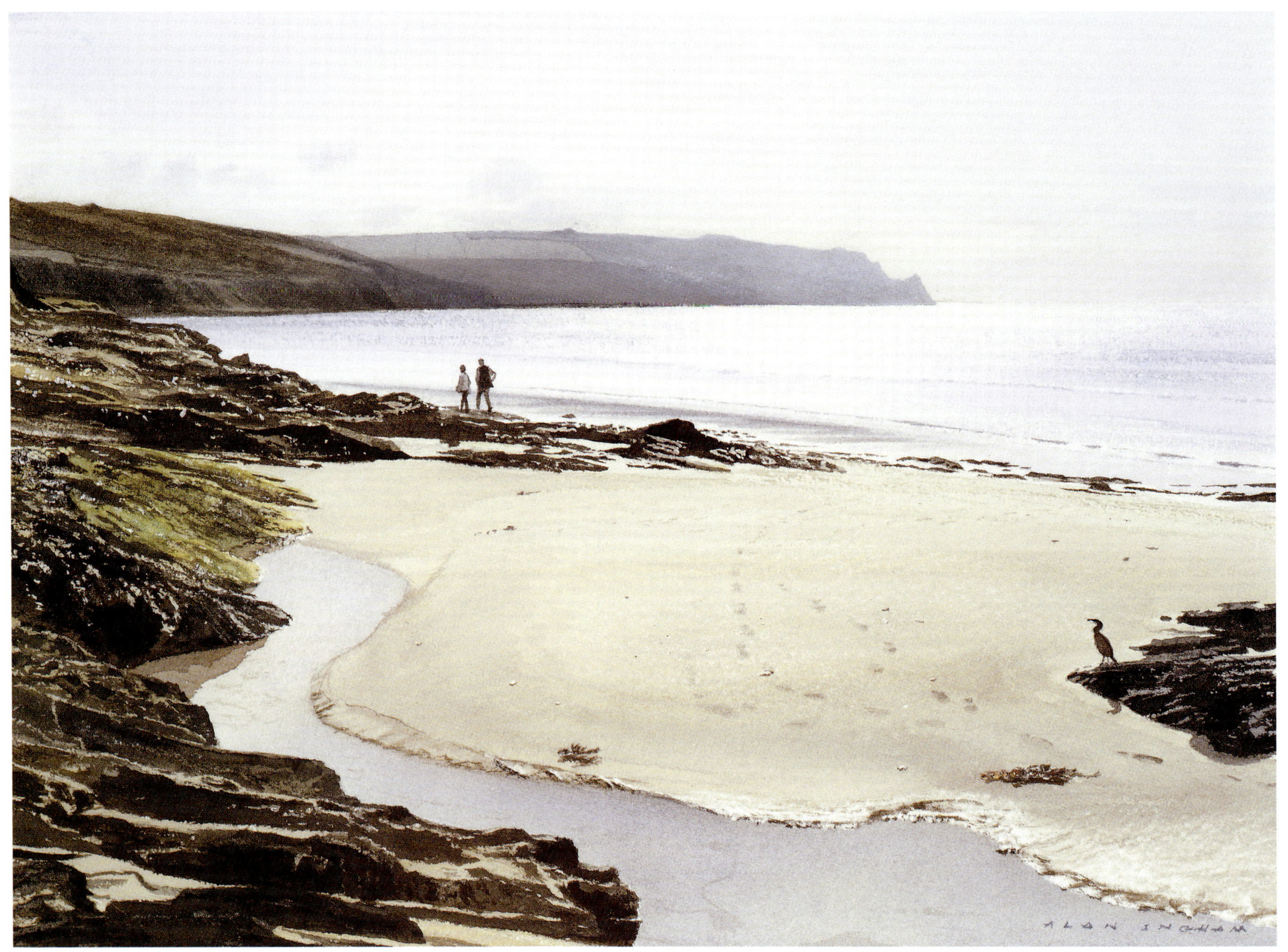

Two's Company, Nare Head from Pendower Beach, Cornwall, 2001.

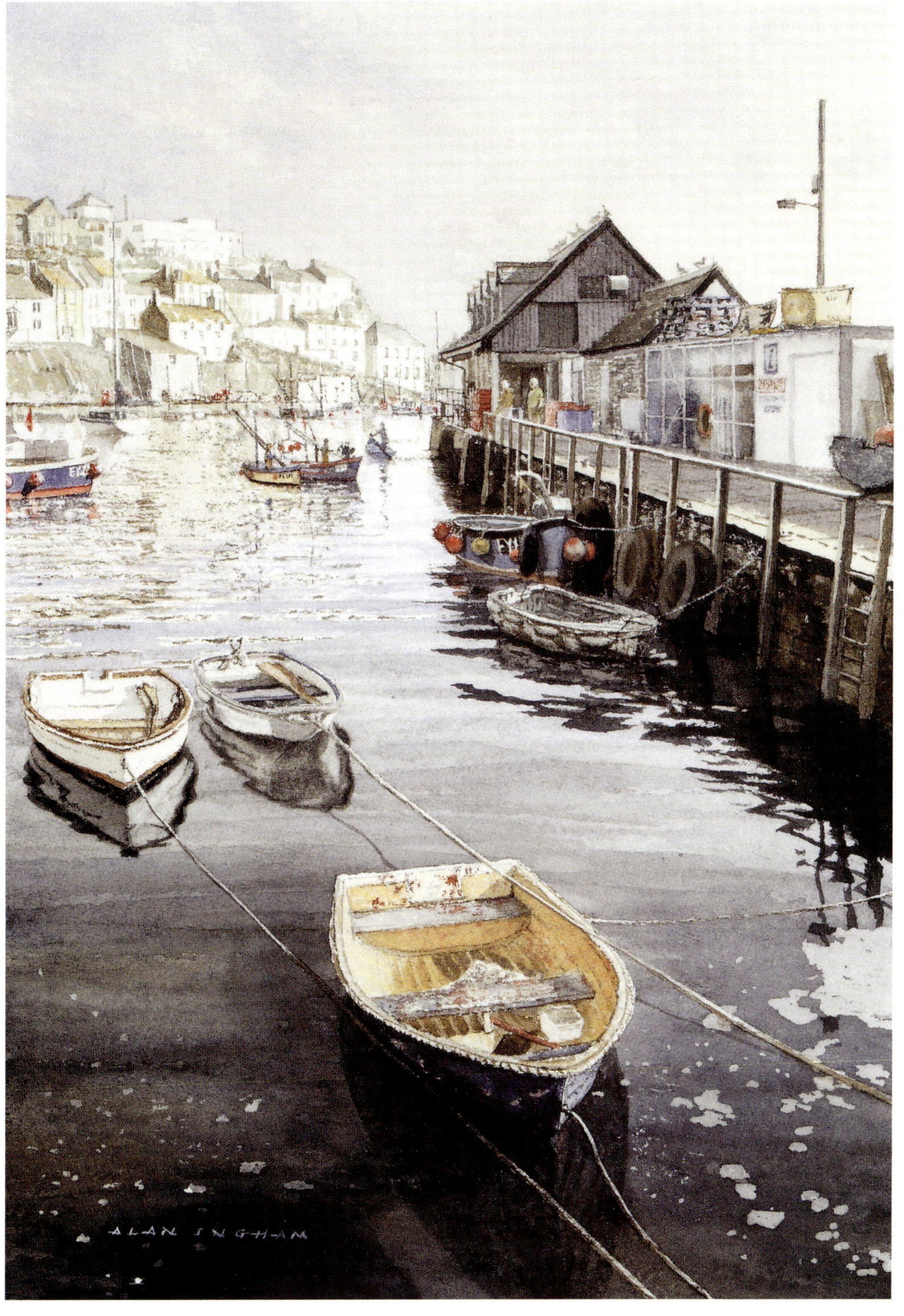

**Messing About,
Mevagissey,
Cornwall, 2001.**

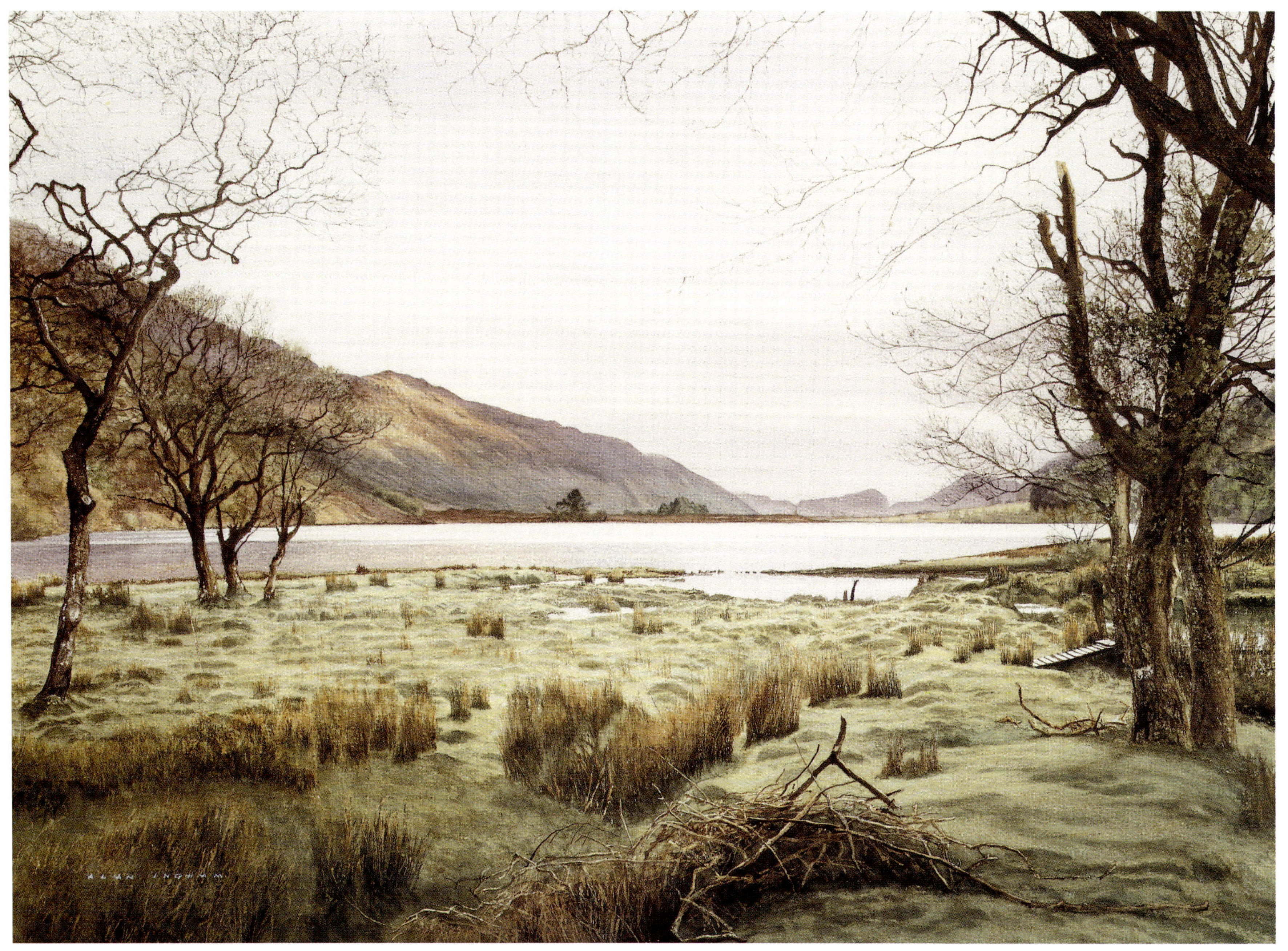

Loch Dughaill, Highlands, Scotland, 2002.

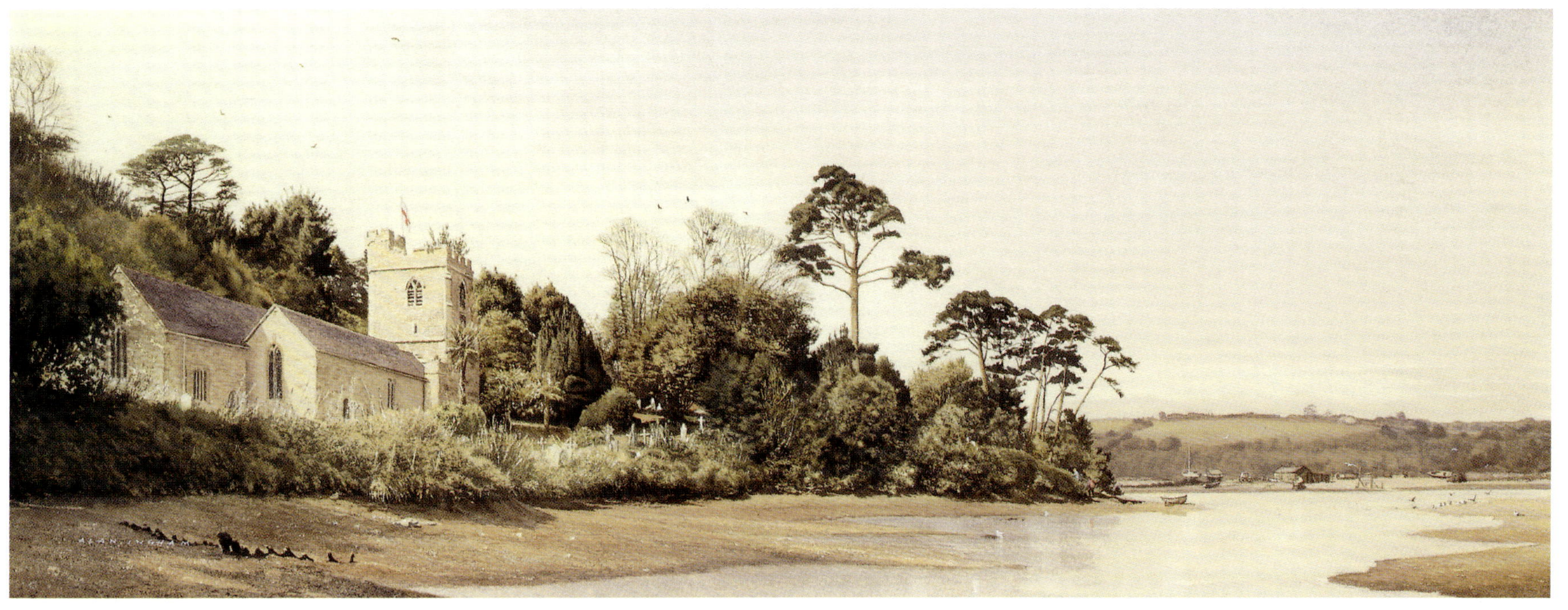

Ebb Tide, St Just-in-Roseland, Cornwall, 2002.

This painting was the last one painted by Alan in 2002 – it was published as soon as it was finished and sold out within one month. The title is so aptly named.

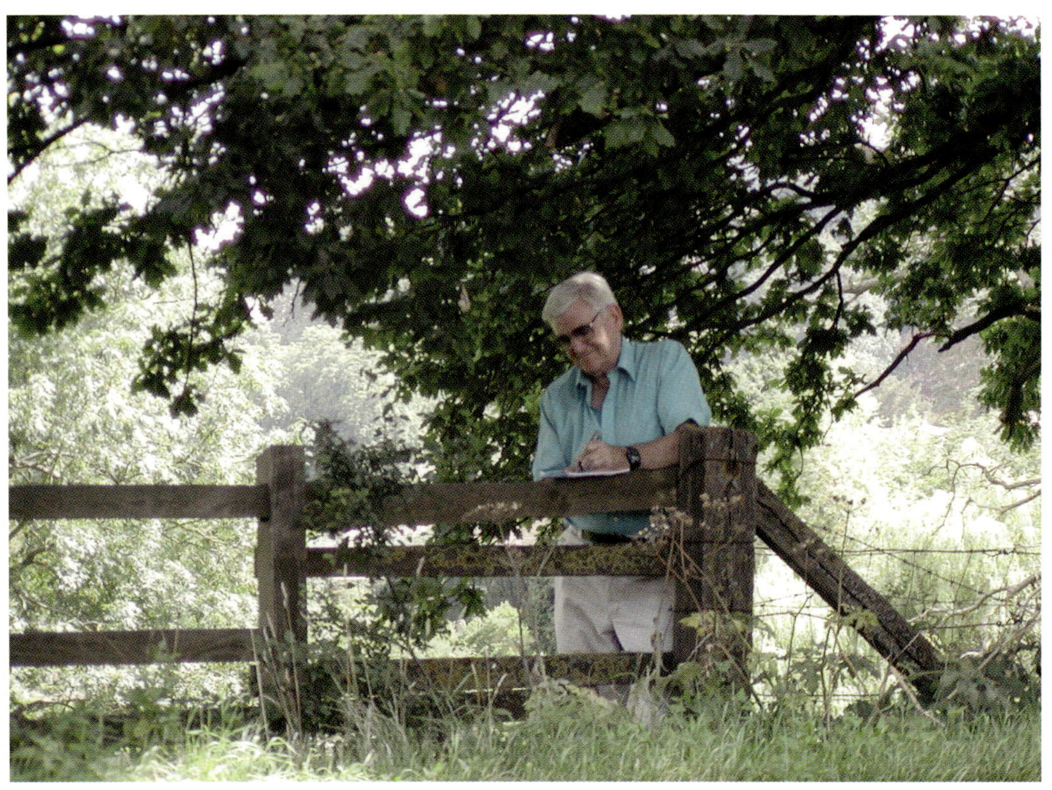

Postscript

This book is a tribute to my husband Alan of whom I am so proud. Unfortunately Alan died in May 2002 before he had quite finished the book. He did not manage to finish the captions and 'thumb nails' as he called them, so they have been completed as best as we may.

During his lifetime he produced many originals all of which were sold for use in some form or another – cards, calendars, prints, some of which are still available today.

My thanks to Halsgrove for publishing this book – it has been a pleasure dealing with them.

I do hope you enjoy the book.

From his soul-mate

Rosie

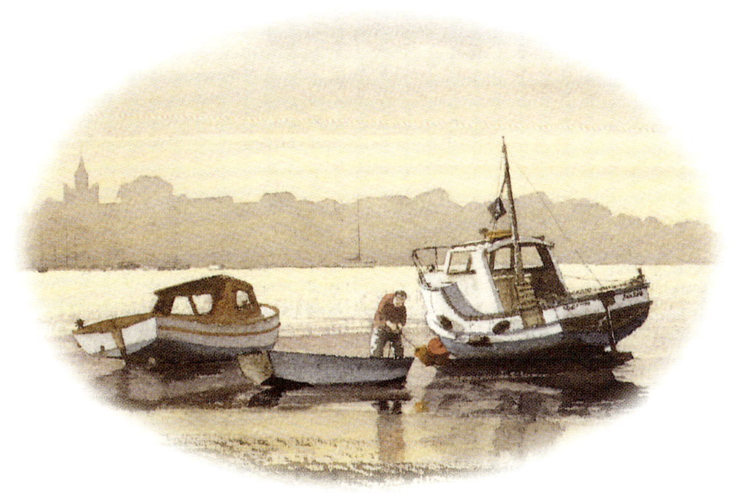